Jewish Latin America
Ilan Stavans, series editor

OTHER TITLES IN THE JEWISH LATIN AMERICA SERIES

passion, memory, and identity

TWENTIETH-CENTURY

LATIN AMERICAN

JEWISH WOMEN WRITERS

passion

memory

identity

edited by

MARJORIE AGOSÍN

University of New Mexico Press
Albuquerque

To Helen Broder Halpern, my great-grandmother

I want to thank my editor, Dana Asbury, for the tenacity and courage of her belief in my work. I also want to acknowledge the contributions made by the Jewish women writers to Latin America. A very profound *agradecimiento* to all of the critics included in this volume, who have created true works of passion so that these writers will no longer be forgotten.

—Marjorie Agosín

© 1999 by The University of New Mexico Press
All rights reserved.
First edition

Library of Congress Cataloging-in-Publication Data
Passion, memory, and identity : twentieth-century Latin American Jewish women
  writers / edited by Marjorie Agosin. — 1st ed.
    p.   cm. — (Jewish Latin America)
  ISBN 0-8263-2045-7 (alk. paper)
  ISBN 0-8263-2049-X (pbk. : alk. paper)
    1. Latin American literature—Jewish authors—History and criticism. 2. Latin
  American literature—Women authors—History and criticism. 3. Jewish women
  in literature. 4. Identity (Psychology) in literature. I. Agosin, Marjorie. II. Series.
  PQ7081.A1 P37 1999b
  860.9'9287'08992408—dc21

                                                                      99-6197
                                                                         CIP

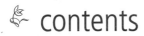 # contents

passion and memory: latin american jewish writers

Marjorie Agosín

Since one feels obliged to write, let it be without obscuring the space between the lines with words.

CLARICE LISPECTOR, *THE FOREIGN LEGION*

My great-grandmother Helena Broder Halpern used to silently descend the stairs from the second floor of her son Joseph's house in Santiago, Chile, every Friday at the time when the stars of the Southern Hemisphere assured us of the beauty and permanence of the firmament. In a Catholic country at the end of the world, my great-grandmother would cover her face and make the ancient gestures of Jewish women when they receive the splendor of the Sabbath. She would pray in Hebrew, Yiddish, and German. At first the maids stared at her, stupefied, then they would speak or hum some strange, always melodious words in the Mapuche tongue. They prayed next to her and recited the rites of other times and other ancestral backgrounds. I would look at my great-grandmother and rejoice because she had the semblance of happiness and memory. Perhaps this scene frames an early meditation on what it is to be a Jewish writer in Latin America. It is to be a type of hybrid of old traditions brought from the Sephardic and Ashkenazic worlds, but also an entity that belongs and inserts itself in the culture in which it lives. It is being like my great-grandmother Raquel, who prayed in Yiddish and then sang and spoke in Spanish and sometimes, when she was happy, in Turkish, and my great-grandmother Helena, who prayed in Hebrew and spoke almost always in German.

The presence of the Jewish world in Latin America is not anomalous. What is anomalous is that it has occupied such a nebulous presence in the cultures of the countries to which these Jews came, escaping persecution. Throughout history, in predominantly Catholic countries, Jews have become the emblematic symbol for the foreigner, the "outsider" who despite being from a family that has resided in his or her country for generations, does not really belong. But neither is he or she really a foreigner. To paraphrase the renowned literary critic of Judeo-Brazilian literature, Nelson H. Vieira, the Jews represent what is alternative; they have occupied throughout history the place of figures who appear in the maps of that which is foreign. It is interesting then that the wandering Jew often has had to compromise, to see himself as a foreign entity in the place he inhabits.

All of these complex and multiple identities remind me of my childhood and adolescence, when I was asked whether I was Jewish or Chilean—somehow I could never be both. Within the Chilean cultural imaginary it seems to be impossible to reconcile that a Jew can be fully Chilean. We were always subject to the fate and classifications of a religion that made it impossible for us to be citizens in the mainstream. This dilemma, which still permeates the lives of many Jews in Latin America, makes me think about destiny, the fate of the Latin American Jewish writer and his or her space within the cultural itinerary of the various countries of residence. Numerous works evidence the hybrid and multifaceted component of Latin American Jewish writers of the twentieth century. Each of these writers places himself or herself in his or her own space and reality, but we can say that the commonality of the Diaspora serves as a link that unifies all of them. The Diaspora is also a source of creativity and reality, a possibility for transcending and reconstructing history, an exile and its multifaceted themes that focus on a time inhabited from exile, linked to a permanent state of memory. The diasporic memory signifies escape and departure. It is constantly associated with the capacity for memories, and it legitimizes remembrance. Thus the Latin American Jewish writer oscillates between the fragile realms of memory and remembrance, but remembrance is not a constant dwelling on one's Jewish identity and past but rather a window to a Jewish future.

This collection of essays, by a most distinguished group of international literary critics, explores the Jewish experience in Latin America. The idea came about as an attempt to define the cultural experience of a Jewish Latin American imagination, as well as its relationship with the various national cultural frameworks. The title sprang precisely from the two keywords that dominate this essay: passion and memory. The poet Chris Wallace Crabb writes:

> All works of literature are to an extent acts of retrieval. Life escapes, it is lost and the writer erects, creates the verbal substitute on paper, a complexity of gestures adding up to a larger, former gesture which is time regained. Not for nothing do writers keep journals and notebooks. These are the halfway houses between life and letters.(7)

Crabb's words serve as a meditation on the unifying themes of this collection. The majority of the writers discussed herein participate in this communal and transnational act through their memories, through what they remember or choose to remember. They have been witnesses to the historical accident of their lives, and the majority of them are daughters of Sephardic or Ashkenazic immigrants. Thus the

Diaspora, the peregrinations and the memories of what it meant to arrive in Latin America, is present in various ways in the texts of almost all of these writers. For example, Margo Glantz views memory from the unique perspective of a family saga. Her *Genealogías* (Family Tree) is precisely an "act of retrieval," an act of retrieval based on the voice of her father's memories, which are the connecting threads to her own memory. Similarly, the Venezuelan writer Alicia Freilich de Segal in her classic book, *Cláper* (Clapper), finds herself in the quasi-Chagallesque villa of her father's childhood in Russia, and she writes about the symbolic condition of the Diaspora, exile, and incorporation into a new Spanish America that grants refuge and asylum. Among the younger generation of writers we see this passion to tell and retell of the arrival to America. Ana María Shua's *El libro de los recuerdos* (The Book of Memories) also exemplifies memory based on the family's trip to America, the wrong America, the poor South America.

If the metaphor for travel is the unifying axis in all of these texts that fluctuate between memories and the present, we also must go back to the ancestral memories that Esther Seligson and Angelina Muñíz-Huberman look for in their writings. I refer to the memories that get us closer to the Jews' mystic search for faith and their relationship with an internal Diaspora, as well as the experience of a nation so closely linked to Genesis and the Old Testament. The works of Seligson and Muñíz-Huberman are close to a mysticism surrounded by magic and a lyrical vision of the Jewish world they re-create.

Another key topic that appears in the texts of these writers is the feeling of being uprooted and displaced, which is seen as part of that atavistic condition of the Jewish people wherein it is very difficult to find lodging and a safe haven. This is why the texts written by Muñíz-Huberman and Clarice Lispector, as well as Esther Seligson, present an almost timeless and mystical universe, a zone where the human being is always condemned to solitude and escape. The gestures of writing become the retrieval acts of memory. To follow Crabb, all literary acts are also acts of remembering.

Another fundamental theme found in the Jewish literature of Latin America is the voyage, either the one that takes us back to the experiences of the ancestors' expulsions or the one that leads to their arrival in America. This theme is particularly accentuated in the literature of the men and women who write as Jews in Latin America. Memories, exile, migration, and the integration to other lands, the American lands, become the main topics of the literary discourse of the women assembled here.

It is interesting to note that for the first time in the cultural history of Latin America, the Jewish writers, and more specifically, the Jewish women writers, talk about their identity and their hybrid condition, but at the same time they analyze their personal experiences vis-à-vis the national culture. These writers get to know each other, and they are not part of the culture of the countries in which they live or from which they write. The words of Samuel Rawinski have a unique resonance in that although male Jewish literature exists in Costa Rica, it does not belong to the official canon:

> Those who know my work respect it and place me within the most prominent writers of Costa Rica, but when it comes to receiving praise, they make me feel like a foreigner in my own country. I would prefer to be less distinguished and to feel that I belong to this world. (Glickman and Di Antonio, "The Authors Speak" 27)

The renowned Brazilian writer Moacyr Scliar says something similar when he is asked what it means to be a Jewish writer:

> Sometimes I think that I am a Jewish writer who was born in Brazil by chance. Other times I feel like a Brazil-

ian writer who happens to belong to a very special group with a very special history and a very special tradition. (Glickman and Di Antonio, "The Authors Speak" 28)

This anthology also intends to explore the tradition of these Jewish Latin American writers and link them to the different cultures in which they grew up and from which they write. I think it is relevant to note that there is a powerful tradition of women writers whose work derives from their Jewish experiences and their symbolic relationship with the dispossessed and marginal. This is to say that Jewish writers not only try to demonstrate their Jewish experiences in their texts, they also write about people who are oppressed and discriminated against, thus forging an even stronger link to this universal experience.

The desire for an identity, for a feeling of belonging to the culture in which one lives, has become an obsession that many of these male and female writers share. In women's literature it is clear that the unifying tradition is the memoir. It is here that Jewish women writers assume their own identities, remember through the voice of the father or the mother, but at the same time feel the world from their position as outsiders. The act of writing memoirs that document exiles and arrivals and that incorporate, through personal experiences, what it means to be Jewish in Latin America is probably the most powerful contribution these writers can make. As Margo Glantz says:

To be Jewish is always to be the other one. It is part of our gestures, our routine, our tastes which persisted. . . . Jews have a different way of feeling fear, which contributes to the mosaic of our lives and all of this makes up our personal palette, the archetype of our memory. (Glickman and Di Antonio, "The Authors Speak" 19)

In Glantz's fundamental memoir, *Genealogías,* we observe that memory is the conducting thread that is glimpsed through the essential gestures of these Jewish women writers in their Latin American Diaspora, but we also have the immense figures of Jews who were burned during Christian Easter celebrations, symbolizing for Glantz the demonic image of the Jews who killed Christ.

Also, the nomadic condition with its metaphorical suitcases and languages is alive within the intimate space of the home. The experience that implies leaving the protective spaces of the home to establish a dialogue with others, those who celebrate Easter and First Communions with all their magic and splendor; that reality which is purely Catholic and visual is juxtaposed and linked to being Jewish in Latin America and Christian in Latin America. The voices of the Kol Nidre unite with the Catholic psalms; the Cross unites with the Star of David. It is in reality a universe of definite and indefinite frontiers that are amazingly different. Perhaps this skein of multicolored threads is what makes the writing of Latin American Jewish women so fascinating.

If the great Latin American writers of the nineteenth century created canonical texts that attempted to talk about Nation and State, an essential contribution of the writers of the twentieth century is to identify and represent the desire to belong: this is the topic that is constantly seen in the texts gathered in this volume. We must not think that belonging signifies acceptance of the dominant culture and eschewing the culture about which one writes and talks. That is to say, identity assumes a historical condition, but it is also a game of multiple projections and an invention of history.

In *Cláper,* Freilich de Segal plays with the images of a Chagallesque Russia but at the same time, a tropical Venezuela. Sonia Guralnik, the Chilean-Jewish writer, laughs at her own story; she often tells me that she landed in Chile wearing an elegant black fur coat during the hottest part of the Southern Hemisphere summer. Identity is a way of being, and integration is not necessarily accepted to its fullest, neither by the writers nor by their readers. However, the great proliferation of texts written by Jewish women creates a new map, a new place within the often homogeneous literature of the continent. Without doubt, this retrieval of personal life histories can be seen in the voices of other women's texts: in Elena Poniatowska's *La flor de lis* (The Lily Flower); in Barbara Jacobs's *Las hojas muertas* (The Dead Leaves), in which she returns to her Lebanese ancestry; in Cristina Peri Rossi's *La nave de los locos* (The Ship of Fools), a lyrical novel that is a deep meditation on the symbolic condition of women and exile; and of course in Margo Glantz's work. Jewish women writers unite their voices with those of other Latin American writers who witness their own histories based on their existence as women. Manuela Fingueret, the Argentine poet, speaks about being a Latin American Jewish writer: "I am the product of the people of Buenos Aires and my Argentine identity substantiates the ancestral stories that make me who I am." Fingueret also states that her poetry and her approach to the Jewish experience are ways of negating authoritarianism:

> For me, it was a way of opposing authoritarianism and the death of an era in which diversity was a dangerous and clandestine activity under the dictatorship. Since the return to democracy, the understanding is that the insoluble nexus between the nature of being Jewish and being Argentine, is essential in a country that is still struggling to grow as a nation. (Glickman and Di Antonio, "The Authors Speak" 16)

In the eloquent texts of the South African writer Nadine Gordimer, we constantly see representations of those meetings in the in-between zones that allow us to get closer to an understanding of the role of the Latin American Jewish writers presented in this anthology as a legacy for the future. For example, when speaking of her own role and that of other South African writers in working against racial segregation, Gordimer says:

> The powers of observations beyond what is normal imply an extraordinary lack of interest or maybe a double process: excessive preoccupation identified with the lives of others and at the same time a huge distancing which bring the most difficult alliances to the truth about that which is hidden and private. The tension between being apart and being completely immersed is what differentiates a writer. (19)

This concept of being a participant but always being apart concerns many of the writers included herein. From Alicia Steimberg's classic *De músicos y relojeros* (Of Musicians and Watchmakers), which narrates the experiences of an immigrant family through the voices of the women who arrived in Argentina, and Ana María Shua's *El libro de los recuerdos*, in which she insists on writing from the margins, to the experience of Rosa Nissán and Margo Glantz, who place themselves amid this constant desire to belong but at the same time to be outside and to see themselves from the outside. I return constantly to the question that I was asked in Chile and that I now ask myself: "Are you Jewish or Chilean?" And I can answer: "I am both."

What is the Jewish writer in Latin America? Is she one more immigrant within a multicultural hybrid society, or is she always the writer who is torn between his desire to be faithful to the past and his ancestors and his desire to incorporate his feelings about the new world? This is the key question posed in this anthology, which is constantly focusing on the state of being, the identity of the Latin American Jewish writer. The Jew is a being who resides in two worlds: the world of the past, which he recuperates through memories, and the world of the present, a very difficult world that contains dangerous and contradictory elements and in which there is a great tension arising from being and not being, from being the same yet different.

Throughout the history of the Americas the presence of Jews has been a constant, from Columbus's arrival in America and the flight of the converted Jews from the Inquisition to the great Jewish migrations of World War II and the cold war. These last represent the key years in the growth and development of the Jewish population of Latin America. This paradoxical history exists precisely because of the destruction of the Jewish world in Europe: it allowed for the consolidation of the Jewish communities in Latin America.

Edna Eizemberg's criticism is essential to understanding the fusion of Jewish writing in Latin America. Eizemberg states that Jewish Latin American literature is a hybrid mix of the past and the present, the folklore of that place and the presence of "here," but it is also a literature that can be tied to the postcolonial discourse of displaced people. Eizemberg refers to all displaced people, and thus the writing of Jewish women would signal a different way to look at them: these are women who do not write as foreigners regardless of the fact that they have foreign ancestry, but rather they try to place themselves within what it would mean to be purely Mexican or Chilean or Brazilian. This is a kind of appropriation of territory, of space from which they can write, because the Old World only functions as an articulation of memory and Latin America is, without doubt, the "now," the present, that on which it is proposed we base our dreams.

The persistence of a fragmented existence, dominated and privileged, is prevalent in the writings of Jewish women in Latin America. I say "privileged" because it is memories that nurture the most fertile areas of inspiration. Memory is also diaphanous and illuminating because it is not only the memory of those who remember and narrate, but in many cases the daughters are the ones who constantly question, and through their questioning memory is transformed; it becomes something different.

Most women who write choose to articulate their memories based on their personal experiences, which they translate into origins. These women have access to the Jewish experience through the poetics of origins and the intimate memories of home, the house and that which they have heard. There is in these memoirs an element of autobiography—a genre that gains more importance starting in the 1970s. The testimonial work of Rigoberta Menchú and the diary of the Brazilian writer María Carolina de Jesús, who lived in the favelas, began to be published in response to that voice which incites memory and remembrance. In the words of Doris Summer, many autobiographies are not only pretty stories.

> At first I assume, innocently, that the testimonials that I had read about Latin American women were autobiographical. As such, the most outstanding features for me were that oftentimes there was an explicit plural subject instead of the individual voice we usually associate with traditional autobiography. (71)

Later, Summer states that the singularity of these texts assumes the condition of the plurality of the collective experience. I would not go so far as to say, for example, that the experience of texts such as *De músicos y relojeros*, Nissán's *Novia que te vea* (I Want to See You a Bride), or *El libro de los recuerdos* could compare to Rigoberta Menchú's text. Let us not forget that the texts of Menchú and Domitila Barros exemplify an experience of the indigenous voice in an Occidental society. While we can think that these autobiographical texts do not identify with any other type of autobiographical voice, they do identify with the voices of those who find themselves in the midst of displacement and alienation. I think that the autobiography of Latin American Jewish writers has a relationship with the autobiographical and testimonial discourse that narrates history and identifies itself with the collective. Jewish women write about their experiences with fascism and anti-Semitism, and they act as loyal transmitters of the social conscience of a people. From this perspective they incorporate an ethnic discourse, and they also talk about the presence of the Diaspora, the passion of memory that is identified with the experience of women who write about that which is Jewish. I would like to point out that being Jewish is an analogy and a metaphor for being displaced, but it has also seemed a privilege to belong to a heraldic and nomadic tribe.

I also want to add about my great-grandmother Helena, the inspiring muse of this text. Helena escaped the SS one balmy evening in her beloved city, dressed in fur and velvet. She often sat in her room in Santiago with a faded notebook. In this notebook she preserved her passions and her memories. I often recall her looking out at the clear, almost electric South American sky and recording her past, which became my future and my legacy. *Passion, Memory, and Identity* is inspired by Helena Halpern's voyage to the New World and the words she nourished in her notebook, words of passion and memory. To my knowledge, this is the first anthology ever to be published in any language that explores the writings of Jewish women from Mexico, Argentina, Chile, Uruguay, Brazil, and Cuba.

This collection of essays by Latin America's foremost critics explores the tradition of Jewish women writers in Latin America and the ways in which they have inscribed themselves in their own cultures as well as the way in which their memory of migrations and often multiple Diasporas has been the essence of their literature and their multiple destinies. The Jewish presence in Latin America presents a fascinating as well as hybrid condition—from the converted Jews who settled in the Northeast of Brazil to the Sephardic colonies in the Caribbean and the massive migration to the Argentine Pampas under the sponsorship of Barón Maurice de Hirsch and, later, the influx of Jews during World War II.

The exploration of what Jewish literature is, is often a complex one. In a thought-provoking article Hana Wirth Nesher writes about the complexities of defining Jewish literature, which is like defining the indefinable. She goes on to write that the common definition of Jewish literature is literature written by Jews and that that is the most unsatisfactory definition. She argues that perhaps the commitment to ethics could be a common sign in Jewish texts (9–12). For the purpose of this collection, I would like to state that although all the writers discussed in this volume have their ancestral origins in Judaism, what really unites them as Jewish women authors is their capacity to participate in and inhabit several literary traditions at the same time. As Wirth Nesher suggests, Jewish literature and civilization has been a universal phenomenon. We do not attempt here to present an exhaustive vision of Jewish women writers in the Americas but to offer the possibility to begin to articulate a complex series of issues, for example, what do Jewish women write about, and how do they insert themselves in their countries and national identities? Why is the theme of autobiography and memoir so prevalent among them and among other women writers of Latin America? How diverse are the writings of these women, and how similar are they?

Each contributor has been asked to explore these issues and to present new ones. For example, although Clarice Lispector has not often been considered a Jewish writer, Nelson Vieira defines her as a Jewish writer embedded in a particular literary tradition that links her writing to the ethical teachings of Judaism.

The reader may be asking, Why a collection of Jewish women writers based on gender? Why create an additional label in this already hybrid presence? I would like to answer in several ways. I am interested in exploring the writings of Jewish women writers in the Americas because of their fascination and obsession with the recordings and the reorganizations of memory as well as the interplay of the personal with the collective. The presence of ancient lineages, the relationships between families and the ways in which these writers have chosen to record their histories, present a truly significant phenomenon in the study of autobiography and memoir writing. These writers as well as their critics often ask: Who writes about women, and how does one write about women? How does one recover the sites of memory? Are these autobiographies written from the position of marginality, or is marginality what allows the women to be and to feel powerful because they are writing their own stories? To this I would add that the memories recorded by women writers in Latin America and elsewhere take different forms and meanings. I was struck by the recently published *In Memory's Kitchen: A Legacy from the Women of Terezin*, a cookbook written in the concentration camps near Prague. Memories of life born from the horrors are also recorded in the Latin American dictatorships. Chilean women, for example, recorded their trauma through colorful tapestries that later were sent abroad to tell a censored history.

These examples go back to my original question and perhaps to the real reason I want to present the voices of these women: I am interested in how women choose to remember and what they choose to remember and how they inscribe in literature the acts of memory. The testimonial qualities of these stories have an almost oral character and a quotidian presence, wherein the sacred acquires a magical meaning, as if the scenes of pre- and post-Holocaust Europe could transfer themselves to the luminous landscapes of the tropics or South America. These women and their stories play through words with the chiaroscuro scenes of their historical and literary visions; they move back and forth, remembering the past and celebrating the present. The Jewish women writers of Latin America retake the testimonies of their ancestors and recover the heartbeat of their lineage. Here there are no intermediaries or collectors, but the author herself retells, speaks, and only approaches the voices of her ancestors, who for the most part are survivors.

Mexico has been the site for this proliferation of writings by and about Jewish women at an extraordinary pace. These texts are mostly autobiographical: memoirs, stories of displacements and homecomings. Curiously, the experience of being foreigners and the anti-Semitic experience do not appear as fundamental elements. Moreover, they recreate the stories of migrations, the desire and the complicity of being and not being part of a country and its official and unofficial histories.

The texts that are discussed in *Passion, Memory, and Identity* are, for the most part, the labors of writers from a privileged elite, middle-class women who recuperate and showcase the voices of their ancestors, of women who arrived in America in second-class cabins or on mules and who assumed their position as immigrants. They narrate and forge alliances of a hybrid past, as well as retake the ancestral voices of those travelers they left behind. Thus all the writers featured here insert themselves in the space of memories and its alliance with history. Margo Glantz's *Genealogías* assumes the identity of a daughter who tells the imaginary and symbolic story of her father, the immigrant Jacobo Glantz. While telling it she also talks about the history of Mexico, she lives it and creates it, she makes it her own. Trotsky and Frida Kahlo are also part of her memoirs—she as a writer, he as a poet, both Mexican Jews, Jewish Mexicans.

This observation presents central aspects of this introduction, for it attempts to explore the rituals of memories, of migration and its relationship to historical memory. If all Jewish migrations to Latin America are centered on the entrance to unknown and unwanted spaces, as well as wanted spaces, the reader must place all Jewish writings of the Americas within historical times, the Holocaust or the dictatorship.

It is through the process of reconstructing memory, as well as the invention of memory, that these texts speak to us. The writer poses the question of how we can keep memory alive. And it is precisely through the process of writing that we create and weave memories. Women elaborate memories through their texts. The indigenous woman remembers through the cloth and in so doing assembles and anchors her destiny. Memory becomes the essence of the feminine. It is the silent net through which the women recover their identities.

This anthology begins with a poetic meditation on Jewish women writers from Mexico. Ilan Stavans, short story writer, essayist, memoirist, and pioneer in the validation of Jewish writings from Latin America, touches on the questions that unite this collection. Like a diligent teacher and student of the Kabbalah, he examines the women writers of Mexico who have produced a true literature of their own, a literature populated by mysticism, secret voices, and whispers. As Stavans points out, this is a kind of "secret" literature, not widely translated, not too available in Mexico City, and mostly interested in the act of writing as an act of defiance and subversion. For example, Stavans points out that the works of Esther Seligson, as well as those of Angelina Muñíz-Huberman, defy conventional narrative and represent a literature inhabited by a haunting theme of mysticism that sets these works in an almost timeless place—a place where poetry and poetic language become a form of truth.

According to Stavans, these writers inhabit a literary universe populated by ancient scribes, visionaries, and poets; a world whose order can be found in the secrecy of mystical texts, like the Kabbalah. Stavans points out that the literary universe explored by Seligson and Muñíz-Huberman, two of Mexico's most intriguing writers, is embedded in mysticism. Theirs is a world of voices and signs, where the personal anecdote is almost nonexistent. This is a peculiar component of these Jewish women writers who have searched the objects of memory, not so much from the point of view of the familiar history of emigrations, but from an ancestry that is beyond the personal, a history that encompasses the Torah, the Talmud, and the sacredness of words.

Muñíz-Huberman possesses a unique originality within the Latin American literary world, and yet she remains unknown. *Huerto cerrado* (Enclosed Garden; 1985) could be considered one of the canonical, decisive, and most beautiful texts about writing as a Jewish woman. Everything is told from the point of view of a closed garden, a garden where medieval literature fuses with the secrets of the Kabbalah and alchemy. It is a garden that goes beyond the literary and historical experience. It belongs to the mystic and thus the secret and ambiguous, rooted in mystery. Muñíz-Huberman calls these texts transmutations, and like a good alchemist she goes on a "pilgrimage" to get closer to the memories of others. This is a pivotal text that creates the history of others and that travels through imaginary and real worlds, through fictions and the great book of life that holds all memories.

Stavans also discusses the more autobiographical works of Glantz, her *Genealogías* as well as the two books about her childhood and adolescence in Mexico as a descendant of Ladinos. The works by Glantz and by Nissán follow a more traditional approach to the autobiographical, and yet their world, to quote Stavans, functions on "separate ground." This ground is occupied by their Jewish ancestry as well as by the Indian-Catholic traditions of Mexico. Their works speak from the marginality of *petit histoires* that are now beginning to be a part of Mexico's literary traditions, and yet they are whispers "added to" the main purposes of literature: to insinuate aspects of life gone unnoticed.

If Ilan Stavans's essay reflects on Mexican writers who are deeply rooted in their mystical experiences, the Kabbalah, and alchemy, we must also explore the Mexican writers who address the issues of memory in order to insert themselves in a pluralistic and multicultural discourse that explores the Jewish issue from the point of view of identity. In chapter 2, Magdalena Maíz-Peña develops a poignant essay on the literary works of Rosa Nissán, Angelina Muñíz-Huberman, and Sabina Berman. She asks how these three writers fit into the discourse of Jewish-Mexican Latin American literature and, above all, the discourse of Mexican literature.

In *Novia que te vea* (Like a Bride), Nissán, a Sephardic-Mexican writer, recovers the voice of her own childhood, that of the girl, Oshinica, and through her narrative monologue and sometimes dialogue, we enter Sephardic-Mexican society. Autobiographical exploration and the challenges of memory are also explored in Berman's *La bobe* (The Grandmother), in which the granddaughter, through her Ashkenazi grandmother, finds her Jewish-Mexican identity. Finally, Maíz-Peña discusses the works of Muñíz-Huberman in terms of what she defines as pseudomemories. That is, created memories, intermittent memories that fluctuate between light and dark, the journeys and the static moments. Through these writings, Maíz-Peña focuses on the strategies and coded representations of a harmonious discourse that is sociopolitical, historical, and cultural. She explores what it means to be a Jewish-Mexican writer as well as the forms in which these writers write and insert their voices of the 1990s into the voice of their societies and their particular histories. She brings to light the unique duality of the sociocultural and the historical. These texts create memories that are both real and invented, imagined and lived. They create heterogeneous realities instead of the monolithic reality of the Mexican literature that proliferated in the 1950s. These writers offer the possibility of multiple discourses in which culture, class, genre, and religion meet. It is noteworthy that in this past decade, the presence of Jewish literature has achieved importance and, most of all, actuality. It is evident that the dictionary of Jewish authors by Darrell B. Lockhart has helped to disseminate the vast and heretofore almost unknown legacy of Jewish writers in Latin America.

Mexico and Argentina have the largest Jewish communities in

Latin America. In chapter 3, David William Foster focuses on writers who have achieved notoriety within Argentine culture: Liliana Heker, Alicia Steimberg, Ana María Shua, the playwright Diana Raznovich, and Alicia Kozameh. Foster points out that all of these writers belong to an urban experience. Buenos Aires with its sophistication and literacy is the site of this experience, but we are also in the presence of the Jewish experience. Heker's novel *El fin de la historia* (The End of History/the Story) alludes to the fact that the Jewish condition is the figure that represents otherness and all that is different.

In Argentina, Steimberg and Shua have written about their identities as immigrant writers. Steimberg was the first woman writer in Argentina to write with subversion and tenderness about the immigrant condition in Buenos Aires. Like Margo Glantz's *Genealogías*, Steimberg's is a fundamental autobiography in the Latin American canon. Shua, following Steimberg's lead, wrote *El libro de los recuerdos*. In an earlier, beautiful text, Shua combined recipes and anecdotes about Jewish cooking with reflections on love, magic, and poetry. In her most recent book, Shua tells us what it is like to belong to an Argentine family whose immigrant grandparents somehow arrived in South America, the wrong America, not North America, the powerful America, as they had intended.

Shua speaks of harmony and broken hearts, of the great and small scandals of life, its colorful men and passionate women. What is interesting and moving in this text is that it presents the constant question of why we have memories and how the author places herself within these memories. Shua constantly presents the ways in which we can articulate history, how it is written and who chooses what to include and what not to include. *El libro de los recuerdos* is the equivalent of a book of the life stories of the other women—women of the fields who tell stories, women who gather and choose certain codes and messages to be remembered. Also, both groups—the illiterate and the literate, those who write their own words—know that the only reliable border is the border created by literature. As Shua wrote in a letter to me of December 7, 1997, "*El libro de los recuerdos* is our only truly reliable source. That is why it is so simple to get angry with it, because what it says is true, but it never says it all, it never even says enough."

The topic of migration and immigration, as well as the constant presence of the Jews as immigrants, can be seen in the works of Shua and Steimberg. Both, like Heker, are consecrated writers. In Shua's *El libro de los recuerdos* and in Steimberg's *De músicos y relojeros* (Of Musicians and Watchmakers), the presence of immediate family is the protagonist. According to Foster, in these novels the space occupied by memories takes center stage, and these memories are the threads that draw us closer to the Jewish experience, to the ancestors and to the urban Jewish experience in Buenos Aires. However, there is also a universalization of the Jewish experience in the writings of these women who are strongly motivated by their experiences as foreigners.

Foster concludes his essay with a writer who has had a significant presence in the political culture of Argentina. In *Pasos bajo el agua* (Steps Under Water), Alicia Kozameh retells her experience as a political prisoner during the Dirty War. Although being Jewish does not appear directly, it is implied in her literature. Through the work of the writers selected by Foster, we can clearly appreciate the eclectic dimension of those writings that unite the experience of the Diaspora with the experience of political repression.

In chapter 4, Regina Igel makes it possible for us to come closer to understanding the literature of four almost unknown women of Brazilian literature, women who are not part of the literary canon: Elisa Lispector, sister of the well-known author Clarice Lispector, Frida Alexandr, Janette Fishenfeld, and Sara Riwka Erlich. As Igel points out, "With the exception of Elisa Lispector, the literary creations of

Alexandr, Fishenfeld, and Erlich have barely been appreciated outside their circle of friends and family."

We see in these writers, all of whom are Russian Jews, a mix of the traditional and the multicultural—the infrastructure of the Jewish neighborhoods and incorporation into Brazilian life. Igel points out that these writers are also united by their relationship with their respective communities and the universality of the migrant experience. With great perception, Igel portrays a cross-section of Brazilian Jewish society: in the work of Elisa Lispector, whose novel *No exílio* (In Exile) brilliantly explores the condition of Ukrainian immigrants to Brazil; in Frida Alexandr's work about the peasant experience of the Jews in the pampas and the aftermath; in the texts of Sara Riwka Erlich, who writes about Jewish mysticism as it is linked to the folklore of the Pernambuco region of northern Brazil; and in the work of Janette Fishenfeld, where we see a greater preoccupation with the problems of assimilation and mixed marriages. In these writers, the hybrid experience is integrated through the geography of Europe, Brazil, and, finally, Israel. Igel presents to us the vision of four women who turn their memories and writings into an exploration of their ancestors as well as a diaspora, an experience that unites their condition as Jewish immigrants with that of the universal immigrant. With this essay we begin to discover these Jewish women and their relationship with Brazil.

Clarice Lispector has been, without doubt, one of the most original and extraordinary voices of Brazilian literature and of Latin American literature generally. Since her death, she has become a literary icon, not only in Latin America, but in Europe as well, especially thanks to the work of the feminist critic Helene Cixous. Lispector's literary presence has been reaffirmed in the last ten years, and not just because of her death, but rather because of her exquisitely sensitive prose. In her autobiographical writings Lispector reveals that few of her friends knew she was Jewish, which makes us reevaluate her literary work and explore the issues of Judaism in her texts. Chapter 5, by Nelson Vieira, is a groundbreaking revision and rediscovery of the Judaic elements in Clarice Lispector's work and a meditation on what Jewish literature means. Vieira makes us realize that Jewish literature is not only literature written by Jews. He points out that Lispector wanted to be considered a Brazilian writer who is Jewish and not a Jewish writer who is Brazilian.

According to Vieira, the strong presence of certain themes in Lispector's fiction and essays—exile, the spirit of the ineffable, the difficulty of language in capturing a reality, the feeling of always being universally foreign—make Clarice Lispector part of the Jewish influence and images of the Diaspora. As Vieira writes,

> In applying the ineffable to Lispector's spiritually motivated writing, I read her work and her universe as bordering on the mystical in her persistent quest for meaning and understanding, despite her awareness of humankind's incapacity to know everything because full knowledge rests only with the Divine.

This vision of Clarice Lispector and her search for a powerful and suggestive lyrical language that would link her to the spaces that go beyond everyday experiences are key elements that motivate her work and originate her constant obsessions. To this we should add the strong presence of the Diaspora in her chronicles, stories, and novels. To quote Lispector: "Perhaps I started writing so early in life because at least by writing I belonged to myself to some extent. Which is a pale imitation" (150).

Clarice Lispector's case is interesting biographically and culturally, for while she universalizes the Jewish experience, her sister, Elisa, writes texts and memoirs that are deeply embedded in Jewish culture.

According to Vieira, Elisa's explicitly Jewish literature testifies to the Judaic spirit of the Lispector home.

The majority of writers included in this volume meditate on exile and alienation centered on certain historical instances in their lives. Yet the work of Clarice Lispector is linked more closely to the narrative of Esther Seligson or Angelina Muñíz-Huberman, for example, writers whose passion focuses on the exploration of literature as a way to approach the ineffable, that which cannot be named, and capturing literature as an experience that borders on the mystical.

Nelson Vieira's essay makes us think about the key question in many of these essays and literary texts: What is Jewish literature, and who is a Jewish writer? The Lispector case points out a way to approach what is Jewish literature—one that focuses on the elements of alienation, the experience of being in exile as an essential condition, and the search for the ineffable and the mysterious in life. Lispector herself states this: "To write is to try to understand, to try to repeat the unrepeatable, to write is to also bless a life which has not been blessed" (151).

In chapter 6, Elizabeth Rosa Horan eloquently addresses the work of three writers from the Southern Cone: Sonia Guralnick, Teresa Porzecanski, and Marjorie Agosín. Unlike Mexico and Argentina, the Jewish population of Chile and Uruguay is very small, less than 1 percent. Horan shows that migration patterns in Chile since 1804 reveal a homogeneous population; Jews were not particularly welcome and were often subject to quota laws like those of neighboring Argentina and the United States. Horan points out the often arduous path to Cape Horn and then on to the Port of Valparaíso. In the case of Uruguay, one imagines the immigrants crossing the Atlantic and then traveling from the port city of Buenos Aires to Montevideo. The topography of Chile and Uruguay and the natural isolation from nearby Jewish communities made the flourishing of Jewish literature invisible and almost secretive. Furthermore, German Jews in Chile had to contend with pro-Nazi communities that already existed there in the early part of the twentieth century. These communities had allied with Hitler's Germany and later on with Pinochet's regime at home. We are left to wonder how Jewish women of letters, and Jewish men of letters too, flourished under these circumstances. They did.

The essays by Foster, Stavans, and Joan Esther Friedman (discussed below) indicate the prominence as well as the abundance of Jewish women writers, especially in Mexico. Chile and Uruguay are only now beginning to forge a Jewish tradition, almost invisible given the closed nature of these societies as well as the extreme difficulties of being a woman writer there. But Jewish culture flourished in the hidden neighborhoods of Santiago, in the boardinghouse that Sonia Guralnik writes about and in my own memory of the south of Chile, which I witnessed through my mother's eyes, and then Quillota, the central valley, through my father's.

Sonia Guralnik is one of the handful of Jewish women writers living in Chile today. She is almost seventy years old and paradoxically began to write in Spanish and identify herself as a Jewish writer during the most turbulent times of Chilean history. Elizabeth Horan points out an interesting fact: during the Pinochet government, many literary workshops for women and directed by women began to flourish. It was a way to engage in a profound dialogue with issues of social justice and the inner life at a time when the "official" dialogue was very secretive. Guralnik began writing her stories in this setting. Her Jewish consciousness, the histories of her past, her arrival in Chile from Kiev with a "coat" in the middle of summer—she tells me of so many stories already brewing inside her, stories that she brought with her from a Russia she remembers through her literature. Thus Horan is right to point out that the writings of these three women are acts of retrieval, engagements with the process of reconstructing a world and a past often re-created through the eyes of relatives. In this instance, Chilean Jewish literature bears similarities to the literature of its sisters in Argentina, across the Andes, but is very different from that of Mexico, so often inspired by Jewish mysticism and pre-Hispanic beliefs.

The work of Sonia Guralnik, Teresa Porzecanski, and Marjorie Agosín centers on a female space, a home, a kitchen, or a door, as the image of the voice that writes, and the characters that emerge exist in the domestic confines of home and in the intimacy of memory. Memory is the thread that unifies these writers, along with the constant presence of the Holocaust that is foreshadowed in the literature of Guralnik, Porzecanski, and Agosín. The struggle involved in building a national identity, the constant "metaphor" of the refugee, the displaced past, and the preservation of rituals and traditions make the writings of these women a kind of threshold between the past and the present, the new and the old.

Teresa Porzecanski, two generations younger than Guralnik, is an anthropologist, short story writer, and professor. She is engaged in a secular world. Her book *Historias de vida de inmigrantes judíos al Uruguay* (Life Stories of Jewish Immigrants to Uruguay) also reveals an intense obsession with and the seduction of recuperating an invisible past. *Historias de vida* is perhaps the only book of its kind to explore the oral history of Jewish immigrants to Uruguay. To my knowledge, this is the only oral history dealing with any immigrant group in Uruguay.

It is revealing that Porzecanski, like her contemporaries, chooses to unveil the voices that made these daring voyages to the New World. The act of their retrieval indicates a passionate commitment to memory. In the case of my own work, I also belong to the generation of Porzecanski, and I have constantly tried to understand the life of Chilean society through the eyes and voices of my own parents. I have used personal interviews, oral histories, and my own recollections of past histories and lives that I heard from my parents.

Horan's essay is both inspiring and challenging. Through the voices of women from Russia, Poland, and Vienna, unto the shores of the Atlantic in Montevideo and the Pacific in Valparaíso, she examines the intricate complexities of immigrant memory through the private histories of each of these authors which somehow become a collective history of nations. Through these memories and oral histories Horan explores how each of these authors has described a world left behind by the Jewish immigrant experience and, further, their tenacious desire to preserve the past.

In chapter 7, Joan Esther Friedman discusses the Jewish women writers of Venezuela. Venezuela's history of migrations is similar to that of most of the American republics. However, we must note that the influx of Sephardic immigrants since the expulsion of the Jews from Spain has had a strong influence on Venezuela. The majority of the writers in this chapter are descendants of Jews who left Turkey, Greece, and North Africa. The Ladino universe and language they carried with them has been fundamental for the understanding of Venezuelan Jewish culture. Another interesting aspect that Friedman discusses is that the Ashkenazi Jews who remained in Venezuela made a key contribution in the persistence of Yiddish in the homes of these immigrants, and, no doubt, they will have an effect on the works of future authors.

The dictatorship of the 1930s and 1940s in Venezuela under Marcos Pérez Jiménez paralyzed the literary production of the country, but it is precisely during these years that Venezuela opened up its doors. Many Jewish and non-Jewish writers migrated to Venezuela. Among these writers was Isabel Allende, who wrote *The House of the Spirits* while living in Caracas.

Friedman's essay explores the work of the playwrights Elisa Lerner and Blanca Strepponi, the novelist Alicia Freilich de Segal, the short story writer Lidia Rebrij, and the poets Jacqueline Goldberg, Sonia Chocrón, and Martha Kornblith. It is revealing that Lerner and

Strepponi had already been part of a third migration. That is to say, they went from the Old World to Argentina and then to Venezuela, which implies an interesting cultural hybridity as well as an enriched Latin American experience. The richness of their writings can be found in their incorporating stories from the past with stories of their lives, which mark the process of their immigrations with the deeply rooted experience of what it is to be Jewish.

Once again we can observe the presence, already noted by Vieira in Brazil, of the dichotomy outsider/insider. In Friedman's work we see how Venezuelan society occupies a border space in which identity is strongly attached to the frontier. However, a key element can be found in all of these writers: the past is a strong and powerful presence that defines each one of these women. It is a very special element of these Venezuelan authors, for although their Jewish ancestry plays a key role in their identity, the past is the link to the future and their writing is the way to cement this link to the present. For example, Strepponi constantly defines herself in terms of having been an immigrant child: "At the age of 24 I emigrated / what a curious family itinerary/always tied to historic reincarnations / Lithuania Reggio Calabria Buenos Aires" (24).

The geographic as well as the historical migration becomes the historical and literary imagination of each one of these authors as well as the defining link to memory. In the case of Jacqueline Goldberg, we see how she constantly refers to the inheritance that defines her as a woman and as an author. In *Luba*, Goldberg's deeply lyrical collection of poems, she honors the memory of her relatives and of a town. When personifying memory Luba (her grandmother) says: "She changes like shadows / to force me to suffer / an inheritance" (14).

Poetry, in ancient times, was the repository of masculine literature, as seen in the tradition of the great Hebrew poets. Throughout history it was like some special incantation that occupied the visionary place where men could find the powerful voice that is rooted in the nebulous zones of memory and personal and collective recollections, the memory of the Jewish people now repeated in the Spanish language as it was before in Ladino. The poet Martha Kornblith especially, in her collection *Oraciones para un dios ausente* (Prayers for an Absent God), weaves the past with the present of a woman who carries the ancestral inheritance of her people: "Nothing hurts me more than my parents' pain, their dead parents" (42).

In the field of narrative drama, Alicia Freilich de Segal and Elisa Lerner are key to our knowledge of Venezuelan Jewish literature, but we must also note the dramatic work of Blanca Strepponi. I think it is fascinating that this woman dedicates a theater piece to Marie Langer, who is recently achieving recognition in the United States. Marie Langer, one of the most important psychoanalysts of our century, was a strong presence against the Argentine military. Strepponi re-creates her by weaving the history of a German immigrant Jew with the history of an American latina as well as including the element of justice and vindication in the realm of human rights, which plays a key role in understanding Latin American culture. Finally, the play reveals Strepponi's condition as an outsider, which links her to her representation of the Jew in a Catholic country.

The works of Elisa Lerner also present the condition of a Jewish woman whose identity is constantly being defined and redefined, but she adds to her female characters elements that result in powerful and controlling external forces. Lerner incorporates in her work the issue of woman's vindication as well as the powerful alliance that exists between being Jewish and being in a world of patriarchal ancestral traditions.

The work of Freilich de Segal, and specifically her book, *Cláper*, which has been very successful in Venezuela and abroad, has many similarities to Margo Glantz's work. Both, through a story and the *petit histoire* of their fathers, trace the history of a migration and the past. Freilich de Segal takes with pride that hybrid position which balances her between two cultures and which allows her to be a key element of both. *Cláper* is a wonderful dialogue between a father and his daughter. Often the structure of this book has a rare and deep lyricism that takes us inside a beautiful and constant dialogue that is reminiscent of the Talmudic question-and-answer form.

Through this important essay, we see in the literature of these Venezuelan-Jewish writers the constant struggle between identity and being part of the dominant culture. However, in the same way that the Ladino culture preserved itself in the language, these writers have continued writing in Spanish, going back to their history, which they translate as the collective history of their people. Interestingly, the element of mysticism prevalent in Jewish-Mexican literature or the strong component of social history found in Jewish-Argentine literature is absent from Jewish-Venezuelan literature.

The concluding chapter is a unique creative work that truly reflects the spirit of this anthology. "In Search of the Cuban-Jewish Woman Writer" questions and presents the destiny of a generation of young Jewish writers, victims of a double Diaspora, as are all Cuban Jews who arrived in Cuba at different times in history, but mainly during the pogroms, and later, in about 1959, abandoned that country for the United States.

Is the history of the Jews who write in Cuba part of the legacy of invisibility? Or is it, as Ruth Behar would point out, that despite the fact that a Jewish presence in Cuba has existed since the Conquest, "the problem is that this presence always inscribed loss, for it remained hidden, repressed, disguised as something else"? This is also the reason for a great absence within the Jewish-Cuban culture, the same absence that leads us to see that there are no Jewish writers in Cuba. The Jewish women who arrived in Cuba and stayed were busy learning Spanish and integrating themselves into a new culture, and those who left had to learn how to live as immigrants again, either in New York or in Miami. So much of the work of Jewish-Cuban women writers is lost (invisible), but there is always the possibility of a new generation. This is definitely a unique phenomenon as there are Jewish writers in most other Latin American countries. Maybe it has to do with demographics: Jewish migrations to the Southern Cone were more massive.

I remember the first time I spoke to Ruth Behar and invited her to participate in this project. She said to me, "But there are no Cuban-Jewish writers in Cuba." I remember telling her she is one of them, as are her friends Ester Shapiro Rok and Rosa Lowinger, of whom she often spoke. I then convinced Ruth Behar to write an essay about the literature of Cuban women. This essay confirms my original conversation about the Jewish cultural presence in Cuba, which can be seen only in synagogues and ruined cemeteries. In a moving article entitled "Los colados," Behar writes:

> Of the fifteen thousand Jews who once inhabited the island, less than one thousand are left in Cuba in 1991. I was not just searching for traces of Jewish life, but trying to find real Jews. One day I went to the daily service held at the small, but well-preserved Adath Israel Synagogue in the old section of Havana, and I found six shabby elderly men wearing threadbare guayaberas. These are the Jews. (125)

This quote makes me wonder, what has become of the Jews who write in Cuba? In this last chapter the reader will experience a powerful dialogue among three women who write, but at first, like their grandmothers and mothers, were afraid to write. Hesitantly, they chose professions that, with time, changed them and allowed them to focus on the arduous work of writing. Ruth Behar is a renowned anthropologist who began to explore her Spanish roots and the understanding of death in peasant societies in her book *The Presence of the Past in a Spanish Village*. Ester Shapiro Rok chose a different path, that of those who listen. She became a psychotherapist. She claims she chose this profession to preserve history. Rosa Lowinger chose a career in architectural preservation. All of these professions seem to me an exploration of lost or broken things and their restoration. Behar says, "For us, the passion of writing seems closely linked to a deep need to make shattered lives whole, to make connections of ruptures."

Each of these women writes and has published creative works. Behar is a poet, Rok writes short stories, and Lowinger is a playwright. They have decided to tell their stories instead of analyzing their own words. Through their conversations, these three writers take us back to a lost time when memories abound, and they bring us to the present, to their desire to preserve, to mend, to retrieve that which is lost, to make alliances through writing and to create bridges between Cuba and other diasporas. Now we can truly say that there are Jewish-Cuban writers. They may be writing outside Cuba, but, as these three women can attest, they have never really left Cuba and the Jewish cemetery.

The essays as well as the challenges found in *Passion, Memory, and Identity* allow us to explore and meditate on the different ways of inhabiting one's self and forging new and old alliances through various migrations. In "How a Samovar Helped Me Theorize Latin American Jewish Literature," Eizemberg asks how one can define Jewish literature and Latin American Jewish literature written by women. Eizemberg returns to one of our own conclusions, that of the universalization of the Jewish experience as well as the pluralization of this experience in the various countries of origin. The experience of being a Jewish writer is made up of multiple identities and visions that are aimed at integrating a nomadic past with a more stable present. Together with this desire to integrate themselves in the culture of their countries, there is also the desire to be the "other," that is, the desire to write about what it means to belong from the perspective of the "outsider." Eizemberg writes:

> Our pluralization from within must also include a move from Latin American Jewish literature to Latin American Jewish literatures, from a definition of what we study as being exclusively in Spanish or Portuguese to one that embraces Yiddish, Hebrew, English, Ladino and perhaps additional languages. (3)

This collection of essays was born at a symbolic and propitious moment for the study of Latin American Jews in America as well as in the rest of the developing world. We are approaching the end of the century, the beginning of a new millennium. It is no coincidence that the voices of minorities in search of collective and personal ethnic significance are being heard. Although the Jewish presence in America dates back to the clandestine arrival of Jews to the New World in the fifteenth century, it is not until the late twentieth century that Jewish literature in Latin America has become visible and gained importance and flourished. To this I must add that the voices of women—including indigenous women such as Rigoberta Menchú and María Carolina de Jesús—are gaining strength and visibility. It is to these voices and this vision of the world that this anthology contributes. The women whose texts we read in this book are second- and third-generation immigrants. Many of their great-grandparents and grandparents, sometimes even parents, arrived in Buenos Aires, Valparaíso, Maracaibo, or Rio de Janeiro. They arrived with little money. They lived in ghettos and were usually street vendors who later began to climb the socioeconomic and cultural ladder. These immigrants created in Buenos Aires several Yiddish newspapers, and the culture of the Old World gained importance in the New World.

Lockhart says it best in *The Silver Candelabra* when he refers to Argentine writings:

> Jewish Argentine writing constitutes a socio-literary phe-
> nomenon that exercises and contributes to the creation
> of a cultural history. Also, as a social text marked by its
> decentered marginal status as a minority discourse, Jew-
> ish writing serves an important function as a countervoice
> to the official discourse. Jewish writings in Argentina like
> all minority literatures, endure a response to the hege-
> monic telling of history. (7)

As I conclude this essay, I have next to me my great-grandmother Helena's notebook that traveled from the port of Hamburg to Valparaíso, and now is in Boston. This notebook survived all these journeys and proves that words are not only knowledge but also mirrors to our future. *Passion, Memory, and Identity* is a struggle against forgetting. As the philosopher Yerushalmy once said, "A people who do not remember stop being a people." As Pierre Vidal Naquet states in *Los judíos, la memoria y el presente*, "Each one of us possesses a memory and it is precisely through memory that one is an individual." (13) This volume attempts to reorganize the memory of the Jewish experience in Latin America as seen by its protagonists, the women who through oral tradition and history have been the most loyal vessels of passions and memories.

REFERENCES

Cixous, Helene. *Reading with Clarice Lispector.* Ed. Verena Conley. London: Harvester, 1990.

Crabb, Chris Wallace. *Falling into Language.* Oxford: Oxford University Press, 1989.

Eizemberg, Edna. "How a Samovar Helped Me Theorize Latin American Jewish Literature." LASS 17.2 (1997): 1–4.

Fingueret, Manuela. *La piedra es una llaga en el tiempo*. Buenos Aires: Botella al
    Mar, 1980.

———. "Ser judía en mi país." *El imaginario judío en la literatura de America
    Latina*. Ed. Patricia Finzi. Buenos Aires: Shalom, 1992.

Gardiol, Rita, ed. *In Memory's Kitchen: A Legacy from the Women of Terezin*.
    Northvale, N.J.: Jason Aronson, 1997.

Glantz, Margo. *Genealogías*. México: Martin Casilla Editores, 1981.

Glickman, Nora, and Robert Di Antonio. "The Authors Speak for Themselves."
    Glickman and DiAntonio, *Tradition* 9–31.

———, eds. *Tradition and Innovation: Reflections on Latin American Jewish
    Writing*. Albany: State University of New York Press, 1993.

Goldberg, Jacqueline. *Luba*. Caracas: Monteavila, 1994.

Gordimer, Nadine. *Writing and Being*. Cambridge, Mass.: Harvard University
    Press, 1995.

Kornblith, Martha. *Oraciones para un dios ausente*. Caracas: Monte Avila, 1985.

Lispector, Clarice. *The Foreign Legion*. New York: New Directions, 1992.

Lockhart, Darrell B. *The Silver Candelabra*. Pittsburgh: Latin American Literary
    Review Press, 1997.

———, ed. *Jewish Writers of Latin America: A Dictionary*. New York: Garland,
    1997.

Patai, Daphne, ed. *In Women's Words*. New Brunswick: Rutgers University
    Press, 1986.

Sheinin, David, and Lois Baer, eds. *The Jewish Diaspora in Latin America: New
    Studies of History and Literature*. New York: Barr & Garland, 1997.

Strepponi, Blanca. *El jardín del verdugo*. Caracas: Monte Avila, 1992.

Summer, Doris. *Foundational Fiction: The National Romance of Latin America*.
    Berkeley: University of California Press, 1991.

Vidal Naquet, Pierre. *Los judíos, la memoria y el presente*. Buenos Aires:
    Fondo de Cultura Económica, 1997.

Wirth Nesher, Hana, ed. *What Is Jewish Literature?* Philadelphia: Jewish
    Publication Society, 1994.

passion, memory, and identity

 # on separate ground

Ilan Stavans

I just spent several weeks reading and rereading novels, stories, and poems by Jewish women from Mexico, and as I make sense of the universe they build collectively one question puzzles me: What makes their message so unorthodox, so moving, so memorable—in short, so unique? This might seem, at first sight, like a superfluous question: Isn't every work of art unique in its own way? Nevertheless, the books piled up in my studio have a texture unlike anything I have read in a long time. Texture is the right word: they have a unique feel to them. As I look at them, one on top of the other, they seem to take the shape of a tower reaching the sky, a tower made of anecdotes where the writer and his entourage become one with their Sephardic ancestry. Obviously, this tower speaks to me dearly; its anecdotes recall an environment about which I know too much perhaps, one I have tried to push away from me to understand it better. But the triumph of these women lies in the way they re-create that environment, not by depicting it with realistic colors, but by fracturing it into pieces, by unearthing its many mysteries. As a reader, I am thankful to them for offering me the key to a handful of undisclosed chambers of the imagination.

For the most part, their counterparts in other corners of the Americas, including the United States and Canada, speak in a very different tone. And even those cases in which women have found a truly singular niche can serve only partially to grasp the contribution of these Mexicans. I am thinking, for instance, of Grace Paley, whose simplicity of style in collections like *Enormous Changes at the Last Minute* leaves the reader overwhelmed with sadness at the solitude her characters are inhabited by; or Clarice Lispector, whose depiction of a complex internal world recalls Virginia Woolf; or Cynthia Ozick, whose meditations on theology and literature in *The Pagan Rabbi* or *The Puttermesser Papers* have a degree of complexity at odds, it seems to me, with all other women writers active in the English language today. These Mexican women, individually and together, share some of these talents, but they deliver a distinct understanding of things. One gets the feeling that they have not embraced gentile society the way Paley and Lispector did, adapting their message to it; nor have they fallen into an easy pattern of complacency, delivering narratives with little personal significance for the sake of sheer entertainment. Their readership is small, but their style has zest: it is exuberant, unconventional; it insinuates itself by talking in a quiet voice.

All of which makes it a pity that only a fraction of their work—and a very small fraction at that—is available in English. For the critic, this is a daunting obstacle: How to describe the beauty they convey in their pages without recurring to easy synopsis and false syllogisms? I feel like the unlucky newspaper correspondent assigned to report from a distant region of Africa: his duty is to explain, in easy, manageable ways, the insider's politics of the place. But how can he succeed if his distant readers do not even know how to pronounce properly the name of the country, let alone have a superficial grasp of what goes on in it? Similarly, I can insinuate how much my reader is missing, and I can try to convey the feeling of enchantment I have experienced; what I cannot do is bring the actual source to him—neither in Spanish nor in Ladino. And so, he must trust me, at least until he himself builds a similar tower in his own studio. The next question to ask, then, is, who are these women? Why is so little known about them outside Mexico? And why have they sprung to life in Mexico, of all places? What have they written that is so singular? By way of an answer, let me offer some context, and I will do so by pointing to tradition as a codifier of literary taste. While Spanish will always resonate with echoes of medieval Jewish prayers and the legacy of Shmuel ha-Nagid, Yehuda Halevi, Saadia Gaon, Maimonides, and Hasdai Crescas, it is not an exaggeration to say that few civilizations abhor essential aspects of themselves as does that which originated in the Iberian Peninsula. Since Jews were expelled from Spain by Isabel La Católica and Ferdinand of Aragón in 1492, Hispanic civilization seems to have been compelled to all but eclipse them forever: they were ridiculed and vilified, even when they were absent; and their impact in science and the humanities was minimized even when such minimization seemed a doomed, irresponsible enterprise in the eyes of its strongest supporters.

It has taken the better part of five centuries for that legacy, the Hebraic remnants in the Hispanic tradition, to come afloat again. It has done so with more enthusiasm on this side of the Atlantic, perhaps because the societies in the Americas know firsthand what its means to be born out of a clash of different world views. In Mexico in particular, Jewish writing has been present, willy-nilly, since New Spain, as the region was known during colonial times, became somewhat of a safe haven for New Christians and, to a lesser extent, for Marranos, conversos, and crypto-Jews. Their existence, it goes without saying, was taciturn and secretive, lived under the shadow of the

Holy Office. Records of denunciations, tortures, incarcerations, and burnings abound in the archives of the Archivo General de la Nación, a portion of which have been studied by scholars like Seymour Liebman in *The Jews in New Spain: Faith, Flames, and the Inquisition*, and by Alfonso Toro in *Los judíos de la Nueva España* and, more memorably, in the long out-of-print *La familia Carvajal*. Any way we conceive of it, the link between Mexicans and Jews was troublesome; and so was their legacy. The literary outpouring of the era still requires exploration, but one thing is sure: little was produced for fear of retaliation; the Inquisition took care of erasing whatever was left, and what is left is mostly legalistic material such as correspondence, promulgations, budgetary notices, and transcriptions of interrogations. The reader must also keep in mind that the very first modern novel written in Spanish in the Americas, Fernández de Lizardi's *Don Catrín de la Fachenda*, did not appear until 1832. This at least partially explains why little by way of Sephardic letters is preserved today, and the echoes that have emerged in the last few decades are a result of the awakening among a small segment of the population to a tradition long forgotten. This awakening is tantalizing: many a Jewish writer in modern Mexico uses characters like Luis de Carvajal and Santa Teresa de Jesús to explore the link between past and present; and medieval and Renaissance motifs are articulated and revamped so as to explain how complex a standing Jews have in Mexico: history runs deep; nothing is as its seems.

By the time the Eastern European Jewish immigration began to set in, the common belief was that Judaism was alien to these lands and that whatever social structure had to be built to make room for it, it had to be done from scratch. In her 1997 book, *Ashkenazi Jews in Mexico*, Adina Cimet has analyzed the development of the modern Jewish community from its foundations at the turn of the century to the present. "The encounter between Mexicans and Jews," Cimet begins, involved many things, including a confrontation with long-standing myths and the clashes of a new reality. The view they had about each other and the context in which they renewed the acquaintance played an important role. Though most of the accounts of immigrant Jews to Mexico highlight the perplexity they felt over the country, the geography, its flora, its folklore, the food, and the strange sound of the language, the confusion deepened because of the newcomers' ignorance of the recent Mexican past and their vague knowledge of an older history of uneasy relations with Jews. Mexicans, having been distanced from Jews for centuries, brought a mixed background to the new acquaintanceship. In addition to strong religious prejudices, Mexicans experienced great difficulty with the idea of and possible intrusion of foreigners—*all* foreigners. Both of these intellectual currents always played a part when judging Jews.

In other words, a doomed encounter, one in which much that is negative has already happened even before the two parties see themselves tête-à-tête. What makes Cimet's study enlightening is not only that it navigates, with patience and accuracy, these troubled waters; it also addresses the cultural politics that served as glue to structure today's community, and thus, indirectly, sets the foundations that would allow the Jewish women writers—Margo Glantz, Angelina Muñíz-Huberman, Esther Seligson, Rosa Nissán, and others—to build their self-contained universe.

Ashkenazi immigration to Mexico began to take place at the end of the nineteenth century, but it reached its height after World War II, owing, in part, to the United States closing its doors in 1924. Thus the arrival of these Eastern European Jews was sometimes fortuitous: Jews had hoped to make it to America but instead were derailed, often waiting for a while in the Caribbean (mostly Cuba and Puerto Rico) until their next stop was clear. Their arrival in Mexico coincides with a radical process of modernization sweeping the nation in the early decades of the century. Textbooks often set the apex of this transformation with the revolution of 1910, a revolt against the dictatorship of Porfirio Díaz. But one would need to be too nearsighted to deny that such modernization actually began with Díaz himself, as he implemented trade with the United States and Europe and sponsored nationwide projects such as the railway system that solidified a sense of coherence in the vast territory. Eastern European Jews began to arrive in Mexico shortly after the fall of Díaz, and it was these Yiddish-speaking Jews who eventually consolidated a community in the nation's capital that would grow to become one of the richest and most solid in the hemisphere. Mexico, it must be said, has never been a paradise for foreigners. A rampant xenophobia and a widespread anti-Semitism, sponsored by the Catholic church as well as by the government, have often worked against the policies of openness the country has repeatedly tried to project. Other national groups— Chinese, Italian, Mormon, Japanese—have settled in its shores, but none has ever assimilated fully to the environment. These groups are ridiculed, harassed, even killed en masse, as in the infamous 1911 incident in the northern city of Torreón, when about three hundred Chinese were massacred. That Ashkenazi Jews have also remained in the margins is thus not an exception but a rule: they have built their lives within an island, Mexicans by language and civil status but Jews by conviction.

The first generation of Eastern European Jews arrived in ports in the states of Veracruz and Yucatán but eventually concentrated in the capital, and to a lesser extent, in Guadalajara and Monterrey. Mexico was interested in keeping them as agents of capitalistic development. Since their own set destination was the United States but immigration quotas were established, in 1921 and up until 1928 it offered them privilege visas so they could wait—first one year, then up to five. But the wait, in many cases, was too long, and so these Jews ended up staying and embracing Mexico as a new home. As soon as the decision to settle was made, their chief task was that of articulating an identity that would alleviate the shock they were exposed to: strangers in an exotic land that suddenly had opened its doors to them, they sought strategies to understand their surroundings and to find a niche where they could grow and prosper. Most of what this generation left behind in literary terms is a record of their arrival. Eventually, though, it produced a couple of Yiddish-speaking male writers, Jacobo Glantz, poet, columnist, bohemian figure, and Margo's father; and Salomón Kahan, a journalist responsible for *Yiddish-Mexikanish,* a 1945 book in which he articulated his vision of Jewish integration without assimilation. Glantz, more than Kahan, served as a bridge between the incipient, undeveloped Yiddish literature in Mexico and that of other regions in the Americas, Europe, and Israel. His friendship with European writers, artists, and politicians, with some of the Yiddish poets belonging to the *Di Yunge* movement in New York, as well as with crucial pioneering figures in Palestine, at least put Mexico on the intellectual map. But neither Glantz nor Kahan—or, for that matter, any other lesser-known writer of the immigrant generation—achieved a wide readership. By virtue of their scope and literary tongue (Yiddish, made useless by the Holocaust and by Zionism), they remained peripheral figures, never reaching beyond their immediate milieu.

This lack of audience is symptomatic not only for the kind of apathy with which Mexican Jews have often embraced their own literati but also as a sign of how different a role these writers have played when compared to their counterparts elsewhere in Latin America, especially in Argentina. Ever since their arrival around 1880, sponsored by the philanthropist Barón Maurice de Hirsch, whose mission it was to turn the Pampas into an alternative Promised Land, Argentine Jews have played an active role in the country's political and cultural development—because of the large number of immigrants, their way of living, and the fact that Argentina, unlike Mexico, is to a large degree an immigrant nation. This role, of course, has not been without its major obstacles, but they have also resisted isolating themselves in a self-sufficient capsule, unlike Mexican Jews. At one point in the mid-1970s, the total Jewish population of Argentina reached a quarter of a million people, almost five times as many as Mexico would ever have. The very first book of literary caliber written by a Jew in Argentina is Alberto Gerchunoff's *The Jewish Gauchos of the Pampas,* and its tone and content announces what was to come: an endorsement of the surroundings as a benign, democratic land. Gerchunoff published his volume in Spanish in 1910, at least a decade before Glantz and Kahan had even arrived in Mexico, let alone switched from the tongue of Sholem Aleichem to that of Cervantes. Expectedly, Gerchunoff as a writer gave birth to many progeny— figures like César Tiempo, Bernardo Verbitzky, Germán Rozenmacher, Alicia Steimberg, Marcos Aguinis, Gerardo Mario Goloboff, and other younger ones, many of whom have enjoyed a large readership, both Jewish and not. Mexican-Jewish letters, in comparison, have been considerably less popular, less involved in national affairs. Their habitat, just like other literatures produced by national minorities, is on the cultural margins and not in the mainstream. It is true that from the 1980s on their audience has grown immensely: their books are brought out by prestigious and well-established houses, with a wide distribution and heavy promotional apparatus; they are discussed nationally in the print media. But with very few exceptions, those books with Jewish themes fare considerably worse than those the same writers produce dealing with more accessible themes.

The first Jewish books by Ashkenazi Jews were not published in Mexico until the 1940s, and it was not until the 1960s that a literature in Spanish began to consolidate itself in the pens of the second generation, one already acclimated to the milieu, less conflicted about linguistic tensions, more conformable in its Mexican self. Ironically, this literary generation is composed mostly of women, led by Margo Glantz (b. 1930), Angelina Muñíz-Huberman (b. 1937), Esther Seligson (b. 1941), Sara Levi-Calderón (b. 1942), and Gloria Gervitz (b. 1943). What these women writers struggled to convey is a universe. Glantz, Muñíz-Huberman, and Seligson are well-established intellectual figures with a much wider readership than their forefathers could ever envision. Why are women in the forefront of this generation? And why have their books acquired such a following? This is the generation that wanted to leave the immigrant mentality aside, to own its place in Mexico, to move from the periphery to a more central spot in national culture. But could it really? What needed to be sacrificed? As it turned out, it was this generation that coincided with a dramatic transformation in the country as a whole and especially in the Jewish community. For one thing, in the 1960s and 1970s the Jewish community became less Ashkenazi and more multiethnic: the size of the Syrian-born Jewish population increased rapidly through immigration and an accelerated birthrate, as did other segments of the Jewish population with roots elsewhere in the Arab world. This generated a tension between religious traditions and even a clash of languages, for Ladino, not Yiddish, was the linguistic stratum of these immigrants. While still predominantly Ashkenazi in number, the overall community ceased to perceive Eastern Europe as its sole place of origin. Simultaneously, Mexico of the 1960s and 1970s, particularly after the student massacre of 1968, gave ample room for women to enter the workforce, which in turn translated into a sense of empowerment. Before this period a number of women writers—for example, Inés Arredondo, Rosario Castellanos—had been active in the national arena, but it was not until the liberating sixties that figures like Elena

Poniatowska and Margo Glantz became fixtures. While machismo still prevailed—could it ever be effaced?—it seemed inconceivable that women would continue to be relegated to domestic affairs. This, after all, was the age of feminism as a revolutionary ideology in Europe and the United States, and Mexico, in its striving for modernity, could not afford to ignore what the main centers of Western civilization were embracing, even if it could only follow at a considerably slower pace. Within the Jewish community, women ceased to play a passive role and began to earn degrees in humanities and in social sciences. They also began to make their feminist voice heard as writers, actresses, columnists, and political analysts.

Enough of context, though. The volumes piled up on my desk vary in length. Some are self-published, while others appeared under the aegis of respected publishing houses: Joaquín Mortiz, Fondo de Cultura Económica, Plaza y Janez, Planeta. They belong mostly to the second generation of Jewish writers in Mexico, the one that turned women's issues into a central theme. Margo Glantz, for one, began her novelistic career with *Las mil y una calorías: Novela dietética* (1978), a domestic novel à la *nouveau roman* made up of puns and quotes. Much of her fiction, up until *Apariciones* (1996), is built as a fractured narrative that uses so-called female artifacts—letters, diaries, journals, postcards, and recipes. In terms of content, the earlier work of Muñíz-Huberman and Seligson moves along similar lines: it uses symbolic figures like Santa Teresa de Jesús, Sor Juana Inés de La Cruz, and the Shekhinah to explore the role women have played in Jewish and Hispanic history and mythology. What is striking about these last two, and to a some extent about Glantz as well, is their ongoing fascination with mysticism. While Mexican society becomes more and more open and cosmopolitan, the artistic direction these women have taken has been in the opposite direction: inward, toward the mysteries and spiritual conundrums of the world. It is as if their voice stands defiant in the chaos of modernity: they will not succumb to the easy rule of mercantilism and, thus, will not adapt their oeuvre to what the reader needs. Instead, they will embrace literature as a tool to explore the recondite, esoteric aspects of reality. By doing so, they delve into a realm approached socially as feminine: the real of the ethereal. In *Huerto cerrado*, a favorite volume among those piled next to me, Muñíz-Huberman explores ancient, medieval, and Renaissance motifs in stories infused by Kabbalah. These stories seem to me like gems: precious, contemplative, unsettling; they remind me of the type of moral tale practiced by Rabbi Nachman of Bratzlav. Her characters are cabalists unearthing the secrets of God, Sor Juana while drafting *First Dream*, unicorns, Greek deities, biblical readers persecuted by the Inquisition, visionaries. The tales have an astonishing, almost mathematical concision: they lose no time in addressing their concerns; and language is pure, crystalline, Borgesian. I know of no other with such optic: numinous, using literature as a tool to penetrate the higher spheres of wisdom. Sephardic symbols abound, as they do in Muñíz-Huberman's outstanding *La lengua florida: Antología sefaradí* (1989) and *Las raíces y las ramas: Fuentes y derivaciones de la Cábala hispanohebrea* (1993), two volumes offering a rich sample of Hebraic poetry, liturgy, and prose from Sepharad by luminaries like Shmuel ibn Nagrella, Moshe ibn Ezra, Shlomo ibn Gabirol, Maimonides, and Shem-Tov de Carrión. Muñíz-Huberman, born into an agnostic family, came to her Jewishness by way of secrecy, when she received candelabras and other paraphernalia from her mother. This led her to trace her ancestry to the pre-1492 Iberian Peninsula (she was born in France, the child of refugees of the Spanish Civil War, and immigrated to Mexico at the age of six), and she eventually converted to Judaism formally, as a means to reclaim this ancestry. Of Ashkenazi background, Seligson has built her work around similar lines: her novels parade a disdain for plot and sequence; instead they are meditations on transhistorical themes, and one in particular, *La morada en el tiempo* (1981), is a lyrical attempt at rewriting the Bible. This disinterest in realism is, in all honesty, her defining quality and stands in sharp contrast to the autobiographical work both Glantz and Muñíz-Huberman have done. And it is in this genre where the reader gets a sharper, more focused view of the travails these three women have embarked on. In *Genealogías* (1981; English trans. 1991), Glantz delivers a portrait of her Ukrainian father, of the Socialist ideology he and other immigrants professed, and of their slow integration to Mexico. Likewise, Muñíz-Huberman, in *De cuerpo entero* (1991), describes her odyssey as the daughter of Spanish immigrants and her early apprenticeship in Mexican schools.

The work of several other women of this second generation—especially Gloria Gervitz, responsible for books of poetry like *Shajarit* (1979), *Fragmento de ventana* (1986), and *Yiskor* (1987)—seeks also to be abstract, intangible, concerned not with the material world but with illusions—or better, with the chambers of memory. But it would be a falsification to suggest that spirituality is the trademark of all of them; a handful have a more realistic, down-to-earth approach to the world, and, expectedly, those that do have had an easier time reaching a wider audience. In the case of Sara Levi-Calderón (aka Silvia Feldman), visibility and notoriety go hand in hand. A classmate of Seligson in Yiddish day school, Levi-Calderón is well known for her autobiographical novel, *Las dos mujeres* (1990; English trans. 1991), a case study of lesbianism in the Jewish community that was controversial when it was first published, to a large extent because the author's father, a wealthy entrepreneur, bought out the whole first edition so as to protect the family from shame. This, obviously, quickly turned it not only into a cause célèbre but a best-seller as well. Written in plain, uninspired prose, the novel denounces patriarchal authority and its condemnation of homosexual love. It is valuable as a kaleidoscope of the type of hierarchical rule that guides Mexican Jews. A more inspired and endearing voice is that of Rosa Nissán (b. 1936), whose first novel, *Novia que te vea* (1992), was turned into an endearing film directed by Guita Shyfter. This realistic narrative chronicles the life of two young Jewish women in Mexico during the 1960s: one of Syrian descent, the other of Ashkenazi ancestry. The ethnic rivalries at the heart of the Jewish community are thus examined, as are the linguistic and intellectual challenges each group faces along the way. Nissán includes whole pages of dialogue in Ladino, the first time as far as I know where the Sephardic tongue becomes an essential part of a Mexican-Jewish novel. And along similar lines is Nissán's second novel, *Hishó que te nazca* (1996), a continuation of sorts of her first novel in which the Sephardic-Mexican protagonist, Oshinica, realizes the patriarchal patterns of behavior that surround her as she undergoes marriage and motherhood.

The literary tradition continues to flourish. A third generation of writers has already made its mark, again mostly women, real or figurative pupils of Glantz, Muñíz-Huberman, and Seligson: Sarah Sefchovich (b. 1943), Barbara Jacobs (b. 1947), Sabina Berman (b. 1954), Ethel Krauze (b. 1954), and Miriam Moscona (b. 1955). Sefchovich, an editor, journalist, and literary critic of national stature, is the bestselling author of the exotic, magical novels *Demasiado amor* (1990) and *La señora de los sueños* (1993), in which romance and dreams, recipes and an encyclopedic compendium of spices and condiments are displayed. Jacobs, of Lebanese Maronite descent and the wife of Augusto Monterroso, wrote about her transcultural and polyglot upbringing in *Las hojas muertas* (The Dead Leaves). Berman, mostly known as a playwright, is responsible for an impressionistic novel, *La bobe* (1990; English trans. 1997), which, like the work of Nissán and Levi-Calderón, chronicles the changes in the Jewish community from the first to the third generation; and she is also responsible for plays like *Herejía* (1991), which chronicles the plight of Luis de Carvajal in his persecution by the Holy Inquisition. Krauze, a novelist, published *Entre la cruz y la estrella* (1990), an autobiographical volume describing the path followed by her family from the Ukraine to Mexico and the many languages and traditions they assimilated; this subject has also been explored in some of Krauze's stories, such as "Niñas de cuento" and "Isaías VII." And Moscona is the author of *El árbol de los nombres* (1992), a volume of erotic poetry, again with a mystical side, in which Jewish motifs are openly displayed.

It is not unfitting, too, to mention a pair of volumes on my pile that are not quite part of this last group, the third literary generation, but share with it an enormous deal. They were written by Alcina Lubitch-Domecq (b. 1953), a Guatemala-born Jewish writer whose *aliyah* relocated her altogether in a different tradition—or perhaps, simply left her as an in-between, a writer without context. In 1983 her novel *El espejo en el espejo: o, La noble sonrisa del perro* appeared under the aegis of Joaquín Mortiz in Mexico, and five years later, the same publishing house brought out her collection of stories, *Intoxicada*. The daughter of an Auschwitz survivor and a gentile Iberian mother, Lubitch-Domecq lived in Mexico in the 1960s and early 1970s, after her parents divorced. Of all the writers I have been reading, she is the one to whom not only the Kabbalah but also the Yiddish literary tradition of Mendele Mokher Sforim, Sholem Aleichem, and Isaac Leib Peretz speaks the loudest. In an autobiographical essay, Lubitch-Domecq talks of reading Gershom Scholem and becoming infatuated with the Zohar, teaching herself to read Hebrew, and finally, for a brief period in her adult years, becoming an ascetic, part of a group of mystics in Jerusalem's Old City. She also describes learning Yiddish to make sense of her father's correspondence after his death in an insane asylum, and then how a passing reference to Mendele Mokher Sforim convinced her that Mendele's soul, like a dybbuk, had transmigrated to her body at her birth in a mutation known to Jewish mystics as *gilgul*. Lubitch-Domecq's stories are minimalist visions of hell. Unlike Muñíz-Huberman, her universe is modern in the cruelest sense of the word: obtuse, chaotic, agonizing. Her characters are constantly undergoing physical and spiritual transformations; they find themselves turned into whales and wolves, trapped in bottles, overwhelmed by a desire to sin—to loot, to attack, to rape, to kill. At the core of her view is the question of belonging: Where do I fit in as a Jew? she seems to constantly ask. Who am I? What is the metabolism of my Jewish body? And why am I so driven to amoral behavior?

It goes without saying that not all the books piled next to me stand equally on their own: some pay less attention to detail than others; a few seem unfinished, unbounded. The cumulative effect is startling though; it makes me think of the oil paintings of Leonora Carrington, one in which the weaver is the theme of her own quilts. What unifies them all is their feminine tone: they speak the language of intimacy. Their mystical trail, their unique texture, their exuberance, their verve is, in my view, result of the unspoken legacy of esoterism that runs deep throughout Mexican history. They deliver side-stepped vistas of a world apart, a universe one is not likely to stumble into by reading mainstream books destined for export.

I said before that not having them in translation is a pity. But knowing they have not yet reached a wide audience also makes me feel privileged: these books are, for the time being, a collector's item, a clandestine pleasure, a spectacle to be enjoyed away from the hordes. It isn't that their authors are silent; they simply deliver their message in murmurs—with undenied conviction, but whimpering it into one's ear. In this they illuminate an aspect of Jewish letters often forgotten: its exclusive quality. For if Jews in the Diaspora are by definition a minority group, their literary legacy should also be a minority affair. This, it is clear, makes these women overconscious of themselves: their religion, costumes, and dream life become their main concern. That they are members of a minority within a minority accentuates this condition even more: they write, as Isaac Rosenfeld once put it, from and about alienation. Should the Jewish writer occupy a prominent, central role in mainstream culture? Sure, but by nature she is best suited for the periphery, a subversive force, a nonconformist. And it is from the periphery where her whispers are heard the loudest. Simply having these books at my side makes me feel confident about one of the main purposes of literature: to insinuate aspects of life gone unnoticed.

mapping the jewish female voice in contemporary mexican narrative

Magdalena Maíz-Peña
Translation by Wendy G. Dunn

The act of reading a Mexican-Jewish or Jewish-Mexican text invokes a fascinating and complex interplay of cultural and ideological realities, intertextuality, and frames of reference that transcend concepts of ethnicity, history, state, or nation. Contemporary Spanish-American and Mexican literary discourses identify multiple and changing identities as a crucial facet of our actual experience: within this domain, such signicly textured Jewish-Mexican literature expresses the uniqueness of a particular sociohistorical and cultural experience, engendering an alternate discourse amid the fissures of the dominant culture.

The Jewish presence and voice in Mexican literature is not a recent phenomenon. The Jewish-Mexican writer Angelina Muñíz-Huberman states that "the history of Judeo-Mexican literature is still being made" ("De las tinieblas" 34), though such fundamental works as the ten-volume edition of the *Jewish-Castilian Encyclopedia* (Enciclopedia Judaica Castellana), edited in 1948 by Eduardo Weinfeld and

Isaac Babani, enabled further generations to transcend circumscribed community boundaries and to meld with the prevalent Mexican cultural discourse.[1]

As the quality and the quantity of the work merited increasing interest, the systematic identification of this Mexican-Jewish corpus as a unique mode of literary expression became a critical task in its own right during the last two decades. Muñíz-Huberman observes the critical role of female Jewish-Mexican writers who explore modernity and women's issues through the portrayal of family relationships, eroticism, the body, mysticism, and spirituality while conveying Jewishness in terms of identity conflict. In this textual space, the narrative becomes a means of affirmation, negotiation, and mediation of dual cultural and national identities and a source of critical reflection on one's heritage, as characters assume their own voice through memory and passion. The crystallization and consolidation of this textual production's significance becomes evident in readings of Margo Glantz's *Genealogías* (1981); Esther Seligson's *La morada en el tiempo* (1981); Angelina Muñíz-Huberman's *Morada interior* (1972), *Tierra adentro* (1977), *La guerra del unicornio* (1983), *Huerto cerrado, huerto sellado* (1985), and *Castillos en la tierra* (1995); Rosa Nissán's *Novia que te vea* (1992), *Hisho que te nazca* (1996), and *Las tierras prometidas: Crónicas de Israel* (1997); and Sabina Berman's drama *Herejía* (1983) and her first fictional work, *La bobe* (1990). Through their aesthetic encoding of individual experiences, Jewish-Mexican writers such as Gloria Gervitz, Miriam Moscona, Perla Schwartz, Nedda G. De Anhalt, Ethel Krauze, and others trace a unique cartography within the textual territory—positively or negatively called national culture—in which they exist and coexist in perpetual dialogue with the dominant cultural discourse through their works of poetry, essay, fiction, and hybrid genres.

The production as well as the reception of Jewish-Mexican literary expression seems to arise from tangential and oblique conditions that mobilized and shifted these voices to the center of multicultural national discourse in response to a yearning for an alternate, pluralistic national expression. Their presence joins contemporary debates about postmodernism, the cultural impact of technology and globalization, the civil movement toward critical reflection and national self-examination, and the disintegration of monological, authoritarian discourse.[2]

Nation as narration, as Homi K. Bhaba states, submits itself to the reader as a symbolic system of cultural signifiers representing and reflecting social life, creating a public interest from a private domain (122). Portraying the Nation as a culturally symbolic composite of times and spaces entails inclusion, exclusion, and legitimization: the narration of a singular Mexican-Jewish experience transforms one individual's story into a multifaceted cultural history of the Jewish Nation. Such pluralistic narrative establishes points of contact with Mexican cultural reality, affirming itself as distinct while forming an integral strand of the national fabric, thus "encoding the Jewish subject into History" (Friedman, *Theory in the Margin* 23).

The textually crafted mosaic of Mexican-Jewish experience engulfs and immerses even the unversed reader in a multiplicity of cultural, social, religious, sexual, and political ideologemes encoded in the works, thus granting access even to the culturally uninitiated. Critical consideration of the narrative markers that produce and articulate Mexican-Jewish literary discourse induces the reader to identify layers of meaning that map different zones of access to the Jewish-Mexican reality portrayed in each of the literary works. This cultural discourse coaxes the reader into an interpretive zone of access to the articulated reality, according to the degree of knowledge or empathy he or she possesses.

This existential texture mediates discourse about identity and difference, about the discovery and recognition of oneself in the Other and the invocation of the present and the past in individual and collective historical memory. The narratives encode sociocultural and ideological themes such as assimilation, resistance, integration, isolation, or affirmation using symbols, motifs, and textual markers that allude to loss, exile, survival, and the search for beginnings and for one's roots.

The experimental and innovative fictional autobiographies and pseudomemories I will discuss here—Sabina Berman's *La bobe*, Rosa Nissán's *Novia que te vea,* and Angelina Muñíz-Huberman's *Castillos en la tierra*—enter into a dialogue with and contest the dominant Mexican imaginary while enriching Spanish-American cultural and literary production. These three works by Jewish-Mexican women writers of the 1990s produce singular creative discourses shaped by their individual experiences, their concrete realities, their positions within the literary-cultural panorama, their hyphenated Mexican-Jewish identities, and their roles as bridgers of two cultures.[3]

Criticism of this body of works plunges the reader into unexplored and uncharted territories, into the realms of identity and difference, unity and diversity, inclusion and Otherness. The discourse about identity and memory materializes in the individual stories narrated by a female character between childhood and maturity who involuntarily recounts a parallel narrative, a story within another story. These hidden accounts recall Jewish history either through the fabulation of the character's own narrative or through other characters' stories: timeless mirrors of mirrors—some indiscreet mirrors—about identity and memory.

I would like to focus on the "narrated" and "textualized" child or adolescent in each work, on the female subject who delineates zones of access to her Jewish reality and invites the reader to decode textual markers as she recounts her life from a unique perspective by retelling stories that evoke her past and the construction of her identity. This female character reveals herself through the voice and vision of a child/adolescent, and this youthful perspective maps and filters her emotional, social, cultural, religious, psychological, and political topography. The child/adolescent assigns names, spaces, locations, and time according to her unique vision in order to be able to comprehend and convey the underlying significance of "her" story.

In *La bobe*, Berman recounts the story of Sabinita (*la que sabe*, the one who knows), an inquisitive and audacious girl initiated into the mysteries of knowledge and awareness via her grandmother. The loss of *la bobe* and the desire to understand her legacy allow Sabinita to transform the mundane into a sacred realm. Sabinita's narrative threads together moments of her own childhood with moments of her mother's and grandmother's lives. In her desire and determination to make *la bobe* live within herself, Sabinita pictures her grandmother embracing death, opening up her testimonial to a multiplicity of stories as she remembers:

> My *bobe* died neatly. My grandmother died in the neatest possible way. I think that she died of an excess of neatness. I do not know; it is something I thought about when I was younger, and I still remember. Anyway, it is better to say that she died of a stroke. Nobody dies because of that: strokes are the culmination of a continuous deterioration. . . . I can imagine my grandma at the moment of her death. She lies in the bathtub, resting, smaller than the long bathtub, she is thinking . . . (My translation 9–10)

In *Castillos en la tierra*, Angelina Muñíz-Huberman recounts the incomplete and fragmented story of the encounters of Alberina, a six-year-old girl newly arrived in Mexico City, dancing with her incredible imagination, loneliness, and nightmares. Alberina uses her marvelous imagination to fight death and the pain of separation, to resist nonsensical reality, to survive the craziness of war and exile. This sturdy and powerful girl bears the burden of traumatic memories, punctuated by nightmares, fears, and an effusive imagination, of her dead brother and parents killed by the Nazis. The omniscient narrator filters the little girl's impressions on a rainy afternoon in Mexico City, March 1942:

> There are some stories that begin in a hotel. The earliest memory does not begin at the moment one departs or leaves home, but at the arrival, at the beginning. A big door made of solid wood. Clean windows. Doormen with uniforms. Solid, dark, heavy furniture smelling of use.
>
> But if the story begins in a hotel maybe it has something to do with a new place which one enters from the outside to the inside. A place of the unknown, and of the different or the unfamiliar. A place that does not impose rules to follow. A place that signifies freedom. No schedule. A magical place. . . . (My translation 9)

Rosa Nissán articulates the life script of a seven-year-old middle-class girl becoming a teenager among five brothers, a father working in La Lagunilla, and a very intelligent mother in modern Mexico during the fifties. In *Novia que te vea*, Oshinica shares her memories about how she came to realize who she was, what she wanted to become and not to become. Translating and redefining tradition, she clearly questions her familiar world and the surrounding Mexican milieu. Oshinica says at the beginning of her story:

> *2nd grade*
> Every night I kneel down next to the window, I see a star directly that might be my guardian angel, I say the Holy Father and the *Ave Maria*. Although I am the daughter of a Jewish couple, I hope one angel will follow me all day as happens to my classmates. Today I ask that I do

not change schools; they want me to go to a Jewish school. Where are they all coming from? Please God, do something so that I can stay in the Guadalupe Tepeyac School forever, do not let me go no matter what, and especially now that I am ready to go to third grade, the hardest one in elementary school. Only with your help will I be able to make it. I promise I will do whatever you want, I will follow the Ten Commandments, I will go to catechism on Saturdays, and the day I die, I will be the angel of whomever you decide. In the name of the Father, of the Son, and of the Holy Spirit, Amen. (My translation 9)

Sabinita, Alberina, and Oshinica tell their own stories, infused with nostalgia, confusion, *naïveté*, loss, and longings, confronting the past as they narrate the construction of their own identities and struggle to be who they are today. These female voices, child and adolescent, probe phantasmagoric worlds, the imaginary realms in which they live, or which they create to survive or to make sense of who they are, and where they are coming from. Sabinita says:

One afternoon I asked grandma how the war had been. She went to the kitchen to check the chicken soup, and I followed her. Tell me what it feels like to be in a war. She went to the balcony to water the plants. . . .

I am going to flunk because of you, I said. You only tell me things in passing, as if you did not want to tell me those things, and you tell me those stories without emotion, besides the fact that I know that you hide. . . . How do you say it. . . . You hide that that. . . .

I closed my fists. Grandma looked at me.

Tell me something about your escape from Russia, I said.

Grandma went to the bedroom to get a sheet from the closet, I went after her. At last, she sat down on the bed.

All right, she said. I am going to tell you something about the most exciting part of the trip. . . .

My mind was full of black uniforms from the SS, gray uniforms, Soviet soldiers, bombs falling down on one side of the train and the other, in the snow all smeared with red blood, fragments of bodies all over the red snow. Images from books, from the movie we were shown every month in school entitled *The Holocaust*, from magazines. . . .

Grandma's eyes were closed. She opened them with her first words. We are on the train, she says slowly, as if each word were a major effort. Your mom next to me, I next to the window. Your grandpa in front of me, asleep. Next to him, asleep as well, your uncle. . . . (My translation 40–43)

These narratives summon affirmations, contradictions, and doubts embodied in layers of a personal, cultural, and national memory made of echoes of experience. The proud silence of *la bobe* who refused to cause more pain for her youngsters while fleeing from *nazismo* in Poland, Alberina's loving brother and parents, perhaps killed by the Nazis, and Oshinica's recognition of the limitations of her own tradition, all generate additional narratives that spring from the main plots. New narratives surface as each of the stories is divided, fragmented, told and retold, invented, or remembered.

These hidden inventories, these unanticipated stories, these unforeseen threads of personal accounts make Sabinita's, Alberina's, and Oshinica's chronicles a macrodiscourse about the Other. Memory becomes the textual impulse that reveals circumstances, contexts, and individual and collective variables, making the identity issue the foundation of these multidimensional, collective, and genealogical

stories. "Who was *la bobe?*" asks Sabinita, or "Who am I?" asks Alberina at the end of her narrative:

> "Yes: I am."
> "I am. And I am I, and the Others." All the possible
> and feasible Alberinas. The ones that remained in Spain,
> the ones that came to Mexico. The ones that lived in
> Caimito del Guayabal. The ones that lived in the Hotel
> Gillow. The ones that lived in Tamaulipas 185. The ones
> that will live in. . . . "I am all these versions of. . . . " (My
> translation 220)

The narrative structure, tone, and viewpoint from which each of
the characters chooses to tell her own story fulfill a unique creative
end: self-affirming fictional autobiography (*La bobe*), journal of self-
discovery (*Novia que te vea*), and pseudomemories and personal ex-
orcism (*Castillos en la tierra*). In each of these texts, memory enables
the characters to shape their own identities. Sabinita recalls her special moments with *la bobe* to keep her alive within herself. Alberina
converts her tragic, ghost-haunted existence into a magical haven,
and Oshinica unites two cultural and national realities into one as
she opens herself to experience both cultural universes. In each text,
the conjunction of an adult memory with the filter of a youthful gaze
forms a textual dynamic that enriches and clarifies the revisited past.

The unadulterated, uncritical voice of the child/adolescent per-
mits a candid reevaluation of the past, free of irony; the adult envi-
sions, revises, and re-creates fragments of her life by giving free rein
to the unbridled vision of the child. As Naomi B. Sokoloff states, child
discourse, "with its peculiarly fictive voice and its acts of literary ven-
triloquism, becomes an apt forum for inventing and sounding new
self-conceptions and for bringing those ideas into dialogue with Jewish traditions and historical transformations" (40).

In a series of vignettes, Sabinita appropriates her own story as she recounts episodes with her grandmother from the perspective of an astute, spirited girl. Her account, framed by the Jewish Holocaust and the Mexican massacre of 1968, gives voice to the stories of her grandparents, her mother and uncle and other family friends. Through her reading of others' stories, Sabinita affirms and enriches her own.

Whereas Sabinita uses the narratives of her family and friends as a mode of awareness, Alberina's naive gaze constructs reality by grappling with the spaces of her new house, city, country, and culture. Through an omniscient narrator, Alberina observes, invents, and re-creates a homeland for herself within the confines of the new nation. In thirty chapters, Alberina documents her strength and survival amid the disorienting echoes of the Spanish Civil War, the Second World War, the flight from nazismo, and her transatlantic trip, ordering her present through voyages into the dreamscape of her past.

Oshinica's vision impels her to forge aspects of both the Jewish and the Mexican cultures into a singular one she may call her own. She chooses and redefines components of each without fear or distance, coming to terms with the values and meaning of both tradition and change. She explores the world that Mexican and Jewish cultures coinhabit, interacting with her own community and exploring her own reality through the choir, the synagogue, the Jewish and Catholic schools, the Zionist youth group, The Universidad Femenina, as well as through the Bas Mitzvah, Purim, and her own wedding at the end of her story as she becomes the bride she was destined to be, yet without surrendering her dreams of furthering her education.

Each of these stories elicits a conscious rendering of the signic texture as well as the modus operandi of the narratives. The reading of each text implies a mapping of the discursive structure, narrative techniques, and shifting positionality of the female character and the narrator in order to grasp the manner in which writing and experience become analogous. *Castillos en la tierra* further displays a theory

about memory that deconstructs the textual dynamics of each intimate chronicle:

> The thread of memory breaks, becomes entangled. Frag-
> ile or invented. It disentangles itself without regard for
> time.
>   Many, many years afterwards, Alberina confuses and
> mixes her own memories. She wants to build a bridge be-
> tween two ridges: yesterday and today. She wants to un-
> derstand. She wants to envelop all. Which is impossible.
>   Memory ignores any measurement. Memories negate
> each other and take on lives of their own without any
> logical order. Without any spatial order. They cannot be
> invoked. They are unforeseen. They become an accumu-
> lation of dreams. . . .
>   That which makes Alberina feel secure at any age and
> assures her that she is alive, are those brilliant images
> shining from the mist. Those impressions. Those revela-
> tions. . . . (My translation 17)

Each work immerses the reader in a textual space intersecting languages, traditions, mythologies, and nations as it encodes an implied
story of the Jewish imaginary and Diaspora. In *Novia que te vea*, the
female narrator transcribes a letter concerning the Jewish communities in Mexico, sent by the *shelíaj* (a person who encourages emigration to Israel) recently arrived from Israel:

> I have noticed that there are significant differences be-
> tween the three Jewish communities in Mexico, which is
> a pity. It is almost natural that this exists, because your
> parents were raised in different parts of the world, and
> when they arrived, they wanted to continue their way of

living, of eating, of marrying, of educating their kids, and burying their dead. Each one believes that their customs are the best.

But the next generations, their children might have been born in Mexico, they might have spoken Spanish, they might have lived the same experience in the new country, they might have gone to the Deportivo Israelita, they might have shared the same story and the same past. Differences will tend to dissolve. . . .

The Russian language is not less valuable than the sweetness of Arabic, neither is Indian music better than Turkish. They are different. Let's think about the word *different*.

We hear each of our relatives talk about their place of origin as if there were no better place in the world. They keep memories that create intimate bonds with the countries where they were born, they will never stop loving their own countries with melancholy. . . . (My translation 75–76)

The reading, interpretation, and encoding of each personal narrative, rather than provide answers, poses a multiplicity of questions concerning the model of representation, the construction and articulation of cultural identity, and the cultural reading process.

The signic textures forged in these three Jewish-Mexican narratives by linguistic, spatial, temporal, and cultural markers sketch blueprints granting even the uninitiated (non-Jewish-Mexican) reader access to the Jewish imaginary. Such schemata invite the reader to venture beyond stereotypes, to map the singular reality fabricated in each work, to approach the topography of references to the Yiddish language, synagogues, sacred texts, the Jewish calendar, rites of initiation, generational differences, the collective sense of loss, persecution, and survival, and the genealogical transmittal of knowledge, among others. The texts record the cultural history of the Jewish Nation, recording in distinct ways the fundamental belief that each individual is part of a cultural continuum—of knowledge, traditions, beliefs, customs, and rituals—extending far beyond mere blood ties.

Narrative voice and gaze coalesce in Sabina Berman's *La bobe*, Rosa Nissán's *Novia que te vea*, and Angelina Muñíz-Huberman's *Castillos en la tierra* to open a critical space that expands the limits of representation of the Jewish-Mexican female subject. In these textual realms, the conjunction of the mature narrative voice with the filter of a youthful viewpoint frames a critical aperture: the voice and gaze of the child/adolescent in each work resists absorption, translation, or appropriation by adults. In this space in between, through the forked voice spanning childhood and maturity, through the lens of bifocal perception, questions supersede answers and the past revisited becomes an affirmation of the characters' Jewish-Mexican identities.

Within the mobile and open contexts of these works, a parallel narrative emerges from the margins of the primary chronicle. The singular personal narratives of Jewish-Mexican females engender an alternate discourse, a macrohistory of the Jewish Nation. These writers mold a culture within another culture and are capable of articulating their realities from "both shores of the border at once" because, as Diana Tey Rebolledo claims:

> Writing after all, is naming, mapping, and leading as well as creating. It forms an explanation of the meaning of experience; it can order chaos, introduce reason into ambiguity, re-create loss, call up the past, and create new modes and traditions. In sum, it orders existence and invents new worlds. It can denounce injustice and prejudice and may function as a focus of a shared experience. (105)[4]

Angelina Muñíz-Huberman, Sabina Berman, and Rosa Nissán place the reader, and their own female characters, in those zones of access that unite cultures and communities. Their history of Histories beckons toward new forms of knowledge and shared worlds of experiences, shattering ideological assumptions and spanning pluralistic cultural frontiers as they invite the reader to know the Other, to appropriate and to share unfamiliar experiences.

Rather than make the unversed reader feel alienated or distanced from the inscribed reality, through the production of zones of access, these three narratives urge the reader to explore, to participate and feel at home in the Other. These zones of access permit multiple readings of the same narratives and coax the reader to the crossroads where fiction and documentary as well as Jewish and Mexican cultures merge, fusing the personal history of each character with narratives of the Jewish Diaspora.

NOTES

1. In her essay "De las tinieblas a la luz," the neomystical vein of literature that begins with her *Morada interior* (1972), continues in her *Tierra adentro* (1977), and is furthered by *La morada en el tiempo* (1981) by Esther Seligson, the Jewish-Mexican writer also comments on the importance of the Holocaust, Sephardic culture, and the Kabbalah.

2. In contrast to the considerably vast and consolidated body of Jewish-Argentine criticism, this mode of contemporary Mexican literature first garnered critical attention in the 1980s. Some of the most fundamental Jewish-Argentine criticism includes Naomi Lindstrom, *Jewish Issues in Argentine Literature* (Columbia: U of Missouri P, 1989); Leonardo Senkman, *La identidad judía en la literatura argentina* (Buenos Aires: Editorial Pardes, 1983); Ricardo Feierstein, ed., *Pluralismo e identidad: Lo judío en la literatura latinoamericana* (Buenos Aires: Milá, 1986); and David Sheinin and Lois Baer Barr, eds., *The Jewish Diaspora in Latin America: New Studies on History and Literature* (New York: Garland, 1996).

3. Sabina Berman, *La bobe* (México: Grijalbo, 1990); Rosa Nissán, *Novia que te vea* (México: Editorial Planeta Mexicana, 1992); and Angelina Muñíz-Huberman, *Castillos en la tierra: Seudomemorias* (México: Ediciones del Equilibrista, Consejo Nacional para la Cultura y las Artes, 1995). It is interesting to

note how each of these voices defines itself and places itself in Jewish-Mexican culture. Sabina Berman engages in a dialogue with the national culture:

> Each person is a unique hybrid, not reproducible, of her or his circumstances. . . . To be a Jew has meant, historically, having a sharpened consciousness of partaking of at least two destinies. I am Mexican and I am Jewish, and I am Jewish-Mexican and Mexican-Jewish. I am Mexican by decision and following many years of studying what it is to be Mexican, I am also Jewish by choice and faith. (Glickman and DiAntonio, "The Authors Speak" 13)

Other writers define this unique narrative form through the concept of *mestissage,* or mestizo culture, the consciousness of a dual citizenship, the unique ways of living and thinking. Esther Seligson defines her writing as the crossing of spatial-temporal realities where Mexican and Jewish cultures intersect: "my writing today, springs from a double source—temporal in its Judaism, spatial in Mexican culture . . . " (Glickman and DiAntonio, "The Authors Speak" 30). Margo Glantz, in *Genealogías,* emphasizes individual and collective memory, the acts of forgetting and not forgetting, revealing or hiding stories and family secrets, and being able to tell a personal story at the same time that one formulates or fabulates other stories.

4. "both shores of the border at once" is Gloria Anzaldúa's phrase as quoted by Rebolledo (128). Rebolledo places Chicano literature by female writers within these same parameters and describes it as a form of acquiring knowledge and appropriating a new voice (117).

REFERENCES

Benstock, Sheri. *The Private Self: Theory and Practice of Women's Autobiographical Writings.* Chapel Hill: University of North Carolina Press, 1988.

Berman, Sabina. *La bobe.* México: Grijalbo, 1990.

———. *Teatro de Sabina Berman.* México: Editores Mexicanos Unidos, 1985.

Bhabha, Homi K. *Nation and Narration.* London: Routledge, 1990.

Bokser de Liwerant, Judith, et al. *Imágenes de un encuentro: La presencia judía en México durante la primera mitad del siglo XX.* México: Universidad Nacional Autónoma de México-Tribuna Israelita, 1992.

Cypess, Sandra. "Ethnic Identity in the Plays of Sabina Berman." Glickman and DiAntonio, *Tradition* 165–77.

De Lauretis, Teresa, ed. *Technology of Gender: Essays on Theory, Form and Fiction.* Bloomington: Indiana University Press, 1987.

Feierstein, Ricardo. *Pluralismo e identidad: Lo judío en la literatura latinoamericana*. Buenos Aires: Milá, 1986.

Friedman, Edward H. "Angelina Muñíz' *Tierra adentro*: (Re)creating the Subject." Glickman and DiAntonio, *Tradition* 179–92.

———."Theory in the Margin: Latin American Literature and the Jewish Subject." Sheinin and Barr 21–31.

Gilmore, Leigh. *Autobiographics: A Feminist Theory of Women's Self-Representation*. Ithaca: Cornell University Press, 1994.

Glantz, Margo. *Genealogías*. México: Martin Casilla Editores, 1981.

Glickman, Nora, and Robert DiAntonio, eds. *Tradition and Innovation: Reflections on Latin American Jewish Writing*. Albany: State University of New York Press, 1993.

———. "The Authors Speak for Themselves." Glickman and DiAntonio, *Tradition* 9–31.

Lionnet, Françoise. *Autobiographical Voices: Race, Gender, Self-Portraiture*. Ithaca: Cornell University Press, 1984.

Mason, Mary. "The Other Voice: Autobiographies of Women Writers." *Autobiography: Essays Theoretical and Critical*. Ed. James Olney. Princeton: Princeton University Press, 1980. 207–35.

Muñíz-Huberman, Angelina. *Castillos en la tierra: Seudomemorias*. México: Ediciones del Equilibrista, Consejo Nacional para la Cultura y las Artes, 1995.

———."De las tinieblas a la luz. La historia de la literatura judeomexicana." *La jornada semanal* 285 (November 27, 1994): 32–35.

———. *La guerra del Unicornio*. México: Artífice, 1983.

———. *Morada interior*. México: Joaquín Mortiz, 1972.

———. *Tierra adentro*. México: Joaquín Mortiz, 1977.

Neuman, Shirley, ed. *Autobiography and Questions of Gender*. London: Frank Cass, 1991.

Nissán, Rosa. *Hisho que te nazca*. México: Plaza y Janés Editores, 1996.

———. *Novia que te vea*. México: Editorial Planeta Mexicana, 1992.

———. *Las tierras prometidas: Crónicas de Israel*. México: Plaza y Janés Editores, 1997.

Rebolledo, Diana Tey. *Women Singing in the Snow: A Cultural Analysis of Chicana Literature*. Tucson: University of Arizona Press, 1995.

Seligson, Esther. *La morada en el tiempo*. México: Artífice, 1981.

Senkman, Leonardo. *La identidad judía en la literatura argentina*. Buenos Aires: Editorial Pardes, 1983.

Sheinin, David, and Lois Baer Barr, eds. *The Jewish Diaspora in Latin America: New Studies on History and Literature*. New York: Garland, 1996.

Smith, Sidonie. *A Poetics of Women's Autobiography: Marginality and the Fictions of Self-Representation*. Bloomington: Indiana University Press, 1987.

Sokoloff, Naomi B. *Imagining the Child in Modern Jewish Fiction*. Baltimore: Johns Hopkins University Press, 1992.

Sprinker, Michael. "Fictions of the Self: The End of Autobiography." *Autobiography: Essays Theoretical and Critical*. Ed. James Olney. Princeton: Princeton University Press, 1980. 321–42.

Stanton, Domna, ed. "Autogynography: Is the Subject Different?" *The Female Autograph: Theory and Practice of Autobiography from the Tenth to the Twentieth Century*. Chicago: University of Chicago Press, 1987.

Zárate Miguel, Guadalupe. *México y la diáspora judía*. México: Secretaría de Educación Pública, Instituto Nacional de Antropología e Historia, 1986.

recent argentine women writers of jewish descent

David William Foster

Given that Argentina's Jewish community is the largest in Latin America, and one of the largest in the world, and that women have come to play a very prominent role in Argentine cultural production, it is no surprise that women writers of Jewish descent figure prominently in any accurate inventory of Argentine literature.[1] Yet the masculinist bias of male historians has tended to result in women writers and women cultural producers being overlooked. Weisbrot's history of Jews in Argentina barely mentions women, except for the infamous story of Jewish white slavery in the early twentieth century. M. Zago Ediciones' picture book on Jews in Argentina includes few Jewish women as independent social subjects: typically, women only appear in pictures as wives and mothers. Feierstein's excellent survey of Jews in Argentine social life includes an appendix on Argentine–Jewish writers in Yiddish and another on writers in Spanish, and the latter does include a good representation of women authors (it is based on

Alperson, Faigón, and Weil's bibliographic work). Not surprisingly, given social customs of the period in which Yiddish figured prominently, Feierstein's appendix includes only a scattering of women. But yet the rather scant narrative section of his book devoted to literature has only the meagerest recognition for women writers (women, it must be said in all fairness, do appear with greater prominence in the section devoted to acting and other performing arts).

While I cannot offer here a thorough survey of Argentine-Jewish women writers, what follows at least can aspire to constituting an examination of some of the most significant.

liliana heker

Liliana Heker (b. 1943) began publishing her writings in the halcyon days of the 1960s in Argentina, when there was a clear sense of the possibility of a committed literature that could contribute to social change. The climate was decidedly international, and many writers who began to publish at this time were associated with the enormous panorama of literary reviews, and many of them were drawn, as was Heker (who came from the sort of petit bourgeois family that underwent social ascendancy under Perón in the previous decade), from nonelite and proletarian sectors. Buenos Aires, like many Latin American capitals of the time, drew people from marginal urban areas as well as the provinces; they came to participate in a cultural effervescence that has yet to be repeated in Argentina. Heker was still in her teens when she joined the staff of *El grillo de papel* (The Paper Cricket), and with her partner, Abelardo Castillo, she subsequently worked with two other influential reviews, *El escarabajo de oro* (The Golden Scarab) and *El ornitorrinco* (The Platypus), the latter founded during the period of military tyranny (1976–83) and surviving until well into the period of the return to constitutional democracy.

Heker, who has worked as a professor of mathematics and the sciences and as a computer programmer, has published numerous collections of short stories in which feminist concerns such as women's issues, the family, communitarian memory, and the sense of the absurd and arbitrary nature of established social life are notably evident. Her novel *Zona de clivaje* (The Cleavage Zone; 1987) won an important municipal award, and it may be considered one of her most important works in its valuation of women's experience. In this sense, Heker may be identified with important developments in contemporary Argentine writing, in the sense of concerning herself with important social issues that are pertinent to contemporary Argentina and in her attention to localist issues in a society that has experienced considerable social readjustments since the period in which she first began to write. The enormous preoccupation in Argentina with questioning and deconstructing the patriarchy, whose violent hand was so clearly evident in recent military tyrannies, has led to important contributions in feminist and, indeed, queer writing, as it has also led to the need to give representation to multiple other social subalternities, with the result that writing by Jewish authors has never been more intense in that country.

However, Heker's most recent novel, *El fin de la historia* (The End of History/the Story; 1996), must be considered virtually a masterpiece in the way in which it brings together the aforementioned issues in conjunction with a narrative discourse of impressive control and execution. It is the story of two women involved with the political events of Argentina over the period of four decades. Leonora Ordaz is a leftist revolutionary who, because of her involvement with a clandestine paramilitary guerrilla group, is arrested and tortured by the agents of the dictatorship. Diana Glass is a Jewish friend of Leonora's. They have known each other since their early school days during the Peronist period, and Diana, whose point of view controls the narrative, recalls the way in which Leonora became involved in political activity, how she dropped out, and the impact on her family of her disappearance at the hands of the special police.

Diana's recollection of Leonora is the reconstruction of an intensely personal relationship that involves the sort of bonding between individuals who sense their mutual social alienation. In one interpretation, such a relationship could be described as lesbian, to the degree that each woman defines herself in terms of the other. Even without any indication of a specifically sexual relationship between them, this exclusivity of sentiment and identity has come to be viewed in some forums of feminist theorizing as a crucial stand of defiance against the patriarchy (here, embodied in terms of the machismo of first Perón and then military tyranny) that strives to exclude a defining masculinist role in the demarcation of a woman–woman pairing. The point is not that there is a "love" story to be told between Diana and Leonora, but a model of bonding that constitutes an important gesture of political resistance.

When Leonora finds it necessary to break this bond, which she comes to consider juvenile, as such bonds are often viewed by parents and schoolteachers by virtue of their generally unreflecting commitment to patriarchal structures (it is bad enough for such a bond to be driven by sentiment; it is viewed as disastrous when it is perceived to be tinged by desire), she leaves Diana with a sense of tremendous loss and the need to reconstruct and recover the sense of their friendship. That Diana sees Leonora "sucked up" by the police only provides an even more acutely pathetic dimension to her abandonment by the other. Diana's story is both a reconstruction of the basis of their friendship and the discovery of what happens to Leonora following her arrest. Part of this story involves the expected themes of abuse, torture, and humiliation. But what Diana also uncovers is how Leonora becomes an accomplice of the repression. In a variation of the syndrome of the bond that emerges between the torturer and his victim (the masculine marking is important here, because torturers are agents of the patriarchy, even when they may be women), Leonora falls in love with the man assigned to her case, and she eventually leaves prison to make a life with him, a life that excludes her parents, the child she is forced to abandon when she is arrested, and Diana herself.

The issue of bonding is important here, because Leonora exchanges the previous "immature" bonding with a woman for a "mature" bonding with a man, but in her passage from one to the other, from lesbian to straight, she becomes complicitous not only with the patriarchy but also with its ugliest face in the form of the agent of torture who literally subjects her to rape and its violent variations because of her political transgressions. It is worth noting that Leonora does have a "normal" earlier relationship with a man, the father of her child, who is killed by the police. However, this relationship does not interfere with the bond she has with Diana, which is significant in modeling intimate female friendships as not necessarily excluding men, not at least when the latter are also opponents of the patriarchy in the form of the military dictatorship.

Silvia Sauter and Mariana Petrea, in their excellent dictionary entry on Heker, underplay the Jewish element in *Fin de historia* (264). Thus they do not mention the way in which Diana, as the excluded Other in what becomes Leonora's inscription in the bosom of the patriarchy, which in Argentina is always marked by institutional Catholicism, ends up standing alone as the isolated cultural and political alien, which is certainly the recurring position of the Jew in unreconstructed societies. And Heker's vision of contemporary Argentina is unquestionably one in which no significant reconstruction that would accommodate the other has taken place. Her title is an ironic allusion to the proposition of a reactionary postmodernism that we have reached the end of history, an end that would nullify any master narrative of ameliorating social change. The history/story (both *historia* in Spanish) that is over here is not just the story that binds/once bounded Diana and Leonora but the history of the Dirty War that reconstructs the once revolutionary Leonora as an agent of her own oppression: Heker here echoes the insistence of President Carlos Menem and reactionary ideologues that one must write an end (the Punto Final—final period) to the attempt to bring the military dictators and their henchmen to justice. That Menem was successful in executing such a finale corresponds with the end-of-history stance that it doesn't matter anymore provides Heker's novel with added layers of resonant irony in Argentina at the end of the century. Finally, that Heker's novel comes after recent violent acts against Jews and Jewish institutions in Argentina indicates that the story may be over for Leonora and her ex-torturer husband, but it is hardly over for the Argentine Jew as sociopolitical Other.

ana maría shua

The bibliography of cultural production relative to Jewish immigration in Argentina is vast, indeed, and representations of diverse aspects such as the difficulties Jews experienced in establishing themselves in the New World, conflicts over religion, language, and social customs (including legal institutions), the drama of preserving cultural and religious identity versus assimilation, Jewish agricultural settlements and urban ghettos, anti–Semitism (including the particularly problematic status of Jews under recent neofascist military dictatorships), and the pertinence of certain themes of Jewish identity to shifting social issues in Argentina can all be found to have been treated with some detail in the cultural record.

The Jewish community in Argentina at the end of the twentieth century has attained a considerable level of acceptance and, for many, notable prosperity. Despite the abidingly horrendous face of anti-Semitism as evidenced in the bombing of the Israeli Embassy in 1992 and of the AMIA (mutual aid society) in 1994, Jews have played prominent roles in government and allied institutions in the process of re-democratization since the return to constitutionality in 1983, and it is safe to say that the general climate of personal freedoms, the respect for individual differences, and the criterion of privacy that have emerged in the last decade have all contributed to significant advances for the Jewish community as a whole.

As a consequence of the social mobility and distributed institutional presence of Jews in contemporary Argentina (which, as always, means predominantly in contemporary Buenos Aires), the one theme of Jewish writers that must necessarily have prominence is that of assimilation, not just of the importance of the participation of Jews in Argentine society as a whole—few would have reasonable reservations about this—or of the difficulty of maintaining difference in a society that has been historically homogeneous and in which neo-liberalism has imposed an overlay of consumerist uniformity. Rather, what is of concern is the inevitability of the loss of important dimensions of Jewishness, whether it be the nostalgic icon of Yiddish or the crucial defining component of religious observance. Yiddish has no more chance of survival in Argentina than it does in the United States, especially as both countries share enormous ties with an Israel for which Hebrew is the language of Jewishness and Yiddish the linguistic correlative of the shame of the Diaspora. And as for religion, if American Jews have the option of Reform Judaism, the lack of a strong Reformist tradition in Argentina has meant that, for most Jews, the turn away from orthodox Judaism leaves only a secular, nonobservant, "cultural" Jewishness.

It is this context into which Ana María Shua's *El libro de los recuerdos* (The Book of Memories; 1994) may be inserted. Shua is not principally a Jewish writer in the sense of making Jewishness and a Jewish problematics central issues in her works. The bulk of her fiction is characterized by an urbane sophistication concerning the day-to-day difficulties of surviving as a human being, the profound vagaries of interpersonal relationships, and the general ineptness of individuals to negotiate the murky waters of social and institutional life (Arango–Keeth). But in *El libro de los recuerdos*, a book whose narrative fluidity and comfortable implied first–person narration may permit one an untroubled assumption that it is essentially autobiographical (or where whether it is strictly autobiographical or not does not really matter), the conventional format of a mosaic of the various generations of personalities of an immigrant family allows for the really very witty exploration of the signs of cultural conflict.

The organizing axis of Shua's novel, as the title directly states, is memory, and "book" is used here first of all in the metaphorical sense of collective memory as constituting a log of shifting entries: material is lost in the transmission from one generation to another or from one member of a generation to another, while new material is added as events take place and history becomes more pertinent. Not everything that gets remembered is momentous, and not everything that happens gets recorded in that shifting log, and part of the interest in an analysis of the book of memory is a determination of what the bases of inclusion and exclusion might be.

Concomitantly, "book" here refers to the novel itself as a narrative less of particular events than of memory itself as a process of human identity and subjectivity. As is widely accepted, life moves forth on the basis of narrative. Not only do we understand the social text and our interaction with it in terms of narrative, but the majority of our interactions with others is on the basis of narratives we tell each other, no matter how fragmentary and incoherent our telling, and interpreting, practices may be. Fiction is only a socioculturally privileged form of narrative, in which the author maximizes both the centrality of narratives in human life and the resources we have evolved for engaging in narrative constructions.

The way in which Shua's text is not a bildungsroman, not a family saga, is important not only to the way in which her writing means to convey the spirit of everyday narratives (rather than the novel as a privileged art form) but also to her interest in modeling the very partial way in which individual/family/collective/societal memory is maintained and communicated. Indeed, *El libro de los recuerdos* is not a novel in the sense of availing itself of the sort of controlling character-based semiotic structure that we associate with a text that tells a particular story in depth and in detail. Such novels have been written about Jewish life in Argentina by José Rabinovich, Bernardo Verbitsky, David Viñas, Gerardo Mario Goloboff, Mario Szichman, and Ricardo Feierstein, for example, and Shua is not interested in duplicating their efforts.

Rather, her work focuses on what one might call metonymic aspects of Jewish life in Argentina that, in somewhat of a fuguelike way, are elaborated around often grotesque individuals and outrageous incidents that are strikingly singular in delineating aspects of Jewish life and identity. The novel centers on the four Rimetka brothers and their respective families. Narrative events concern the usual struggles for survival and for dominance and influence within the group. But what is particularly striking about Shua's handling of this material is how she relates it to sociohistoric events. This is done no longer in the Lukácsian sense of making novelistic characters the embodiments of historical processes but rather in describing the system of impingements whereby personal stories exercise an antiphonic relationship with the swirling social events in which they are immersed. For example, one section deals with how one of the uncles, impressively overweight and lamentably impotent, begins to take diet pills prescribed by a refugee physician from Gdansk. Described as "bombs," these pills provoke in him a case of amnesia, and he disappears. The pills may have been a pretext for some time out from the family and the pressures of his business activities, or it really may have been a medical reaction. Whatever the real cause, this disappearance provokes a family crisis, which in turn brings to the fore a whole range of conflicts of existence. However, Shua moves this event outside the direct realm of high-tension interfamily conflict by adding in a footnote (hardly a conventional novelistic device) that at a later date, in the Época de Miedo, the period of fear (i.e., the so-called Dirty War, ca. 1976–79, waged by the military dictatorship against armed subversion), the verb *desaparecer*, to disappear, will assume a completely different meaning—indeed, as Shua does not note, it will cease to be strictly an intransitive verb and become a transitive one whose subject is obligatorily an agent of state terrorism.

Language is a recurring motif of *El libro de los recuerdos*, as well it should be, since our interpersonal communication and the records of our lives are inscribed in language. Language conflict is an abiding feature of the immigrant experience, and it is often an eloquent marker of the difficulties of accommodation, the nature of assimilation, and the negotiation undertaken between different cultural establishments. The family is presided over by Babuela, a clever melding of the respective words for grandmother in Spanish and Yiddish, *abuela* and *bobe*. The narrator attributes to Babuela the rhetorical question "¿Pero acaso se pueden decir cosas de verdad en este idioma?" (But can you say real things in this language? [165]), which implies that, of course, you cannot. The proposition that Spanish is not a "real language," at least from one individual's perspective, is an outrageous proposition in terms of the society that individual inhabits, and this is even more apparent because Shua is relating the grandmother's attitude toward the Spanish language in a text written in Spanish: "Castellano, bah: qué clase de idioma es ése" (Spanish, phooey: what kind of language is that [165]).

To be sure, what is at issue here is the way in which anyone has difficulty relating to a foreign language. Nevertheless, the question for Shua is not strictly a psycholinguistic one, but rather it relates to language and cultural politics. Yiddish has an undeniable subaltern relationship to Spanish in Argentina. In addition to being a language that is structurally very different from Spanish, unlike the Italian of the other major immigrant group in Argentina, with virtually no incidence of cognate words, Yiddish is primarily a spoken language and a medium of domestic communication. While Yiddish does, of course, have a rich literary and oral cultural tradition, it is only minimally a written language among immigrants, and those who speak it are enveloped by the overwhelming presence of Spanish as, in addition to its spoken representations, a written language as it appears in all the trappings of modern urban existence, completely the opposite of Yiddish as a premodern language of the isolated ghetto and rural shtetl life. But the Yiddish–Spanish divide also marks the boundaries of assimilation, and the fact that Babuela cannot envision real life taking place within the structures of Spanish also refers to the impossibility of meaningful life existing in the full domain of Spanish in which cultural and religious oblivion, the unlearning of the native tongue and the native culture, has taken place. In this way, language is underscored as the quintessential locus of memory.

alicia steimberg

The writings of Alicia Steimberg (b. 1933) are also marked by a keen sense of humor and, to the delight of her readers, by a frequently exquisitely malicious wit. In *De músicos y relojeros* (Of Musicians and Watchmakers; 1971), she too has written of questions of Jewish identity, the family, issues of cultural and linguistic assimilation, and, particularly, on the position of women. *El árbol del placer* (The Tree of Pleasure; 1986) deals with a uniquely Jewish cultural institution in Buenos Aires, psychiatry, which Steimberg reinterprets, following certain feminist interpretations, as a uniquely patriarchal enterprise. Psychiatry reappears in *Cuando digo Magdalena* (When I Say Magdalena; 1992), but more in terms of the construction of personal subjectivity and the deceptive securities of fixed identities, a proposition that has as much to do with the hypostatization of national values by the right wing in Argentina as it does with the notion of Jewish essentialism. Finally, with *Amatista* (Amethyst; 1989), Steinberg joined a select group of Latin American women writers who have experimented with what can be called a feminist pornography (Foster, "The Case for Feminine Pornography").

All of these works demonstrate Steinberg's particular engagement with the city and urban culture. Steinberg cannot really be said to have written to be identified as a Jewish writer in the sense that, unlike a writer like Mario Szichman, she has not created a dense narrative world centered on Jewish life and driven by a family saga extending over several generations (see, however, Schneider). Her novels are intensely urban, many of her characters and situations are clearly Jewish, and more than anything else, her writing is marked by a sense of sacrilegious irony, irreverence, and smart–girl sassiness that can be generally identified as a Jewish—and, in this case, feminist Jewish— point of view (see Barr's comment on the use of irony in Steinberg, "Alicia Steinberg" 502). Steinberg has written both short stories and novels, and her principal focus has been on the misadventures of middle-class women in their efforts to make their way against the odds of the city. These odds could be synthesized in terms of the masculinist codes that predominate as the ground zero of Argentine social life, although they are not always personified by male characters. Indeed, in her autobiographical first novel, perhaps the one most anchored in the immigrant ghetto, *De músicos y relojeros,* the household in which the narrator grows up is essentially the domain of women. Yet it is clear that that domain serves to enforce patriarchal law, whether in its specifically Jewish form or as the prevailing social code, and forms of resistance are purely tactical skirmishes. In her second novel, *Su espíritu inocente* (Her Innocent Spirit; 1981), Steinberg writes about being a Jewish student in the predominantly upper-middle-class and therefore profoundly Catholic teacher training school,

Lenguas Vivas, which specializes in language teaching (Steinberg is formally trained as an English teacher, and she worked many years as the translator of English-language fiction, most often best-sellers). That Steinberg was able to attend Lenguas Vivas in the early 1950s is the consequence of the changing fortune of Jews under Peronismo, and the title of the novel refers to a principal ideologeme of the school's anthem and the way in which a proper social education allows for overcoming the illusions, and dangers, of female innocence in the masculinist patriarchal jungle.

La loca 101 (Madwoman 101) was published in 1973 during the brief period of cultural euphoria between the temporary withdrawal from power of the military and the return to power of Peronismo; the euphoria was short lived—the military resumed power in 1976, less than three years after turning the government over to civilian control— but while it lasted, some of the best of recent Argentine literature was published and publishers were eager also to bring out socially progressive and revolutionary culture from other Latin American countries as well. In large measure, in the period since the return to constitutional democracy in 1983, Argentine cultural production has yet to recover the sense of euphoria and creative intensity that characterized the early 1970s.

Saúl Sosnowski, in an article in a special issue of *Folio* on Latin American Jewish writers, speaks of Steinberg as "enhebrando pequeñas historias"—stitching together little stories ("Alicia Steinberg" 49). His comment is allusive in two ways. In the first place, it stresses the "domestic" quality of Steinberg's writing. By contrast to the large social canvas typical of the bourgeois—and masculinist—novel, Steinberg's texts deal with more everyday, even mundane matters. Whether it is paradigmatically feminist to back away from the great themes of masculinist culture, the fact is that Steinberg focuses on details of experience that are synecdoches and metonymies of human existence. Such details may have a particular Jewish flavor about them, but they are more important for how they provide resonances to the common-places of daily life. Sosnowski's title stresses how Steimberg's writings are *petits récits*. Again, it may be a feature of feminist writing to renounce master narratives/the narratives of the master, but also for the way in which they articulate interpretations cast as Big Issues and Major Themes.

For example, *La loca 101* is described as a novel. Yet in 109 pages there are 44 chapters: each is given a separate titled identity in the index, although that name is not repeated as part of the heading of the actual division. Most of the texts run two to three pages; many are shorter. Thus what Steimberg presents possesses a loosely jointed continuity (the rejection of the sort of complex narrative structure of the latest modernist fiction of the boom) tied together by a feminine narrator who is underspecified beyond the suggestive nature of the title. In Argentine Spanish, *loca* applied colloquially to a woman means someone who is "daft" or "batty" but not strictly "mad" or "crazy." It is also used in the sense of someone who is overly talkative, sassy, unconventional, too loud, undemure—in a word, someone who is not sufficiently feminine in a conventional reserved and self-effacing way. The result is someone who not only sees more than she should but who talks openly about it as she should not, analyzing it aloud in the process in a way that is highly improper.

What one receives, then, is one young woman's discomforting observations on the world around her: as Barr has stated, "the text reveals the author's underlying terror of everyday life. It is a bloody business to live where she lives (*Isaac Unbound* 59). Because in a society in which there is an overdeterminedly constructed gender system, a woman sees things and experiences them differently than a man does (assuming that individuals are conforming appropriately to that gender system). A loca will speak that difference out loud, when, although her difference is not denied, she is supposed to keep it to herself. Steimberg's text functions both on the basis of that difference and on the fact that it is spoken out loud. And, of course, as a result of her outspokenness, she does in fact make the transition from "daft" to "mad": the designation "101" refers to her identification within the insane asylum in which she is held. Steimberg's ability to focus on minimalist aspects of behavior and thought and to wryly and wittily develop them into symptoms of significant issues of the individual's interaction with the social text, particularly as women and then also frequently as Jews, is the abiding hallmark of her fiction.

diana raznovich

Jews have long played a major role in the Argentine theater (Foster, "Argentine Jewish Dramatists"), and I would like to turn now to a particularly strong dramatic voice whose work has been important during the period since the return to constitutional democracy in 1983. One will recall that theater was a powerful forum of cultural resistance during the final years of the military dictatorship, and Diana Raznovich (b. 1943) was included among the Teatro Abierto '81 group of twenty-one dramatists whose works were organized into a theatrical cycle that openly defied censorship and cultural repression.

I have written elsewhere about Raznovich's fiction and included her, along with Steimberg, in the inventory of those engaged in producing a feminist pornography ("The Case for Feminine Pornography"). Raznovich's interest in sexual politics is evident in one of her best-known plays, *Jardín de otoño* (Autumn Garden), which also includes the lesbian dimensions that may also be associated with her writing. As Glickman has pointed out, Raznovich's work involves extensive parodies of Jewish themes of identity and social customs ("Paradojas y mitos," "Diana Raznovich").

An excellent example of Raznovich's recent work is *Casa matriz* (Dial-a-Mom), a complex play built, on the one hand, around the metaphor of the brothel as a microcosm and, on the other, around the myths of maternal origins and maternal dependency, particularly the Argentine ideologeme "Madre hay una sola" (You only got one mother). Demonstrating that the individual does not, in fact, have one mother and that the biological mother is an elusive and fragmentary link in one's life, Raznovich promotes the proposition of an enterprise where one can go to contract the services of a woman who will perform the maternal role one requires, enact the interpersonal relationship one could wish to have with one's mother, and provide, if only for a fleeting moment and at cost, the sense of solid biological, psychological, emotional, and affective link that real, everyday life, lamentably, does not provide.

Raznovich's play turns on the conceit that such an enterprise might exist for the same reasons that brothels exist: the latter (and, in turn, their alternative embodiments) supplement, often to an extensive and dominant degree, the range and depth of sexual fulfillment often lacking with conventional sexual partners. As the demands for attention and compliance are limited in the case of conventional sexual partners (whatever the actual boundaries of definition are to be placed on this concept), by contracting the services of a professional, the individual can make demands that life, in its customary course, does not fulfill. Real mothers have their own lives to lead, have other demands on their minds and their bodies than just those of their children, and are psychically and psychologically incapacitated in many and uncontrollable ways and thus are prevented from complying with the role social conventions and hegemonic ideologies are viewed as placing on them.

In a clever move to enhance the dramatic texture of her play and to bring out both the juxtaposition and the continuity between "real" mothers and "contracted" mothers, some of the Mother's clients in *Casa matriz* are willing to pay for an enactment, not of their ideal of a mother, but of the specific details of how their real mothers are perceived as falling short of the specifications of the former. Thus the scripts demand—and the play also works off the proposition that our social roles are, in fact, dramatic scripts—that mothers be selfish, distracted, absent, cruel, arbitrary: in sum, that they manifest all the unsavory characteristics of mothers who are seen to fall short of the overdetermined images of the perfect mother and the virtues she is seen to model as the source of individual biological and social linkages.

Raznovich's play clearly parodies certain motifs of the paradigmatic Jewish mother, both in the sense of the mother as constituting the line of transmission of a proper racial identity and in the sense of the *idische mame* as a comic, and often tragic, figure of the deficiencies of the ideal. But Raznovich's play is also feminist in its exploration of the bond between mother and child, particularly between mother and daughter, with the latter including intimations of the lesbian dimensions that are never far removed from Raznovich's texts. It is also feminist in its dissection, through grotesque reenactment and parody via the medium of theater, of the oppressive weight of hegemonic definitions of motherhood. The clients who turn to the Casa Matriz are agents of a patriarchal oppression that the Casa's personnel are obliged to reconfirm through the services they perform. What is cruelly ironic about this arrangement is that the substitute mothers must not only reenact the terrible and terrifying role of the perfect Mother, but they must also comply with the scripting requirements that force them to play out the deficiencies of the mother figure. These deficiencies are as much brutal evidence of the impossibility of attaining the ideal prescribed by the patriarchy as they are signs of the way in which the clients of the service personnel perceive that mothers can never be, given the circumstances of their social positioning, anything other than failed human beings. Like a good Argentine, Raznovich knows her Lacan, in the sense of the imperative of enactment of the Oedipal sexual dynamic, in the complex aporia and ambiguities of ever getting that dynamic right and, most of all, of the null or vacant sign that the woman as mother is called on to embody. That the identity of the mother is transitory, incomplete, and, in the final analysis, ephemeral is marked by the fact that the client's time is up and the role of Mother the Casa Matriz employee is playing ceases to exist, because there is another client with another script waiting to be serviced. In this sense, Raznovich's play has no Aristotelian structure of resolution but is rather an open-ended series of sketches that could be continued indefinitely.

alicia kozameh

Jacobo Timerman, perhaps the most internationally famous political prisoner of the military dictatorship in Argentina in the late 1970s, has insisted that Jews received special attention from torturers and experienced even harsher conditions of imprisonment than other political detainees. The accumulated record of testimonials, official reports, and general agreement among experts would tend to bear this allegation out, along with similar circumstances for women and those alleged to be homosexual: Jews because they were claimed, by definition, to be anti-Christian and agents of international conspiracies against the integrity of the Argentine nation, women because by being involved in subversion they violated the sanctity of their womanhood (certainly, women must also have received special attention since they were available as victims of rape of an unimpeachably masculinist enterprise), and homosexuals because they violated the pact of manliness demanded by the authoritarian ethos (and, too, like women, to whom they were assimilated because of their nonmanliness, they were available as victims of rape).

Pasos bajo el agua (Steps under Water; 1987) by Alicia Kozameh (b. 1953) is representative of the extensive testimonial and documentary literature that has come out of Argentina since the return to constitutional democracy in 1983 (Foster, "Argentine Sociopolitical Commentary"; Bergero and Reati). Like many of the testimonial works,

Kozameh's text is a personal story, as she herself was a political prisoner in Rosario and Buenos Aires beginning in 1975 (by contrast, other testimonials are based on interviews with former victims, and some are explicitly fictional). And like many former prisoners, her subsequent life has been characterized by alienation and separation; Kozameh has lived for the past several years in the Los Angeles area.

Much of the standard information is available here: the circumstances of arrest, the humiliation of the treatment by agents of the state, the abuses and torture, the imprisonment under degrading and terrifying conditions, the circumstances of interpersonal relationships with other prisoners, and the profound sense of loss regarding one's previous life and what will remain of it after release. *Pasos bajo el agua* is especially eloquent in its transmission of the degree to which it is impossible to return to life as usual following such an experience. As David E. Davis notes, writing for Kozameh "is not a catharsis" (316), because, indeed, it is difficult to see how writing, no matter how determinant it may be in the life of an individual, can resolve the traumatic conflicts imposed by the conditions of political imprisonment.

Kozameh's text is particularly feminist in its adherence to the principle that the "personal is political." Thus she does not discuss political matters as such (as, say, Timerman does) but rather construes her personal story as, on the one hand, allegorical of the complex political movements of Argentina in the 1970s and, on the other, as interpretable in terms of those movements, since, after all, were it not for those movements she would not have ended up in police dungeons.

But *Pasos bajo el agua* is notably feminist in another regard, and this is in terms of the representation of the body. Although most testimonials describe the details of the rites of torture and abuse, Kozameh is concerned to inventory the body as an organic phenomenon beyond the specific circumstances of interrogation. Woman's body is "problematic" for a masculinist culture, which is here not just a general Argentine readership but more precisely the indirectly implied readership—but which is yet never likely to actually provide readers of her text—composed of the agents of state terrorism, whose military authoritarianism directly results in the torment, literal and figurative, of the bodies of its victims. Kozameh's violent figurings of the body portray in harshly material terms multiple levels of the manipulation, transformation, and destruction of the body as a living organism placed, as the legal jargon goes, at the disposal of the state. Moreover, Kozameh's text is written in such a way as to capture both the materiality of the body and its transformations. Written in brief segments that signify a clandestine process of creation, the fragmentary nature of the text is a direct objective correlation of the fragmentation of a sustained personal identity under prison conditions. Concomitantly, the narrative text is composed of various forms of discourse, represented alternatively by roman and italic type: "Letters, diary entries, notes surreptitiously passed from one to another facilitate a communication that has effectively been cauterized by imprisonment and exile" (Davis 317).

Buenos Aires continues to be a major focus of Jewish culture in the world and, because it is also a major center of cultural production with a high degree of femininist consciousness, a major point of reference for the production of a literature that is signed by both the Jewish and the feminine, despite the fact that this production has yet to receive anything like an adequate recognition.[2]

It is not possible to speak of a specific unity for such writing in Argentina, precisely because it is so extensive and therefore so diverse. Certainly, these authors manifest common concerns for motifs associated with Jewish culture, such as identity, collective interpersonal relationships, and the problems of religious and cultural (including linguistic) survival in an environment that, no matter what the random evidence of tolerance and acceptance may be, is still very much of a hostile environment for Jews. The crisis of assimilation is in-evitably a theme, even when writers like Shua and Steimberg ironize and parody it. But despite valid observations regarding the margin-alization of women in Latin America and the marginalization of women in traditional Jewish culture, there is little case for either in the writers I have discussed here. Buenos Aires is simply too sophis-ticated a venue for women (and I say this without meaning to deny very real practices of gender discrimination) to make it possible to generalize about an across-the-board subordination of their creative efforts. Buenos Aires is, after all, the home of strong feminine figures like Victoria Ocampo in literature and Eva Duarte de Perón in poli-tics, and their public personas as much put in evidence the opposi-tion to women's rights as it underscored the real changes that were possible within the sociohistorical parameters of modern Argentina. By the same token, one cannot diminish the evidence of religious and ethnic discrimination against Jews in Argentina, especially since it is quite literally physical evidence in the case of the bombings of the Israeli Embassy and the Jewish mutual aid society. But the sheer presence of Jews in Argentine social, cultural, and institutional life, a presence that is shared extensively and equitably by women, at least in the realm of cultural production, makes it unadvisable to speak from the position of any significant marginalization as a group. All five of the authors studied in this essay are in their prime and likely to continue to produce a record of impressive accomplishments in several genres.[3]

NOTES

1. For example, in Darrell B. Lockhart's *Dictionary of Latin American Jewish Authors*, 118 authors are included, 74 of which are Argentine. Of the latter, 24 are women writing in all literary genres: Cecilia Absatz, Alicia Borinsky, Aída Bortnik, Eugenia Calny, Perla Chirom, Alicia Dujovne Ortiz, Manuela Fin-gueret, Luisa Futuransky, Nora Glickman, Liliana Heker, Tamara Kamenszain, Alicia Kozameh, Rebeca Mactas, Alejandra Pizarnik, Silvia Plager, Diana

Raznovich, Reina Roffé, Hebe Serebrisky, Ana María Shua, Alicia Steimberg, Susan Thénon, Paula Varsavsky, Elina Wechsler, Clara Weil.

2. For example, three major studies on Jewish authors, by Lindstrom, Sosnowski, and Senkman, make virtually no reference, beyond passing comments, to women authors.

3. Two other authors must at least be mentioned: Alicia Dujovne Ortiz and Cecilia Absatz. I have not discussed their work here because I have recently written on them elsewhere, in my *Buenos Aires: Essays on the City and Cultural Production* (unpublished). Particularly noteworthy is Dujovne Ortiz's biography of Eva Perón, *Eva Perón: La biografía*. Dujovne Ortiz makes specific reference to Perón and the Jews.

REFERENCES

Arango-Keeth, Fanny. "Ana María Shua." Lockhart 483–89.

Barr, Lois Baer. "Alicia Steimberg." Lockhart 499–504.

———. *Isaac Unbound: Patriarchal Traditions in the Latin American Jewish Novel.* Tempe: Center for Latin American Studies, Arizona State University, 1995.

Bergero, Adriana J., and Fernando Reati, eds. *Memoria colectiva y políticas de olvido: Argentina y Uruguay, 1970–1990.* Buenos Aires: Beatriz Viterbo Editora, 1997.

Davis, David E. "Alicia Kozameh." Lockhart 315–21.

Foster, David William. "Argentine Jewish Dramatists: Aspects of a National Consciousness." *Folio* 17 (1987): 74–103.

———. "Argentine Sociopolitical Commentary, the Malvinas Conflict, and Beyond: Rhetoricizing a National Experience." *Latin American Research Review* 22.1 (1987): 7–34.

———. "The Case for Feminine Pornography in Latin America." In *Bodies and Biases: Sexualities in Hispanic Cultures and Literatures.* Ed. David William Foster and Roberto Reis. (Minneapolis: University of Minnesota Press, 1996): 246–73.

Glickman, Nora. "Diana Raznovich." Lockhart 414–19.

———. "Paradojas y mitos judaicos en dos obras de Diana Raznovich." *Noaj* 9 (1993): 83–87.

Heker, Liliana. *El fin de la historia.* Buenos Aires: Alfaguara, 1996.

Kozameh, Alicia. *Pasos bajo el agua.* Buenos Aires: Contrapunto, 1987.

———. *Steps under Water.* Trans. David E. Davis. Foreword Saúl Sosnowski. Berkeley: University of California Press, 1996.

Lindstrom, Naomi. *Jewish Issues in Argentine Literature: From Gerchunoff to Szichman.* Austin: University of Texas Press, 1989.

Lockhart, Darrell B., ed. *Jewish Writers of Latin America: A Dictionary.* New York: Garland, 1997.

Ortiz, Alicia Dujovne. *Evá Perón: La Biografía.* Buenos Aires, Aguilar, 1995.

————. *Eva Peron: The Biography.* Trans. Shawn Fields. New York: St. Martin's Press, 1997.

Raznovich, Diana. "*Casa matriz.*" *Salirse de madre.* Ed. Hilda Rais. Buenos Aires: Croquiñol, 1989. 163–86.

————. *Dial-a-Mom. Women Writing Women: An Anthology of Spanish-American Theater of the 1980s.* Ed. Teresa Caijiao Salas and Margarita Vargas. Albany: State University of New York Press, 1997. 100–130.

Sauter, Silvia, and Mariana Petrea. "Liliana Heker." Lockhart 260–67.

Schneider, Judith Morganroth. "Alicia Steimberg: Inscriptions of Jewish, Female Identity." *Yiddish* 9.1 (1993): 92–104.

Senkman, Leonardo. *La identidad judía en la literatura argentina.* Buenos Aires: Pardés, 1983.

Shua, Ana María. *El libro de los recuerdos.* Buenos Aires: Editorial Sudamericana, 1994.

Sosnowski, Saúl. "Alicia Steimberg: Enhebrando pequeñas historias." *Folio* 17 (1987): 104–10.

————. *La orilla inminente. Escritores judíos argentinos.* Buenos Aires: Legasa, 1987.

Timerman, Jacobo. *Preso sin nombre, celda sin número.* Barcelona: El Cid Editor, 1981.

————. *Prisoner Without a Name, Cell Without a Number.* Trans. Toby Talbot. New York: Knopf, 1981.

✒ brazilian jewish women writers at the crossroads

Regina Igel

In contemporary Brazilian Jewish literature, scholars and readers alike have shown a tendency to examine almost exclusively the works of three fictionists, Samuel Rawet, Clarice Lispector, and Moacyr Scliar. Besides these significant personalities and their writings, however, there are a considerable number of Jewish-Brazilian authors who have wafted almost unperceived in the literary lanes of Brazil. Among them are the four women—Elisa Lispector, Frida Alexander, Janette Fishenfeld, and Sara Riwka Erlich—whom I have selected as representative of a special literary approach to Jewish experiences lived in Brazil. They stand among those whose affinities, allegiance, and critical perspective on the many facets of Judaism are explicitly indicated in their writings. Although they do not belong to the group of canonized authors, these four women present in their texts a distinctive level of communication and artistic elaboration. Moreover, they are consistent with a subliminal, if not almost elliptical, recognition of their status as representatives of a double disadvantaged condition: as women writers and as part of a diminutive literary Jewish community.

That the Jewish community in Brazil is rather small in comparison to the country's population[1] may have a connection with the scanty readership and also with the negligible attention given to these women by the critical establishment. As women authors of Jewish origin, however, their experience as writers conforms to a situation lived by non-Jewish female writers too. Female authors have been tacitly denied opportunities to realize their potentialities, a predicament parallel to the situation lived by women in general. Leila de A. Linhares Barsted observes that "our historical mark, as women, has been the silence to which we had been forcibly submitted, resulting in the hiding of our actions and our isolation, therefore making communication among us impossible" (101).[2] As Ana Miranda states, the roots for such a condition are as old as the times when the Portuguese settlers landed south of the equator, thus before the arrival of Jewish women onto the literary scene: "Since the arrival of Cabral's naval fleet to the Brazilian shores [1500] until almost two hundred years later, there is no mention of any woman's name in our official History" (129).

The slow emergence of female Jewish writers in Brazil can be understood within the complexities of a patriarchal environment that has shaped the Brazilian social system, not yet exhaustively discussed but denounced by the two scholars mentioned. Moreover, it has been suggested, not surprisingly, that Jewish traditional restrictions on some dimensions of women's freedom and growth have also contributed to the slow pace at which women writers have emerged among the Jewish population.[3] Another factor contributing to the scarcity of women writers among Brazilian Jewry is probably the relatively recent arrival of immigrants, mostly between the two world wars. As the emergence of Brazilian Jewish women writers is connected to the status of Brazilian women writers in general, it bears noting, too, that the pattern of discrimination against women started to change only in the 1930s.

Nelly Novaes Coelho indicates three important moments of "conscientization" of women, as evoked in their literary creations, that marked the stages by which they progressed from victims to challengers confronting a hardened system of inequalities between men and women. According to Coelho, the first moment of women's social consciousness took place in the 1930s, as reflected in women characters, created by women authors, who began to denounce the situation of being denied free will by the patriarchal system; the second moment occurred in the next decade, with the publication of Clarice Lispector's *Perto do coração selvagem* (Near to the Wild Heart; 1944), a novel that conveys the ambiguities of a female character who is beginning to know herself and who is implicitly demanding recognition for her feelings and thoughts; the third period, encompassing the decades 1960–80, is one of multiple social and political transformations, including a constant renewal of the fictional language, initiated and stimulated by Lispector; from then on women have been organizing themselves in popular movements, academic and professional associations, and nongovernmental organizations. Though still opening trails through the jungle of a lingering patriarchy, women are having their rights and plights recognized and are influencing new policies and changing laws incompatible with modern times. By all accounts, the election of a woman, Nélida Piñon, to the coveted position of president of the Brazilian Academy of Letters (December 1996) epitomizes an achievement for the female gender that was unthinkable a few years ago.

The main plight of women authors is that literature or any other artistic production by women had seldom emerged in the Brazilian cultural landscape, either during the colonial period (1500–1822) or even for a long time after independence from Portugal (1822). Although some creative works by women began to appear on the artistic scene early in the twentieth century, it is rather recently that females have been part of the intellectual, artistic, and literary circles in Brazil as scholars, artists, and writers. Still, Brazilian women authors are in a minority. Although there has been no statistical study of the participation of men and women in contemporary Brazilian life, the general consensus is that women are much less included and incorporated than men in many areas of Brazilian arts, particularly in the administrative and political sectors. Cristina Bruschini observes that "the methods traditionally used to measure work and the methodological procedures for gathering data, based on economic activities performed by men, covered up women's contribution instead of conveying it" (124).

It is within such a context that the writings of Jewish women authors started to emerge. With the exception of Elisa Lispector, the literary creations of Alexander, Fishenfeld, and Erlich have barely been appreciated outside their circle of friends and family. Their work was published in one edition only, and with very limited commercial distribution. The public and critical recognition received by these writers can be characterized as ranging from almost none to scarce to a certain degree of appraisal. Although the subject of their neglect by established critics is not addressed here, suffice it to say that their predicament is the same as that endured by Brazilian women writers in general. A code of good social conduct, not spoken yet understood by all, would have prevented women from expressing themselves through the many artistic avenues that were traditionally taken by men.

These complex attitudes present in Brazilian society engendered another intricate question. As Tânia Regina Oliveira Ramos observes, there is

a feminine silence in the Brazilian memoirs . . . an absence of texts by women in the most feminine of genres:

the memoir. In Brazilian literary and cultural history [there is]. . . a predominant representation of books of memoirs written by men. . . . The female gender is smothered by a discourse emphasized ideologically by History and by a social attitude that perpetuates the recognition of statements by males. (21)

The writers here presented did break down the tacitly imposed restrictions on women and did compose memoirs. They also are among the first to convey, in Portuguese, a profile of Jewish immigrants in Brazilian territory from a woman's perspective. This inaugural characteristic of their writings is complemented by an autobiographical identity and by an aspect of orality that permeates most of the stories narrated. Although none of these works is centered on issues related solely to women, and although none espouses a political feminism or presents a gendered argument, they all demonstrate strong links with a feminine view of the world. This can be detected in their places within their families, in the kinds of banners they metaphorically lift in their writings, in the sense of community they impart, and in their reverence for tradition and respect for innovation. In their chronicles, fiction and poetic prose, to be examined further, women are portrayed as field workers, wives, mothers, daughters, and sisters, caretakers of members of the family, bearers and dispensers of tradition, and as solitary spirits, lonely and marginalized in their own milieu. Narrators similarly describe their habitat as a form of enclosure: in the country, it is a territory materially limited by fences, like a farm; in urban areas, it is the elusive boundaries of a budding *bairro judeu*, the Jewish district taking shape in some cities at the time of the narrated experiences. Other affinities perceived in most of the texts examined here are related to the emphasis on the roles played by women in the formation of the communities and the specific pressures exerted on them under the circumstances of being Jewish immigrants or first-generation descendants of immigrants. The authors share equally a similar sense of living in a dual culture: the one brought from Europe by themselves or their ancestors and the other Brazilian. The differences noted among their texts, in terms of substance and style, are discussed below.

Representing different times and communities and distinct geographic areas, these women defy societal challenges by the mere fact of producing literary creations—albeit represented by a lonely book, in some cases. Their foreign names not being a deterrent to creativity or publication (by coincidence, three of them were born in Brazil and are descendants of Russian Jews; Lispector was born in Ukraine), they are women who were little encouraged by their times or environment to aspire to writing or any other occupation that would prevent them from marrying, bearing children, and taking on the responsibilities of raising a family.

The publications of these four women, who represent a cross-section of a budding Jewish society in Brazil, spring from and reflect some of the country's different regions: Elisa Lispector, setting her novel initially in Europe, portrays a burdened family of refugees in Rio de Janeiro during the 1940s; Frida Alexander conveys the lifestyle of Jewish immigrants as peasants and cowboys in the southern Brazilian Pampas at the beginning of the twentieth century; Janette Fishenfeld creates pieces of short fiction about family and generational conflicts among Jews in modern surroundings; and Sara Riwka Erlich relives, in poetic prose, aspects of the Jewish folklore and traditions of her young years in the northeastern city of Recife.

The capture of the past, in most of these writings, is colored by perspectives ranging from mistrust to bitterness. Paradoxically, since many of the narratives are blanketed by feelings of nostalgia, the authors' gaze tends to distort reality in favor of an amiable atmosphere that might or not have existed. Therefore, beneath reflections of despondency and in spite of the exceptions, the spirit found in the writings of these authors suggests a conciliatory judgment of the past, revealing their perceptions to be inclined rather toward a serene view of history.

Included in some of these general characteristics is Elisa Lispector's novel *No exílio* (In Exile), published in 1948.[4] Born in the Ukraine in 1911 (later she obtained Brazilian citizenship), the author personally experienced most of the passages described in the story. She was fourteen when she and her family arrived in Rio de Janeiro, where she died, at age seventy-eight, after a modestly recognized literary career. After graduating in sociology, Lispector was selected to work in the Department of Labor in the federal government, where she soon became interested in women's working conditions and influenced certain government decisions related to women's rights in the workplace. She published ten books, both novels and short stories.[5]

No exílio is the only fictional work by Elisa Lispector that mentions her Judaic roots. It establishes a time-space link between Europe and Brazil, starting soon after the Bolshevik Revolution in 1917. The story continues through the Second World War, with the family already settled in Brazil, and comes to a halt on the day the birth of the state of Israel was announced (1948).

In an interview granted to me, Lispector said,

> *No exílio* has many autobiographical traits, and has to do with my attachment to my ancestors. It represented, for me, a form of release. I had the urge to disclose the anguish, the sadness, the terror felt by a girl who saw the pogroms, the attacks of the crowd and the systematic destruction of her home and of other Jews there in Russia. That girl, who understood nothing of what was going on, remained inside me. Sadness accompanied me during all the time I was writing this book, but I finished it on a happy day, when the foundation of the State of Israel was approved by the UNO.[6]

Admittedly autobiographical, the characters' names in the novel barely disguise the identities of members of the author's family: Lizza, the protagonist, is a modified version of Elisa, the writer's own name; Pinkhas is the Yiddish version of Pedro, her father's name in Portuguese; Marim, his wife's name, is a slight variation of Marieta, the real name of Elisa and Clarice Lispector's mother. Her famous sister is called Ethel, and Tânia, the youngest, is represented by the character called Tina.

The novel revolves around the sense of solitude, frustration, sadness, and despair felt by Lizza's family in their forced move from one country to another and across the Atlantic Ocean. As she openly linked the history of the book itself with the story narrated, Lispector is represented, on her own account, by the oldest daughter of the couple who is also the reflexive voice in the novel. In it, Judaism is seen as a target of the suffering endured by the family whose members were often howled at as *bejentzy*, a Russian word meaning "fugitive," equally applied to outlaws and to refugees. The narrative is a flashback that starts its voyage in time from the day Lizza is released from a hospital and is getting ready to turn over a new leaf in her life. The first nine paragraphs focus on the woman sitting in a train that has stopped at a sleepy station somewhere in Brazil, where a "sluggish and sad paperboy came closer and shouted, with a tenacious effort, but with no enthusiasm: 'Read this paper! Latest news: The Jewish state has been proclaimed!'" (7).

Lizza's reaction to that moment is verbalized in a language that denotes a uniquely female identity. The narrator tells of a growing sensation of "lassitude that spreads all over her being, as if a fountain of tepid water was flowing inside her, impregnating her body to the last cell" (8). Lassitude, fluid, impregnation—the prevailing images selected by Lispector to describe that moment—are definitely associated with natural or conventional insemination. This was being experienced by the woman at the precise moment when a new life was being inaugurated by and for the Jews. The gynocentric metaphor that explains Lizza's personal connection to the political moment is conveyed in a language that is linked to women's experiences in intercourse. Elisa Lispector may not be the first writer to use a woman's possible experience of sexual relaxation to interpret her organic reactions to strong emotions. However, by making use of a language that relates to a distinctively feminine experience—of being impregnated—during the sexual act, she inaugurates, among Jewish writers in Brazil, a language and a literary vision that can be labeled as specifically feminine.

Similar images are reiterated in the course of the novel, as in (emphasis mine) "in the tepid cozyness of the homes, men rested from the day's struggles, and the soil, apparently inanimate, in the lethargy of latent energies, went on materializing, in the *depths of its entrails, the fruitful miracle of sap and life*" (9), and, when describing a certain phase of the exodus in which the protagonist's family participated, "Midway, many stopped for a while, in order to overcome an obstacle, as if they were going to be born again. And inside themselves were whirling the pains of childbirth that would strenghten them for life" (15). Still, she extends another metaphor for women's experience: "She felt the ship piercing through the dark waters, its itinerary associated with the boat's rhythmic swinging from one side to the other, like *an old woman's weeping, weak and insignificant*, in an endless desert" (89).

Regardless of the author's personal life, whether she went through labor or not, the metaphor of birth may function as a sort of a distinctive line of communication between the narrator and her women readers. However, her use of the image of an old woman as a way to describe an unstable ship testifies to the societal norms prevailing during her time, a view that remains to be dispelled: an aged woman equals an insignificant object.

The eventual death of Lizza's ailing mother results in a shift of the protagonist's (and the narrator's) focus to the father. A large part of the narrative is, therefore, concentrated on the father, who is viewed from two different angles: as a lonely and wise man, always dispensing advice and suggestions to his daughters, and as a sort of announcer of world events, about which he gives long and tedious commentaries. Most of his speeches, related to events occurring at the end of the Second World War or the emerging problems between Arabs and Jews, burdens the text with a didactic tone that hinders the flow of the narrative. However, the father is the only male character in the novel whom the author endows with dignity, sensitivity, and understanding. In one scene the oldest daughter proclaims to her widowed father that she does not want to follow the conventional course for women, to get married and procreate. The narrator shows him as a Jewish father facing a resolute daughter who goes against his basic principle of maintaining Jewishness in the next generations. Nevertheless, hesitantly at first, he ends up accepting her reasons.

By capturing the sense of isolation felt by the immigrant and the feeling of exclusion imposed on the Jews, Elisa Lispector disclosed her skillfulness in dealing with the theme of solitude and marginality that would be extensively developed in her later novels and short stories. A sense of distress envelops the protagonist's mind, further described in her spiritual and emotional struggle, whose origin is revealed to be the inferiority complex imposed by others:

> She returned to the first source of her bitterness, to the statement that a Jew is someone marginal, someone who has to struggle and to suffer. To suffer always, even when praising God. In the Church, where Eudóxia took her one afternoon, the atmosphere was joyful: the icons in the profusely decorated altars, an organ, incense, the peasants wearing intriguing and colorful dresses. In the Synagogue, no bells, no images. No decoration, no joy. (128)

As if intended to soothe the jolting series of disturbances that intervened in Lizza's and her family's history, the author brings the novel to a jubilant close. Lizza learns of the founding of the state of Israel, thus returning the story to its beginning. As the train resumes its journey, Lizza personalizes the machine and turns its rhythmic progress into a tune of glory: "'. . . So they didn't die in vain . . .' the wheels on the tracks began to sing, while the train started to move again and immerse back into the immensity" (8). Lispector's Zionist zeal, which would not be brought up in any of her other fiction, led her to link the historical birth of Israel to Lizza's rebirth: after eighteen months in a hospital, her health restored, she has the possibility of beginning a new life. The converging of these two moments are, as other tropes used by the author, a move that might symbolize a connection between the woman and her destiny as a Jew in the Diaspora, where moments of elation may be mere stops in an internal voyage through solitude.

A much less pessimist tone is given by Frida Schweidson, later Alexander, to her novel *Filipson*. It depicts the experiences suffered by her family and many other Jewish immigrants in the first twenty years of their settlement in rural southern Brazil. Alexander was born on December 29, 1906, in Filipson, one of the farms subsidized by the Jewish Colonization Association (ICA), founded by Barón Maurice de Hirsch. *Filipson*, her only known book, which bears the name of her birthplace, was published when the author was sixty-one years old. She died in São Paulo in 1972. According to her son Leon, the bedtime stories she used to tell him and his siblings, Riva and Marcos, led them, when they reached adulthood, to request that she write down her memories.[7] So she did, thus becoming the first woman to publish about life in the Brazilian fields for the Jewish immigrants and their descendants.

Frida lived in the country until her marriage to Boris Alexander, a Russian émigré and formerly a conductor, who worked as a pianist for silent movies in the theaters of São Paulo. When her husband started a job as representative of international companies, Frida became a typical housewife, sharing her time among their three children, chores at home, and social and charitable activities in some areas of the local Jewish community. They never moved away from São Paulo, where, many years later, she would pen, as Frida Alexander, the book of chronicles, based on reminiscences of her youth.

Composed of fifty-six short chapters, each with a brief title directly relating to its content, the stories concentrate on the almost two decades the author spent on the farm, from her birth until her departure. She also tells of happenings that took place before her birth, with the help of spontaneous storytellers living on the farm. Thus there prevails, in her writings, a floating atmosphere of oral communication, further emphasized by her choice of a vocabulary filled with local colloquialisms. The chronicles convey a steady search for fidelity to the acts she witnessed and a language that, in addition to being cultivated and articulate, features some attributes of storytelling. The oral character of Alexander's writing is apparent in the use of verbs that indicate the habit, in the community, of passing information "by word of mouth." So as to locate a story not resulting from direct observation, she constantly applies the verb "to tell" while providing the identity of the source (emphasis mine): "*Mom* used to *tell me* how well she was received by the sisters in the hospital" (17); "*Golde,* the oldest daughter of the Averbacks, *told me* that, when they arrived in Filipson, they were guests of my parents" (22); "*Sturdse,* right now in his eighties, but in total command of his mind, *told me* the following" (23); "*Jacques,* later on, *told us that* . . . " (about a dispute between a peasant and her father; 71); "*My little cousins told me* that Nenén . . . " (about an incestuous relationship; 123); "*Professor Budin . . . informed us,* very formally, that Brazil had decided to enter the War" (128).

The descriptions offer a detailed view of her horizon of plantations and pastures, inhabited by traditional gauchos, South American cowboys, and the newly conformed Jewish cattle handlers and sowers. It also uncovers the coexistence among the old folks of the shtetl, such as the *felcher* (a sort of pharmacist) and the regional healers, midwives, and spiritual guides. Though schooling for the children was provided by Jewish teachers imported from Europe, and technical instruction was provided by emissaries of the ICA, the whole community learned lessons of a practical nature from the local inhabitants: how to read the direction of the winds, how to measure the fertility of the soil, and how to cook using the resources found in the region. Érico Veríssimo, the renowned author from Rio Grande do Sul, wrote, "The narrative is done with simplicity and clarity, two fundamental qualities of a writer."[8]

Many elements distinguish Alexander's book: a candid attempt by the author to bond with the readers; a view of a collective past, encompassing activities of a social, spatial, and temporal order, independently of the narrator's participation in the events; an implicit feminine perspective on the plantation's world inhabited by a variety of people; and a survey of some Jewish celebrations, within the limits and rigors of the plantation area. The chronicles cover the farmers' lives from their very first activities on arriving at the land to be plowed to the period of collective frustrations to the decay of the plantation's agricultural production.

Still in the same storytelling vein, the narrator directs herself toward invisible readers. She rhetorically communicates with them, as if attempting to include them in the atmosphere of reminiscences (emphasis mine): "*Have you* heard of Filipson?" (15), and stimulating their potential creativity, "*You may imagine* the discomfort felt by those wretched people" (15).

The moments in which she participated directly and those in which she was an onlooker or bystander are equally portrayed. She tells of the slaughter of animals for the Jewish farmers' consumption, of the handling of food, and of the folklore and traditions carried on in that faraway and isolated region. The narrative is a dynamic construct intersected by people in constant movement, in a continuous verbal exchange and in a never-ending curiosity for all things demanding their attention for survival.

The observations on the farm's social universe are continuously alternated with personal remarks, therefore focusing on both collective events and individual behavior. She describes the plagues that destroyed harvests, the diseases that killed adults and children, and the lack of medical care that resulted in the shortening of the life span for children as well as for adults. On a lighter note, Alexander refers to the non-Jews living and working in the area, honoring the memories of the local chiefs of police (34), of the workers at the train station (195), and of employees that served in the plantations and pastures (160).

In spite of the scanty descriptions of her physical traits, Alexander's itinerary as a young peasant confers to her writings some characteristics of a mini-bildungsroman. She dedicates an entire chronicle to registering her passage from childhood to puberty ("Adolescência"—Adolescence, 158–59). She emphasizes the importance of her biological evolution, referring to herself as a twelve-year-old who suddenly became a frequent consultant to a mirror. Otherwise, she transfers to others the disclosure of the changes occurring in her, as in the observation of a working man in the farm: "You are different from all other women" (206).

Although she avoids burdening her narrative with manifest criticism against the ICA (a common practice among many others who wrote about the experimental farms in Brazil and Argentina), Alexander uncovers, nevertheless, problems that developed between the peasants and the administrators. She implies the indifference with which the Jewish farmers were treated by contrasting the two modes of comfort coexisting on the farm, one enjoyed by the representatives of the ICA—

"a white house, with all possible amenities, typical of those who are used to living in Paris, . . . surrounded by a huge and well-maintained garden full of flowers, . . . a large orchard with a variety of fruits, . . . all protected by a barbed-wire fence" (17)—and the other endured by the immigrants on their arrival—"[these houses] were not ready to receive [their] inhabitants. . . . It was an absolute discomfort. Everybody had to sleep on the floor, in a depressing promiscuity" (17).

The social, spatial, and religious dimensions of the feminine perspective are evident in Alexander's writing, though not with the same emphasis found in Elisa Lispector's novel. My examination of *Filipson* led me to perceive the results of the limitations the author had to endure, due to a social structure circumscribing women to predetermined physical and social roles. Within those limits, Alexander writes about the cosmos found inside the fences of the farm, with her family's house serving as background and sometimes as her bridge to the world. By coincidence, it was situated on a privileged plot of Filipson: "Our house was located on a promontory, facing the main road" (199). On one of its flanks there was a creek that, transposed to a metaphorical language by the narrator, summarizes the lives of the inhabitants of Filipson: " . . . our modest creek. It rolled year after year, fulfilling its destiny, quenching our thirst, cleansing the newly born, washing our wounds, sweat and tears of frustration, and changing itself into the golden and aromatic broth at the table of the newlyweds" (200). Alexander's view of the world was supported by her close connection with her parents, since most, if not all, of the people she associated with on the farm were also people with whom her parents had a relationship. Once aware of this support, she roamed, with the lack of discipline typical of young, healthy people, all quadrants of her territory. That was her reign, though it was not hers to rule.

While the women could leave the farm only on the arms of their husbands (or with this prospect in mind), the men were free to try different skills in the nearest town or to leave the farm for good. The separation of customs and roles between men and women was tacitly followed. Women would remain on the farm's grounds and hear about the outside universe through the perceptions of their men: "young and old, meeting in the train station on Saturday afternoons. The older ones exchanged ideas about politics and agriculture. . . . And returning home, they used to tell their wives, who stayed behind to care for the children, the news about the world" (72).

The author does not present formal grievances by the women in Filipson, though she refers to "different" females who either chose or were impelled to lead their lives alone and independently from a man's support. Those women were ostracized by the community, as it happened to a woman, conveniently called "the crazy one," who had been abandoned, with three children, by her husband ("Ratzel Amonis," 149–57).

Though Alexander's reminiscences are varied and colorful, they are restricted to the limits of the farm. She was vivacious and could be found everywhere as a keen observer. Still, she was a woman in a cocoon, while the men, including her brothers, younger and older, were able to brave the world beyond Filipson's fences. Apparently not personally hurt by this division, in the text she occasionally acknowledges the restrictions she felt: "After Adélia [the older sister] got married, my chores in the house were doubled, I hardly found time to study. I would return from school in a dash, then would run to meet my parents in the plantation in order to help them in the sowing or in the harvest" (147).

Since these harsh routines were justified by the times, she expanded her limited world by verbally plowing the farm in all directions, recreating a cosmos that she was able to relive with its old crusted structure and the division of roles between men and women. The refreshing approach of the girl who lived in that world has an expected ending: she leaves the farm on the arm of her husband.

Janette Fishenfeld, born Janette Diamant in Niterói, Rio de Janeiro, in 1927, was the daughter of a Jewish immigrant from Bessarabia and a Jewish-Brazilian native. Her upbringing was traditional, but at the same time, she was liberated from the usual restrictions that have been the major obstacle to the development of a career among women in the first quarter of this century. It was in high school that she began pursuing an inclination toward literature, by working on the school newspaper. In her senior year in high school, she earned first prize in a fiction and poetry contest. She graduated in biological sciences from the Faculdade Nacional de Filosofia but relinquished the chance to pursue a teaching career in her field. Soon after graduating, she married Luis Fishenfeld, with whom she had two daughters. She died in 1990, in Rio de Janeiro, of leukemia.

After her marriage, having given up teaching, she devoted her energies to the preservation of Jewish values and Zionism. In keeping with her concerns, she became a dedicated volunteer in the local chapter of Wizo, a women's international Zionist organization. Though she had studied science, Fishenfeld soon began to distinguish herself as a good communicator and speech writer. Resuming her interest in writing, she started to contribute to Jewish journals in Rio de Janeiro. In time, she became an "official chronicler" through regular contributions to *Aonde Vamos?* (Where Are We Going?) and *Menorah*, the most popular magazines in the community. For many years she had a regular column, "Imagens no meu espelho" (Images in My Mirror), in *Aonde Vamos?* in which she also published short stories, some of which were later collected in *Os dispersos, contos* (The Scattered Ones, Stories), her only published book.

Fishenfeld's columns and the short stories took a forthright stance on the preservation of Jewish religious values, belief in Zionist ideals, and her view that the family is the essential institution for sustaining Judaism. In "Uma estória que se repete" (A Story that Repeats Itself), published in the mid-1960s, she describes the reactions of the parents of a young man when they find out that their son, in order to become the husband of a non-Jewish girl, is going to be married in the Catholic church.[9] Their bewilderment has tragic consequences: When he found out about it, the father had a violent reaction, which brought him his first heart attack; some months after the wedding, he died. The mother ended up getting used to the new situation: embittered, she saw her daughter-in-law baptizing the two children who were born to the couple, with the husband's approval. The author gives an ironic stitch to the narrative: "Now I hear that the couple is getting a divorce, after some years of a marriage that looked good. A friend of the wife, unaware that I know the situation, observes: 'Marriage to a Jew does not end well . . .' In the end, the balance is, as usual, negative."

In the same monthly column, Fishenfeld published "Casamentos mistos" (Mixed Marriages), in which she again writes of marriage between Jews and non-Jews. The impetus for this article is the announcement that "the Catholic church publicly acknowledges that 'it opposes the marriage of its followers to people of another faith.'" Based on this news, the writer states that the fear of assimilation is reciprocal, for it exists among Jews and non-Jews alike. She ponders on the "pope's pronouncement about mixed marriages," through which "the Pope will give authorization between Catholics and non-Catholics once the spouses respect their respective religions." It seems that Fishenfeld's intention is to deconstruct the popular voice that emphasizes that only Jews avoid mixed marriages. Her posture on this newly articulated position of the Church is thus summarized: "Therefore, the pope's declaration exonerates the Jews from one more accusation: that mixed marriages are unilaterally avoided."

In the short story "Os dispersos," which appears in the book of the same title, Fishenfeld refers to the scattered Jews, reformulating the meaning of "scattered" to invoke those Jews who have separated themselves from the mainstream of Judaism. The narrator in the story, a young man who is never named, has strong religious beliefs. He falls in love with Ruth, of Jewish descent, whom he met while both were attending the same art school. She belongs to a family of Jewish atheists, politically involved with Socialist ideas. Bringing to the forefront of the story the contempt the young man's father has for "the others," that is, those Jews who have renounced the rituals and prayers, like Ruth's father did and taught her to do, the dialogue discloses their mutual lack of understanding and lack of acceptance of their differences.

The narrative describes the couple's eventual separation and then brings them back together when Ruth is about to get married to a non-Jew. When she reveals that her father does not approve of her plans, the unnamed narrator suggests that the father will suffer because of it. Fueled by a rhetoric that supported her development into a woman alien to Judaism, she retorts: "My father is a cultivated man. He understands. Because I am his daughter it is difficult for him to accept my reasoning. I am the product of his concepts, his philosophy, the mirror of a new youth, without roots or ties, as he dreamed of. In any case, he cannot do anything anymore" (31). In the face of her arguments, the young man remains silent. However, as in the final act in the theater, he offers a last comment on Ruth's father: "On Yom Kippur I saw him on the veranda of his home, somber and distant, plunged in his old rocking chair, where Ruth used to wait for me. There was in his features a terrible bitterness. I think that if it were possible for him to pray, there would not have been a prayer more contrite than his" (32). Fishenfeld seems to take the position of the young man who tried his best to attract Ruth back to the folds of Judaism. Unable to realize that, she/he blames Ruth's father for the loss of the object of his love and for her straying away from Judaism.

In the article on mixed marriage and in this short story, the author makes a dual argument against mixed marriages. Her focus on this subject emphasizes the danger of dissipation of the Jewish faith and cultures in the Diaspora. Coming very close to openly opposing mixed marriages, she stresses the threat of assimilation that hangs over traditional Jewish homes, through marriage, as in "Uma estória que se repete," or through political and cultural affiliations, as in "Os dispersos." Although we are left without knowing how Ruth's marriage to a non-Jew turned out in the latter story, we are assured that a divorce occurred in the former. Taking the two stories together, with both situations carrying tragic consequences for the fathers of the youngsters, one is led to conjecture that Janette Fishenfeld intended them as fables whose moral was a warning to her readers.

Sara Riwka Erlich, the last of the authors to be examined here, is the only one alive at this writing. Erlich was born in Recife, Pernambuco, the daughter of Polish immigrants. There she graduated in medicine, with a specialty in child and adolescent psychiatry. She has published many articles and essays in her field, and belongs to several professional associations in Brazil and abroad. Her semifictional and semiautobiographical books are mostly about her experiences as a child of immigrants and as part of the first generation born in Brazil.

No tempo das acácias (In the Time of the Acacias; 1978) conveys the elements of exchange and acquisition that are typical of cultural transactions. As the daughter of foreigners, she was immersed, from an early age, in both cultures: the one belonging to her parents and the one acquired in Pernambuco, where she was born, to which they also partially adhered. To this interchange, Sara added a third one, her experiences in Israel, therefore creating a multifaceted cultural world to which she adjusted without any major difficulty.

The main component in her writings is her desire to combine, fuse, or juxtapose all cultures to which she had been exposed throughout her life. Thus the ecumenical, comprehensive aspect of *No tempo das acácias*, which revolves around reminiscences of her psychological and spiritual formative years. The author describes her multidimensional world, which ranged from the dominant Catholic religion to Judaism, from Pernambucan to Jewish cuisines, and from Brazilian to Yiddish songs. Her style has a polyphonic rhythm of images, when she changes the focus of her description through short and concise sentences, some of them devoid of a verb. The ellipses that appear at the end of many of the sentences in the text seem to convey the feelings of suspension that the author is supposedly experiencing while reminiscing. The stories refer to a third person, "the girl," who is obviously herself, given the biographical similarities of the author and her character:[10]

> The Gloria street. The Brazilian-Hebrew school . . . The Gloria Convent . . . The Woodmen's club . . . Every year, the roller coaster, the carousel, the little boats, the ferris wheel, the stands with little trinkets . . . The Church, all lighted up and perfumed. Traditions whose beauty and mysticism wrapped up the girl and merged with her feelings and memories, with the deep chants, old as the times, that reverberated in the old Synagogue of the Leão Coroado Street . . . during the Jewish religious and historical celebrations. (*No tempo das acácias* 47)

She imaginatively strolls along the streets where she feels the harmonious coexistence of Catholicism and Judaism, and in her home in Pernambuco, she feels the presence of an old Europe and the echoes of the adaptations made by the Jews:

> The big and yellow samovar, polished and glistening, that would "warm up by itself" belonged to the grand-grandpa. The samovar in the backyard, on the ground, the kerosene, the charcoals as embers, the water, the black tea . . . And the sliced dry fish, the potato, the black bread and the butter made out of melted chicken fat . . . along with the black beans and rice, the sun dried meat and the cod, the pudding of coconut milk, the tapioca, the hominy . . . The "borscht," the carrot "tsimes," the chicken liver . . .

"kreplach," pickled cucumber, cheese "blintzes," the "glo-
rious" "gefilte fish" . . . and the renowned "feijoada," the
black bean soup, the sun dried meat, the "macacheira,"
the flour eaten in the backlands, the minced meat with
vegetables, roasted loin (not the pork loin, forbidden) . . .
(47–48)

Erlich reminisces about the past and observes the present through
concrete object-symbols, such as pots and other utensils, as well as
through music abstractions. Her home is represented in the kitchen—
source of a nurturing process through actual food and spiritual nour-
ishment, a place traditionally reserved to women. While merging her
ancestral inheritance with the newly acquired cultural ambience, she
tells of the latter as a way of constructing a new life, yet based on and
emerging from Brazilian and Jewish foundations:

To the copper pans that crossed the ocean, we added new
pans, of aluminum, generators of different kinds of food
and energy. In the kitchen, the melancholic, sweet and
millenary folkloric and religious songs in Yiddish, Hebrew
and Polish, alternated with *samba* and *frevo*, songs that
reflected almost always a great and hidden passion, un-
reciprocated or not understood and missed. (60–61)

The author's experience in Israel, where she lived and practiced
medicine, went in an opposite direction in relation to the exchange
of cultural traits. Whereas her parents brought with them across the
Atlantic the objects, food, and songs that were transformed into shrines
by her nostalgia, when she went to Israel she took her Pernambucan
background. Therefore, the Northeast region and Recife, where she
was born, met Jerusalem in her very personal world, vast and pluralistic, mingling all landscapes in one: "Brazilian Northeast and Israel.

Not the Israel for tourists, that looks in despair and bravery to hide its pains and whose screams are forbidden from polluting the chain of luxurious hotels and their colorful audiovisual programs, cheerful and filled with joy and rhythm . . . " (72).

The similarities of climate and topography between the area where Sara Erlich was born and most of Israel surpasses, in her text, their resemblances and are transported into a mystical dimension:

> Walking along your streets, Jerusalem, entering through your gates, I felt and better understood the city of Recife that I had already described for you. Recife and the live memory of my companion, of my dear friends, so far away and yet so near. It was in you, o Jerusalem, that the merging was complete, integrated and harmonious, more than in Tel Aviv, in spite of its beaches and of its sun. (77)

The threefold alliance—Europe, Brazil, and Israel—is gently revived in the poetic prose of Erlich, who does not tell a story that might lead the reader through meanders typical of fiction. Her story draws a circle, a convergence of cultures that, if it does not exist in practice, is of an unconditional reality for her. The transposition of the old home to Brazil through pots, pans, and food and the transportation to Israel of her memories of a companion and friends are coherent with her vision of life as a circle, not a linear itinerary. The cycles are repeated, starting with the Jewish education, viewed as fundamental in her life, that she incorporates into non-Jewish Brazilian culture, in order that both can merge in the curved hills of Jerusalem. From a diasporic perspective, she dives into a vision that dissolves the division learned in the Diaspora itself. Erlich undoes what is done, blurring the separation of religions and cultures in the world, by melting its boundaries, at least in her mind.

These four Jewish Brazilian women present in their discourses different topographical landscapes and distinct styles of writing. From the fictionalized biography of Lispector to the chronicles of Alexander and of Fishenfeld to the inspiring prose poem of Erlich, the representation is complete. Lesser- known writers than Elisa Lispector, Frida Alexander, Janette Fishenfeld, and Sara Riwka Erlich are yet to be discovered. Nevertheless, all four of them have discovered us, women (and men) in the Diaspora, in our act of balancing the past and the present, in control and being controlled by the order and the chaos of the new worlds.

The four women, representing diverse regions of Brazil—Alexander, Rio Grande do Sul; Lispector and Fishenfeld, Rio de Janeiro; and Erlich, Pernambuco—also convey a diversity of perspectives on Judaism. While Alexandr's writings suggest an informal study on the adjustment of newly arrived immigrants not only to a new land but also and mainly to a new style of life, Lispector emphasizes the condition of loneliness shared by immigrants in general. And while Fishenfeld maintains a Judaism that should not admit a crack in its walls, Erlich opens up her religion and culture to better understand the others' beliefs and ways of being.

Several dimensions of Judaism are thus represented by these authors: undeviating instances in relation to tradition, as indicated in Fishenfeld's writing, imply a self-absorbing attitude, not unknown in some Jewish circles; a jubilant Zionist discourse, permeating Lispector's novel, is a rupture from common stories on wretched Jewish characters; the uniqueness of a world thrust into the flat southern lands of Brazil, as depicted by Alexander, uncovers the struggles of the multifaceted Brazilian Jewish gauchos and, finally, the encompassing ecumenical gesture, as suggested by Erlich. All these viewpoints, converging in the fictional arena, represent not only different regions where Judaism has settled in Brazil but also a manifold Portuguese-speaking facet of Latin American Jewry.

1. Though not submitted to an official census, Jews in Brazil number 150,000, with a large concentration in the cities of São Paulo, Rio de Janeiro, Belo Horizonte, Porto Alegre, and Curitiba. The total Brazilian population is officially counted as close to 149 million.

2. All translations in this chapter, unless otherwise noted, are mine.

3. The restrictions seemingly universal, it is interesting to compare Susan Weidman Schneider's thoughts, in "Our Minds for Ourselves," on the limitations felt by Jewish women immigrants and natives of America when it came to improving their education. Keeping in mind the cultural and social distances between both societies, Brazilian and American, they coincide, nevertheless, in what concerns the first Jewish communities. During that period there was little, if any, freedom of choice for women; they had to choose between marriage and education, for combining both was not considered practical.

4. All quotations here are from the second edition, revised by the author: Elisa Lispector, No exílio. Brasília: Ebrasa, 1971.

5. For a brief biographical note and primary bibliography, see Regina Igel, "Lispector, Elisa," in Lockhart 356–58.

6. Regina Igel. "O Tigre de Bengala, Os Polos Invisíveis da Solidão Humana," O Estado de S. Paulo, 264.5 (July 7, 1985): 7.

7. Interviews with Leon Alexander (New York, February 1997) and with Roberta Alexander Sundfeld, the author's granddaughter (São Paulo, August 1997).

8. Érico Veríssimo. Letter dated September 5, 1952, in São Paulo (on back cover of edition being examined).

9. Copies of this story and "Casamentos mistos" were given to me by the author when I interviewed her in her home in Rio de Janeiro in April 1985.

10. I spent many hours interviewing the author over a span of five years (1988–92), in Recife, Pernambuco, and in São Paulo and Israel. When I visited her in Recife, Erlich took me on a tour through the city and showed me all the places mentioned in No tempo das acácias, and, among friends, she sang some of the tunes whose lyrics are printed in the book.

REFERENCES

Alexander, Frida. Filipson. São Paulo: Editora Fulgor Limitada, 1967.

Barsted, Leila de A. Linhares. "É falando que a gente se entende." Mulheres em movimento. Org. Projeto-Mulher do Instituto de Ação Cultural. Rio de Janeiro: Editora Marco Zero, n.d. (possibly 1984).

Bruschini, Cristina. "Mulher e trabalho. Uma avaliação da década da mulher (1975–1985)." *A condição feminina*. Ed. Nanci Valadares de Carvalho. São Paulo: Vértice, Editora Revista dos Tribunais, 1988.

Coelho, Nelly Novaes. "Tendências atuais da literature feminina no Brasil. *Feminino singular. A participaçãoda mulher na literature brasileira contemporânea*. Ed. Ana Maria de Almeida Camargo. São Paulo: Edições GRD/ Arquivo Municipal de Rio Claro, 1989. 6–13.

Erlich, Sara Riwka. *No tempo das acácias*. Rio de Janeiro: Editora Civilizaçao Brasileira, 1978.

Fishenfeld, Janette. "Casamento mistos." *Aonde Vamos?* November 4, 1965.

————. *Os dispersos, contos*. Niterói: Wizo do Brasil, 1966.

————. "Uma estória que se repete." *Aonde Vamos?* November 4, 1965.

Igel, Regina. "Lispector, Elisa." Lockhart 356–58.

————. "*O tigre de Bengala*. Os polos invisíveis da solidão humana." *O Estado de S. Paulo* 5 (July 7, 1985): 7.

Lispector, Elisa. *No exílio*. 2d ed. (rev. by author). Brasília: EBRASA, 1971.

Lockhart, Darrell B., ed. *Jewish Writers of Latin America: A Dictionary*. New York: Garland, 1997.

Miranda, Ana. "Ser mulher." *VEJA 25 Anos-Reflexões para o Futuro* (n.e.). São Paulo: Fundação Odebrecht, 1993.

Oliveira Ramos, Tânia Regina. "'Meninas atrevidas. O que é que não dizer?'" *Feminino e Literatura, Tempo Brasileiro* 1.1 (1962): 21.

Schneider, Susan Weidman. "Our Minds for Ourselves." *Jewish and Female, Choices and Changes in Our Lives Today*. By Schneider. New York: Simon & Schuster, 1984. 149–97.

clarice lispector's jewish universe
PASSION IN SEARCH OF NARRATIVE IDENTITY

Nelson H. Vieira

> *For everything alive is searching for something or someone.*
> CLARICE LISPECTOR, "SEARCHING"

> *Writing is a curse, but a curse akin to salvation. . . . To write is to try and*
> *understand, to try and repeat the unrepeatable, to savor to the last that senti-*
> *ment which would otherwise remain vague and oppressive. To write is also to*
> *bless a life which has not been blessed.*
> CLARICE LISPECTOR, "WRITING"

If writing has the capacity to bless a life that has not been blessed, then Clarice Lispector's life was most assuredly blessed by art, in her case, by her passion for delving into the mysteries of beingness and salvation. As a fervent writer whose prose manifests a burning quest for ontological knowledge through writing, this Brazilian Jewish woman, one of Latin America's premier female authors, invented an original way of using words that revealed an intense search for understanding the enigmas of existence, the problematics of subjectivity and difference, and the experiences of displacement, exile, and alterity as well as the paths toward the unsayable and the spiritual. The inspirational quality of her writing, described as spontaneous, intuitive, introspective, and lyrical, generated from an inner drive, emblematic of her lifelong search for her own literary voice.

This search was influenced by her own life experiences of exile and migration—her Russian Jewish heritage and its drama of emi-

85

gration from the Ukraine, her identity as a naturalized Brazilian, a Northeasterner as well as a Carioca, and her sixteen years of living abroad in the uncomfortable role of diplomat's wife. All these episodes in her life are emotionally marked by dislocation and exile, beginning with her "exiled" birth during her immigrant family's trek to Brazil. As her biographer, Nádia Battella Gotlib, states: "Clarice accumulated spaces as if she were in no place at all, motivated by the sensation of not belonging to anything and to anybody, in a constant state of exile—she came from exile, lived in exile and leaned toward exile" ("Ser ou não ser" 317).

Did the trauma of exile leave its mark in the form of a silence about her early life experiences and her roots? As a Brazilian Jewish, middle-class woman and uncommon writer intuitive to the existential depths of the human soul, her public silence about her Jewish heritage may indeed be rooted in the terrain of exile, just as the Bible's Queen Esther kept silent about her heritage by not disclosing her family and race. Moreover, was Clarice Lispector's aesthetic preoccupation with silence, as an allusion to the unsayable and the limitations of language, linked to her own enigmatic feelings about displacement and exile? Since Lispector's writing only discloses her Jewish voice in an oblique manner, for many years her Jewish cultural heritage remained unacknowledged by critics and readers. Consequently, it is prudent to refer to her as a Brazilian writer who was Jewish rather than a Jewish writer who was Brazilian. Nonetheless, this essay examines Clarice Lispector's fiction within the context of her Jewish heritage and the Jewish Diaspora in Brazil. When referring to her Jewish immigrant home culture, her own study of Hebrew and her parents' Yiddishkeit lifestyle, Gotlib also observes: "But Hebrew culture, metaphorically transformed, will be manifested in her future work" (*Clarice* 66).

It is my contention that Clarice Lispector transposed her sense of the uprootedness and unfixedness of life-in-dispersion to her identity-questing narratives in which she explores and searches for what the Jewish Diasporist painter R. B. Kitaj calls "the Diasporist pursuit of a homeless logic of *ethnie* [that] may be the radical (root) of a newer art than we can yet imagine," one striving for a universal artistic expression that speaks to many people.

In this vein, Clarice Lispector wrote to reclaim for herself and for her readers a form of expression representative of the ontological struggle she experienced in trying to understand the human condition, a compelling quest related to women as well as to men, one bordering on the metaphysical, as the above epigraph on writing evokes. In her strong urge to write and communicate her protagonists' profound sensations of personal and sociocultural displacement, Lispector experienced through narrative a pulsating force that became a spiritual search for understanding and redemption. In a related fashion, Gotlib sees Lispector's struggle with the word as her being "occupied throughout her life with the labor of writing as a process of search for her identity" (*Clarice* 98). The Brazilian critic Olga de Sá refers to this fundamental proclivity in her work as "ontological questioning" ("Clarice Lispector" 272). This ontological "quest" is apparent in her major novels, especially those told in the intimate first person in which the lines between autobiographical fiction and autobiography appear to be blurred. In such works as *A paixão segundo G. H.* (The Passion According to GH; 1964), *Agua viva* (The Stream of Life; 1973), and *A hora da estrela* (The Hour of the Star; 1977), her narrators' monologues are frequently internal discourses or quests on the phenomenon of "being" and "being other," simultaneously. These quests are also evident in the interior monologues of the protagonists of her third-person novels such as *Perto do coração selvagem* (Near to the Wild Heart; 1944) and *A maçã no escuro* (The Apple in the Dark; 1961). Consequently, Lispector's writing derives most profoundly from a sensibility linked to an acute sense of alterity as well as to the myriad tribulations within the experience of *galut*,[1] one remarkably in tune with another of Kitaj's statements:

> A Diasporist picture is marked by Exile and its discontents as subtly and unclearly as pictures painted by women or homosexuals are marked by their inner exilic discontents.
>
> If some of us cover up (or raise up) our discontents in the name of universal art, I can see no reason why others should not make memorable pictures in another name, not 'art' but, say, (Diasporist) Commonality—as I choose to believe Kafka did. And then it can be called art . . . risen from universal connectedness. (96–97)

Clarice Lispector's search does spring from a sense of exilic connectedness, groundlessness, and homelessness that was translated into many levels of meaning inspiring a spiritual affinity with her readers whose own sense of exile went beyond the geographic. Her spiritual quest also lies in her being a Jewish woman of spirit, an independent-spirited writer who was open to a form of mystical reception and, above all, to the experience with the ineffable. Transcending the concreteness of the written word, Lispector frequently evokes what words are incapable of saying—the ineffable—an ingredient also integral to Judaic philosophy and religion. Her work calls to mind the teachings of the Jewish theologian Abraham Joshua Heschel who, in *Man Is Not Alone*, describes the sense of the ineffable as the "distinction between the utterable and the unutterable, to be stunned by that which is but cannot be put into words. It is the sense of the sublime that we have to regard as the root of man's creative activities in art, thought and noble living" (4). Lispector's prose repeatedly alludes to the insufficiency of language to grasp and to relate the feelings she experienced. Heschel goes on to describe further the ineffable in a way that not only recalls Lispector's "unsayable" but also conveys her special brand of spiritual insight in its acknowledgment of the unreachable, a feeling also related to the sense of "not belonging completely," one often associated with diasporist and female situations:

> The attempt to convey what we see and cannot say is the everlasting theme of mankind's unfinished symphony, a venture in which adequacy is never achieved. . . . A sensitive person knows that the intrinsic, the most essential, is never expressed. . . . The stirring in our hearts when watching the star-studded sky is something no language can declare. What smites us with unquenchable amazement is not that which we grasp and are able to convey but that which lies within our reach but beyond our grasp; not the quantitative aspect of nature but something qualitative; not what is beyond our range in time and space but the true meaning, source and end of being, in other words, the ineffable. (4–5)

In applying the ineffable to Lispector's spiritually motivated writing, I read her work and her universe as bordering on the mystical in her persistent quest for meaning and understanding, despite her awareness of humankind's incapacity to know everything because full knowledge rests only with the Divine. In this vein, the mystery of her writing is commensurate with the hermeneutical idiom of the Old Testament: the imperfections of language and meaning are continually searching for an answer, a hidden one that is ungraspable. Her spiritually motivated prose strives for answers and meanings that are always elusive, but, in so doing, she frequently uncovers new and hidden meaning in the language of everyday life. In this sense, one may read her work as a form of modern Midrash in the tradition of the Talmud. In addition, she relies on the nonrational means of love and spirit to attain an imperfect sense of the attainable that parallels undeniably the imperfections of the human condition.

In describing her spiritual approach to life and writing, Clarice Lispector indirectly addressed her own view of the ineffable in one of the many notes she scribbled for possible inclusion in her fiction:

> I could narrate all the facts, but of what I felt I could not speak: there are more feelings than words. There is no way of saying what one feels. One can allude to them mysteriously. . . .
>
> Spirit spirit spirit spirit spirit spirit spirit. In the final analysis what is spirit? Is it what I feel inside the non-me? More. Morphologically it's a word that's a flash and audacious, like the flight of birds. Spirit: and then it takes off. (Borelli 77)

However, Lispector does indeed convey her sense of the ineffable and the spiritual most directly in a very famous and frequently quoted passage from her tour-de-force novel, *A paixão segundo G. H.*, where she illustrates how language and the ineffable are linked:

> Language is my human endeavor. I have fatefully to go seeking and fatefully I return with empty hands. But—I return with the unsayable. The unsayable can be given me only through the failure of my language. Only when the construct falters do I reach what it could not accomplish. (170)

Interestingly, in Hebrew, G-d's name is unsayable, and thus one has to employ other means to allude to the divine presence. In a similar vein, Lispector's struggle with words and their meanings, also reflected in the poststructural problematics and gaps between the signifier and the signified, parallels the process that acknowledges the unsayable or the unattainable. In her work, her allusions to the hiddenness of meaning imply that the ineffable in existence and signification is also related to the emotional enigmas of exile or separation and, by extension, to the element of "search" as a condition of these experiences. Along these lines, one can appreciate how the ineffable is related to the exegetic legacy of her Jewish culture. This concept is movingly illustrated in her chronicle "Belonging," where she reflects on the unreachable in her search for a spiritual homeland within her personal and social circumstances. This chronicle manifests her emotional exile in the desert of solitude as well as her undying need to belong, which she pursued in order to nurture herself as well as others:

> Perhaps I started writing so early in life because, at least, by writing, I belonged to myself to some extent. Which is a pale imitation. (. . .)
> An intense desire to belong often comes from my own inner strength—I wish to belong so that my strength will not be useless and may serve to strengthen some other person or thing. (*Discovering the World* 32–33)

And then Lispector makes an even more personal confession, revealing not only her primal need to belong but also how the exilic circumstances she repeatedly encountered in life were linked to a specific event:

> Yet my birth was planned in such a pleasing way. My mother was in poor health and there was a well-known superstition which claimed that a woman could be cured of illness if she gave birth to a son. So I was deliberately conceived: with love and hope. Only I failed to cure my mother. And to this day I carry this burden of guilt: my

parents conceived me for a specific mission and I failed them. As if they had been relying on me to defend the trenches in time of war and I had deserted my post. . . . I wanted to work a miracle: to be born and cure my mother. Then I should truly have belonged to my father and mother. I could not even confide my *solitude of not belonging* because, as a deserter, I kept the secret of my escape which shame forbade me to reveal. (33)

Lispector closes this chronicle with a moving statement that conveys her emotional and spiritual homelessness:

Life has allowed me to belong now and then, as if to give me the measure of what I am losing by not belonging. And then I discovered that: *to belong is to live.* I experienced it with the thirst of someone in the desert who avidly drinks the last drops of water from a flask. And then my thirst returns and I find myself walking that same desert. (33–34)

The focus on images of exile, belongingness, quest, diasporism, Judaism, and writing as well as the ineffable and the metaphysical serves as a fitting prelude to a discussion of Clarice Lispector's spiritual and aesthetic universe. With this perspective, one can glean the myriad issues and insights embedded in her narratives, such as her Jewish heritage and her undying interest in women's conflicts vis-à-vis the surrounding society, situations that projected her own intense identification with the dilemmas facing women in the modern world. To render a meaningful picture of Clarice Lispector's cosmos within the context of these above issues, two aspects of her life and writing warrant further development—her literary vision or nonreligious spirituality and her Jewish heritage. This focus will illustrate how her

Jewish background and experience with diasporism contributed to her art.[2]

As a form of spiritual and mystical quest, her narratives explore creation and existence by incessantly challenging traditional concepts of God, woman, humanity, and beingness. However, it is important to reiterate that the spiritual in Lispector does not translate into traditional religiosity; rather it suggests ideological or metaphysical questioning (and often defiance) in relation to conventional forms of subjectivity, thinking, religion, and behavior. The Brazilian critic Alfredo Bosi stresses the metaphysical thrust of her vision as a force stronger than the psychological. And in referring to her aesthetic vision of subjectivity, Olga de Sá affirms Bosi's perception by recognizing her "desire to live or to interpret the density of life; to take part in the thick blood of existence or to throw [herself] into the game of writing" ("Clarice Lispector" 272). In her essay "Paródia e metafísica," Sá also underscores Lispector's spiritual orientation in her discussion of the novel *The Passion According to GH:* "She privileges certain metaphorical-metaphysical nuclei which as poles or 'pulsations' attempt to retrieve within the abstract of 'rational language' the sensitive concreteness of the human being" (213).

Underscoring the ironic, mocking, and sometimes parodic voices of her narrators who scorn the human struggle "to know" about life, solely in rational terms, Sá believes Lispector's goal was "to highlight the essential, a mystical vision of the world which dispenses with religion . . . without dispensing with the deepest religious experiences of Judaism and Christianity, of the Bible's cosmic vision" ("Paródia" 988, 219). Therefore, although she was publicly reticent about her Jewish background, not being predisposed to social realism or rigid categorizations such as being considered an ethnic writer, she nonetheless did incorporate, albeit subtly, spiritual and hermeneutical aspects of her Jewish cultural legacy into her unique style and thematics. In so doing, she transcended the parameters of literary mimesis, focusing on interpretive openness and unconventional narration while simultaneously propelling thought and feeling from the contemplative toward the ineffable.

Clarice Lispector (1920–77) was born in the Ukraine and emigrated to Brazil as a baby with her parents and two sisters. This household and the family's Yiddish-Russian cultural heritage are mimetically portrayed in the semiautobiographical novel *No exílio* (In Exile) written by Clarice's older sister, Elisa Lispector (1911–89), an accomplished novelist with her own reading public. Published in 1948 at the time of the birth of the Jewish National State of Israel, this novel, a paean to the new homeland for Jews, captures the brutal realities of a persecuted Russian-Jewish family "in flight." Interspersed with many Yiddish and Russian words, this narrative traces the exodus and exile of a Jewish husband, his wife, and their three daughters from a violent and cold Russia of the steppes to the stifling heat of an underdeveloped world in the tropics of Brazil. Told from the point of view of the older sister, this roman à clef is relentless in its depiction of Jewish fate and exile, twentieth-century anti-Semitism, episodes of Russian history, Nazism, the controversy over the foundation of Israel, and the family's valiant resistance to obstacles that attempt to destroy their cultural identity. Imbued with a strong Jewish/Yiddish flavor, Elisa Lispector's semiautobiographical novel confirms the presence of an ardent Jewish cultural ideology in the Lispector household, one commensurate with Clarice's personal sense of social justice, which she undoubtedly inherited from her father who, in this novel, is depicted as a passionate ideologue of social freedom for all Jews.

For purposes of understanding Clarice Lispector's cultural, ethnic, and spiritual ethos, it is significant to note that the profoundly Jewish worldview presented in her sister's novel testifies to a more than superficial acquaintance with Jewish mores and rituals on the part of the Lispectors. What emerges is the dramatic portrait of an immigrant family deeply immersed in a shtetl mentality and culture of Jewish faith and ethics as it confronts the cataclysmic and cross-cultural conflicts of the twentieth-century Jewish Diaspora in Brazil, today the home of 120,000 to 150,000 Jews. Modern-day Brazilian Jews are primarily Ashkenazi who emigrated in the early part of this century, given that the Sephardic population from the colonial period eventually disappeared via their forced assimilation as New Christians.

Clarice Lispector became the youngest daughter of Jewish parents who had already started their emigration to Brazil when she was born.[3] In 1923 they arrived in Brazil, settling for their first three years in the underdeveloped northeastern state of Alagoas and then moving on to Recife, at that time the provincial capital city of Pernambuco, where the family lived until 1937, when Clarice was seventeen. Gotlib's literary biography provides documents attesting to her attendance at a Jewish school between the ages of nine and thirteen where she studied Hebrew. In reconstructing the scenario of the Lispector family in Recife, Gotlib furnishes details that describe the Jewish ambience of Clarice's years in Recife, placing her in the neighborhood where many Jewish families resided (Clarice 95). Being the youngest of the family, Clarice appeared to her relatives to be unaware of the poverty and difficulties her immigrant family first encountered in their new land. It was her older sister, Elisa, who was to document the family's tribulations in that semiautobiographical novel metaphorically inspired by the theme of exile, a subject that was to emerge in Clarice's works in the form of displacement and otherness. However, on the occasion of several interviews, Clarice was to recall the family's struggle and pain as well as her attempts to overcome that harsh reality by pretending to be happy, mischievous, and gregarious.[4] According to Clarice, although the family almost starved, they managed to eke out a living until her father improved his situation by going into business. Her upbringing in Recife, in the underdeveloped Brazilian Northeast, left many lasting impressions about social injustice that were recorded in several chronicles and articles. In one piece she is quoted as saying: "to live in the Northeast or the North of Brazil is to live more intensely and nearer to true Brazilian life. (. . .) My beliefs were learned in Pernambuco."[5] She returned to her northeastern roots in 1976, one year before her death, in addition to another trip, albeit literary, via her unsophisticated, northeastern, and seemingly anti-Maccabean eponymous heroine, Macabéa, of her last novella, *The Hour of the Star*. In revisiting her cultural roots by way of this very ironic narrative with its subtle Judaic motifs, for the first time in literature, Lispector also returned more openly to her Jewish roots and to the various social classes she experienced during her life. As a more evident coming-to-terms with her Jewishness and with her innate sense of social justice, this last work first appeared during the last months of her life and incited even greater interest in her work as well as in the enigmatic figure of its author.

Moving to Rio de Janeiro in 1937, she completed a high school preparatory curriculum in law and enrolled in the National Faculty of Law in Rio de Janeiro from 1940 to 1943, hoping, somewhat naively, as she later commented, to pursue her goals of social reform and justice, interestingly in the area of penal law. Her initial interest in this area of study was sparked by her serious commitment to social justice. During her first year of law school, she worked as a translator and copy editor for the Agência Nacional. Enjoying the excitement of coming into contact with many different and often famous people and intellectuals, in 1942 she acquired another journalistic position in the evening newspaper *A Noite*, at which point she began to write, with considerable angst and over a painful ten-month period, her first novel, *Near to the Wild Heart*. As she was to remark repeatedly, this novel "pursued" her, forcing her to jot down notes and ideas wherever she was. It was this habit of taking notes, reminiscent of the heroine Joana and her note taking, or jotting down ideas on any form of paper at hand, that became Lispector's unique inspirational method of writing, one she employed throughout her life.

Clarice Lispector's auspicious literary debut was even more remarkable because much of the critical reception to her first work was imbued with an air of mystery and wonder that something new was happening in Brazilian literature. At the time, the Brazilian critic and scholar Antônio Cândido characterized her innovative use of language in an unadorned style in his pathbreaking essay, "No raiar de Clarice Lispector" (At the Dawning of Clarice Lispector) as "an impressive attempt at taking our awkward language style to realms barely explored, forcing it to adapt to a way of thinking filled with mystery" (127). In describing her literary production throughout most of her life, critics usually avoided mentioning her Jewish heritage and for the most part never considered, until after her death, that her work actually harbored any Jewish overtones. Rather, her prose was primarily linked to the modernist tradition of James Joyce and particularly Virginia Woolf because Lispector's early fiction revealed an experimentalist bent with extensive use of interior monologue and stream-of-consciousness aimed at portraying moments of heightened introspection and perception. And later, as Clarice Lispector's writings became recognized as more philosophically and metaphysically evocative, she was also viewed as an author who reflected much of the thought of Kierkegaard and Sartre, ergo the existentialist interpretations critics gleaned from some of the stories about women in the 1960 collection, *Family Ties,* and from the 1961 novel, *The Apple in the Dark.* More recently, several literary studies have reevaluated her work within the poststructuralist position of linguistic "displacement" and postmodernism's literature of Silence.[6] All of these interpretations—existentialist, feminist, poststructuralist, postmodernist, and Judaic—are viable readings and rereadings of Lispector's work.

As alluded to above, it was not until her last piece of fiction, *The*

Hour of the Star, a novella published just months before her unexpected death from cancer, one day before her fifty-seventh birthday, that critical commentaries began to emerge about the oblique use of Jewish myths in her work.[7] This new way of looking at her fiction stemmed from this novella's symbolic use of the apochryphal Maccabean legend, personified in her eponymic protagonist Macabéa. Inspired by the biblical Maccabeans who resisted against Greek oppression in their refusal to disregard Jewish law, this novella was especially motivated by an image of a poor, unknown, northeastern girl, "exiled" to Rio from Alagoas, who was seen by Lispector in the Saint Cristóvão market fair of Rio's northern suburbs. Placing herself subtly within the multilayered narrative scheme composed by her fictional upper-middle-class male writer, Lispector evokes the hardships and resistance of a deprived soul who is seriously disadvantaged by an unjust and inhuman social system. Ergo, the indirect link to the Maccabeans, albeit the seemingly unheroic nature of her protagonist. According to Lispector, the novella in one way represents a "catharsis for a partially repressed childhood" (Gotlib, *Clarice* 465). And according to Gotlib, "the character may also be a catharsis for a Jewish past of suffering, an evocation of Hebrew culture" (465).

New insights into Clarice Lispector's writing from the Jewish motifs in this novella, however, were for the most part eclipsed by this narrative's surprisingly overt social theme, an unusual feature in Lispector given her predominantly lyrical, intimist, metaphysical, and psychophilosophical proclivities. As a result of its timely publication, the novella was seen by many as Clarice Lispector's swan song, where she was making an open and final social statement about Brazilian society, herself, and supposedly her ethnic background. With no overt social element in her previous work, she had been frequently taken to task by Brazilian interviewers and critics accustomed to a literature heavily oriented toward social and realist mimetics, a tradition stemming from the naturalist literary strain and from the social realism and neonaturalism promoted by Brazilian Regionalist writers of the 1930s, a prose movement developing out of Brazilian modernism of the 1920s.

As a response to the many misconstrued interpretations of her apparent lack of social concern for her fellow man, in a 1975 interview with Celso Arnaldo Araújo for the magazine *Manchete,* Clarice Lispector emphatically stated: "There isn't a writer, painter or any artist whatsoever who doesn't mirror his times. In my own way, I am participating. I talk about anguish, joys, human feelings. Is there anything more *participatory* than that?" (48–49). Nevertheless, it was evident that in this late work Clarice Lispector had indeed afforded her fiction a new feature, one dramatizing the social plight of the impoverished people and migrants of Brazil's Northeast, symbolized by the barely literate Macabéa. In fact, in 1977 in the *Suplemento Literário Minas Gerais,* the Jewish writer Samuel Rawet underscored Eduardo Portella's statement about a new and socially concerned Lispector: "We ought to be talking about a new Clarice Lispector, outward and explicit, the *wild heart* committed northeasternly to the Brazilian scene" (8). However, Rawet believed that the northeastern as well as the Jewish impulse in Clarice Lispector had always been in her work. Thus we must remember that although Lispector never allowed her fiction the limited or deterministic parameters set by overt sociopolitical themes, she nonetheless was a very socially concerned and committed individual, as she emphatically declared in a 1968 interview[8] about her participation in student protest marches and her preoccupation with the general social conditions in Brazil. In the newspaper *A Gazeta,* in an article by Lígia Monteiro published one year after her death and entitled "Nostalgia for Clarice and Her Love of the World," a statement discussing her social commitment and sense of justice is included under the subheading "Literature and Justice,"[9] the title of one of her chronicles. This chronicle warrants attention because it infers a type of social commitment, reflective of, though not exclusive to, Judaism's

Golden Rule of loving thy neighbor and stressing ethical behavior[10] as well as Jewish radical socialist and political thinking.[11]

This discussion on the absence of a concrete social and ethnic context in Lispector's fiction serves to illustrate how her sensorial, inspirational, evocative, introspective, and lyrical writings, concerned as they were with ontological themes laced with a mystical quest, were evaluated as unique to Brazilian literature and therefore at odds with the neonaturalist style, current at the time she began to write. One could say that for Brazilian literature, Clarice Lispector was heralding a new way of expressing the "stream of life," one that sprang from a very individualistic vision. By internalizing the external, her prose responded more to an inner reality than to an exterior one explicitly preoccupied with social, cultural, and nationalist concerns, which, by the way, she did voice overtly in her chronicles, written for the *Jornal do Brasil* between 1967 and 1973 and published in the volumes *A descoberta do mundo* (Discovering the World; 1984) and *Selected Crônicas.*

As an adult, she was constantly reminded of her foreign birth—the paradox of being both a nationally famous Brazilian writer and a naturalized Brazilian citizen. Her childhood in a Jewish immigrant household sparked the double perspective that gave her insight into the dynamics of cultural difference. Moreover, Lispector's father was a self-taught student of the Bible and Talmud who according to her "leaned toward spiritual matters" (Lerner 66). Similarly, in speaking of their father, Clarice's other sister, Tânia Kaufmann, states:

> My father possessed much biblical culture. We used to celebrate three or four holidays of the Jewish calendar. My father knew the rituals. He knew Yiddish very well. And he used to receive the New York newspaper, *The Day*, in Yiddish. He had very forward ideas. He was a progressive man. He never hit any child of his. He was exceptional.

If it weren't for the circumstances, he could have had a better position in life. (Gotlib, *Clarice* 84).

In view of her cultural background, the domestic ambience of her Jewish home and its emphasis on scholasticism—biblical interpretation, Talmudic thinking, and Jewish mysticism—contributed significantly to her innovative use of language with its oxymoronic motifs as well as its polysemic stance toward signification, and, ultimately, to her understanding of difference and alterity. To deny or ignore the Jewish impulse in her fiction is to deny the impact of her cultural upbringing, her early fascination with the word, and her subsequent defiance of lexical absoluteness and supremacy. And so from my viewpoint, her ethnic experience did indeed fuel her ideological and pluralist stance toward life and language.

After her father died in 1940, her daily ties with Yiddishkeit life ended somewhat abruptly. In 1943 she married Maury Gurgel Valente, a fellow law student at the National Faculty of Law. In the same year she became a naturalized Brazilian citizen, published her first novel, and graduated from law school. She began her career auspiciously— with a law degree and the 1944 Graça Aranha prize for her novel *Near to the Wild Heart*. Her husband had embarked on a diplomatic career, and Lispector became displaced again, this time as a world traveler. Her husband's career of protocol and tradition, however, never changed her independent attitude toward life. She fulfilled all her duties as a diplomat's wife but was unhappy in this role. At the time of her death, the writer and psychiatrist Hélio Pellegrino said, "She was anti-diplomatic. This was funny because she married a diplomat . . . . No false refinement. She didn't put on airs. She was incapable of being conventional."[12]

Her first son, Pedro, was born in Berne in 1948 and her second, Paulo, in 1953 in Washington, D.C., where the family lived from 1952 to 1959. During this period she continued to write, working on her famous short story collection, *Family Ties*, portraying the social ties that frequently bind and stifle individuals, especially middle-class women. She also completed many drafts of her existential novel, *The Apple in the Dark*. Problems in her marriage eventually led to a legal separation in 1968, but by 1959, Clarice had already returned to Rio with her sons. The 1960s and 1970s were an especially productive period for Clarice—six novels, seven collections of stories, and four children's books. However, she always experienced financial difficulty during this period, being obliged to work as a journalist in order to survive. And except for an occasional short trip for tourism or to attend conferences, she made Rio de Janeiro her home until her death in 1977.

Clarice Lispector's spiritual universe stems in part from a Jewish sensibility that often adopts metaphors and motifs frequently connected to the Judaic Diaspora experience, from biblical times in the desert to the modern-day sense of displacement experienced in immigration. While not exclusive to the Judaic experience, these motifs and images do evoke a culturally Jewish frame of mind in their drive toward personal search and incessant questioning. To demonstrate how Clarice Lispector's passionate search through narrative is illustrative of her Judaic spiritual impulse, I will discuss, in addition to the above commentary on *The Hour of the Star, The Passion According to GH*—narratives that manifest the process and passion of search as well as psychological, social, and cultural exile.

In *The Passion According to GH*, Lispector explores the issue of cultural and ontological otherness by using the desert as a metaphor for evoking displacement as well as a necessary process of struggle for something called redemption, grace, or, in this case, a spiritual passion. The metaphor of the desert and an individual's passionate search are dramatized by the character GH in a particularly telling passage that reverberates with images of the wandering Jew and the ineffable:

In prehistory I had begun my march through the desert, and without a star to guide me, only perdition guiding me, only error guiding me—until, almost dead from the ecstasy of fatigue, lighted by passion, I finally found the strongbox. And in the strongbox, the sparkle of glory, the hidden secret. The most remote secret in the world, opaque, but blinding me with the radiation of its simple existence, sparkling there in a glory that hurt my eyes.

(. . .) I hadn't found a human answer to the enigma. But much more, oh much more: I had found the enigma itself. (129–30)

The first-person narrator of this novel is only known by her initials, GH, thereby turning the text's compass toward an ontological direction of identity that points to universal issues of self, otherness, nothingness, self-knowledge, exile, action, and possibly redemption. The minimal plot of this retrospective and subjective narrative merely revolves around a seemingly innocuous domestic event of a Brazilian bourgeoise's account of what happened when she entered the *bas-fond* of her apartment and into the tiny quarters of her maid who recently and unexpectedly left her employment. Ironically, the *empregada* Janair was for all purposes ontologically invisible to GH prior to this experience in the maid's room, which in the course of the narrative becomes a metaphorical "desert." Expecting to find a dirty mess in a cubicle that was intended to serve as storeroom *and* living quarters, GH is shaken to find the room as (other)wise: "Instead of the jumbled shadows that I was expecting, I encountered the vision of a room that was a quadrangle of white light" (29). It is in this metaphorical desert/room where, as GH states, she will "walk forever through the desert with a shepherd's staff. Many have been those who have walked in the desert with a staff" (64). In the course of her narrative search,

GH's perspective on difference and cultural otherness will be altered significantly by being in this disturbing desert: "What I hadn't expected was that the maid, without saying anything to me, had fixed the room up the way she wanted it, and acting as though she owned it herself, had done away with its function as a storage area" (29–30).

This observation by GH the narrator, but engineered by the author, casts doubt on GH's ethics because she is sincerely shocked by the supposed audacity and will of the *mulatta* maid to transform her sleeping quarters, or the *dona de casa's* version of a storeroom, into a tiny room of her very own—"ousadia de proprietária" (the audacity of ownership). Janair's action of transforming the room, and moreover leaving it blindingly white, upsets GH's benumbed view of Janair as the dark, silent cultural other. (On another level, the novel hints at the self-serving and often insensitve behavior of Brazilian housewives toward their maids.) As a result of seeing the maid in a new light, GH is eventually forced to recognize that Janair's own sense of self, *not* her otherness as first perceived by GH, stirs unexpected feelings and perceptions: "had it never occurred to me that in Janair's silence there might have been a criticism of my life-style, . . . Janair was the first outside person whose gaze I really took notice of" (32). This consciousness obliges her to resee the maid's "quiet, black face" (33) and to recognize how Janair's manner and clothing made her "all dark and invisible" (33) in GH's eyes, thus obliging the reader to be suspicious of GH's overwhelming self-containment within her own subjective shell. This self-containment exists at the expense of a fuller and deeper perception of others and of herself: "I shivered to discover that till now I hadn't noticed that that woman was an invisible woman" (33). Here, we should read the last sentence as Janair being *made* to be invisible by socially dominant people such as GH. Ironically, this sudden awareness instills in GH a suspicion as to how Janair may have really perceived her, perhaps seeing only the surface and not the substance, a disturbing idea she entertains when on the wall she sees Janair's charcoal outlined drawing of a woman figure: "And was it inevitable that just as she herself was, so she saw me? abstracting everything unessential from the body that was me drawn on the wall and also seeing only my outlines. Curiously, however, the figure on the wall still reminded me of someone: myself" (33). From this event and the others that all take place within a short time and the limited space of that small room, which metaphorically becomes a vast desert, GH will begin a narrated "voyage within" that will dismantle her single/same constructed identity of immutable subjectivity. As she emphatically states:

> And, in my great expansion, I was on the desert. How can I make you understand? I was on the desert as I had never been before. It was a desert that called me like a monotonous, remote canticle calls. I was being seduced. (. . .) Hold my hand tight, because I feel that I'm going. I am again going to the most primary divine life, I am going to an inferno of brute life. (52)

GH's reading of herself and her newly uncovered feelings of rage, misunderstanding, and dislocation will finally lead her to refocus her search for identity on her grasp of her own otherness. This refocusing process becomes concretized via her narrative quest and via her creation of an imagined interlocutor, gradually provoking within her, and within the reader, diverse perspectives that will forge individual, social, cultural, and spiritual awakenings and insights.

Having occurred prior to GH's narrative, this incident has stirred within GH a new condition of being that constitutes the motivation for her retrospective tale. And this new condition, based on enlightened feelings about disorganization, disorientation, and disintegration, constitutes states opposite to her well-ordered and neatly arranged world of an unmarried woman and amateur sculptor whose existential subjective optic (her Satrean *en-soi*, "being-in-itself") has never been seriously questioned. Up until now. On account of her maid's unexpected action, GH's *discours* explodes into her newly disturbed state of being and feeling, which she attempts to examine consciously via narration in an effort to understand what has really happened to her on the deep structural level of life. The novel begins in midsentence with "I keep looking, looking. Trying to understand. Trying to give what I have gone through to someone else, and I don't know who, but I don't want to be alone with that experience" (3).

This text reminds one of Paul Ricoeur's view on the significance and implications of the examined, narrated life—his take on Socrates' "an unexamined life is not worth living"—as it points to other elements of his treatise on discourse, consciousness, and narratives that grapple with self, subjectivity, otherness, and mediation, cogently inferred in GH's statement: "living isn't courage, knowing that you're living, that's courage" (16). This mediated perception is also evident in GH's disillusionment of no longer belonging securely to a staid, single system of living such as that of a rigid patriarchal society, and thus she is forced to examine her life by giving it a form—a narrative form as Paul Ricoeur would advise, one that may lead to a new narrative identity: "And my struggle against that disintegration is just that: is just trying to give it a form. A form gives contours to chaos, gives a construct to amorphous substance" (6). While the issue of narrative mediation surfaces throughout the novel, it is dramatically crystallized once GH's subjective world gives way or opens up to otherness via the construction of her imagined interlocutor: "What was happening to me? I shall never be able to understand it, but there must me someone who can. And I shall have to create that someone who can inside myself" (37). This "tu" interlocutor serves as discursive and feigned dialogic support throughout GH's quest as she frequently enjoins "Give me your hand" (90), that is, until she reaches a spiritual and loving level of reciprocity with her sense of her own alterity, enabling her to declare late in the novel: "And now I am taking your hand into my own. I am the one who is giving you my hand" (163).

Interestingly, GH's personalist narrative is a struggle toward depersonalization and deheroization and away from an obsessively subjective (narcissistic and selfish) ego that is counter to Jewish ethical behavior and the Golden Rule's commandments. Her newly discovered state, optic, vision, is thus primarily provoked and symbolized by her unexpected killing and tasting of a cockroach, the *barata* in the maid's room, a forbidden and primal act—"I was for the first time being the unknown figure that I was" (45). The age-old, exogenous social experience of the Jew as Other is mirrored here in the discovery of the narrator's own alterity. The act of tasting the roach enables her to ontologically kill her old self and transgress certain cultural (biblical and Talmudic) taboos such as the eating of the unclean: "I had committed the forbidden act of touching something impure" (64). The latter suggests Lispector's never being too distant from the precepts of her ethnic and religious heritage. Furthermore, with intertextual intimations to Kafka, to my mind, Clarice Lispector, via her own selective ethnicity with her Jewishness, is symbolically "eating Kafka" in her attempt to go beyond the fatal circumstances of Gregor Samsa's tragedy as depicted in "The Metamorphosis." By forcibly nourishing them(selves) with alien matter, both Lispector and GH are behaving anthropophagically, the cultural theory promoted by the Brazilian modernist Oswald de Andrade in his "Cannibalist Manifesto," which points to Brazil's unique ethos, developed after having consumed the foreigner/alien and his culture. GH's "cannibalistic" or anthropophagic act will eventually lead her to treat the "tu" interlocutor (of "give me your hand") less dependently because to face and taste the Other that is the barata, or any other form of alterity, she must become dispossessed of the hierarchical and conventional trappings of her former self so that she will be open to another form of discovered self: "I am finally moving toward the opposite path. I am moving toward the destruction of what I have constructed, I am moving toward depersonalization" (167). In the Ricoeurian sense, this depersonalization is really "a self deprived of assistance from sameness—identity" (Wood 198). GH has forsaken the identity of sameness that is so indicative of woman's traditional and insidious function in a society that relegates her to domestic roles. In so doing, she is acknowledging her own alterity as a woman as well as the subalternity represented by the maid.

What is actually occurring within GH is the expansion of selfhood and, ultimately, subjectivity (to include otherness, alterity), epitomized in the following sentence that highlights her increased empathy and dialogue with others and the world beyond the narcissistic 'I': "My life is used more by the earth than it is by me, I am so much greater than what I have called 'me' that just by having a life of the world I would have myself" (115). As GH becomes more socially conscious and engaged with the world beyond the selfish ego, she states: "He who lives totally is living for others" (162). While GH's search is never-ending, its mini-revelations have led her quest for enlightened narrative to the raw material of life and an altered personal identity.

With this narrative Clarice Lispector brings her strong sense of social justice to the foreground via a spiritually evocative discourse that heralds the need for acknowledging difference, or rather a sense of alterity, that is frequently wanting in a society inured to the behavior of exclusion, resulting from a dogged adherence to hierarchical structures and social taboos. In other words, both Lispector and GH appear to be grappling with the discovery of a new voice and self-identity via narrative discourse. Related to this process, Ricoeur articulates the concept of applying literature to life in his famous essay "Narrative Identity," where he declares

> that the self does not know itself immediately, but only indirectly by the detour of the cultural signs of all sorts

which are articulated on the symbolic mediations which always already articulate action and, among them the narratives of everyday life. Narrative mediation underlines this remarkable characteristic of self-knowledge—that it is self-interpretation. (Wood 198)

In the case of GH and Clarice Lispector, their co-narration manifests revelations about race (the black Other as subaltern), gender (female subjectivity), ethnicity (embedded Jewishness), and taboos (censured cultural behavior); in short, cultural signs that disclose one of the "performative" times of Brazil's everyday life. Albeit centered around women, Clarice Lispector's narratives reach beyond gender binary by speaking to the self in both men and women, thereby transcending issues of gender toward the neuter state of the human spirit. In a similar sense, Lúcia Helena's recent study is relevant to my observations for she reads Clarice Lispector's positionality as "intermediate" instead of binary: "Alluding to Muses and Medusas, in narrative form as much as in the thematics which it conveys, the process of textuality in Lispector constructs itself as a place of inbetweens" (112).

In conclusion, I have presented Clarice Lispector's passionate search for a literary voice and identity as stemming in great part from her deep-rooted sense of displacement, of not belonging, which harks back not only to her experience as an immigrant Jewish child but also to her identification as an artist and woman of beauty and spirit who was unable to function in the conventional role prescribed by men and society. Like her, all her protagonists struggle with Others and otherness, a situation leading to perspectives that offer a glimpse of who they are or can be. In this vein, Clarice Lispector's writing illustrates how literature can be applied to life and, in so doing, represents an homage to an enlightened sense of exile (geographic, social, and psychological), belongingness, identity (mutable and transitory), and existence, conveying to us the genesis of her metaphysical questioning and spiritual stance. In her chronicle "Belonging," with its metaphor of the desert as a spatial metonymic trope for existence-in-process, she hints at her personal and spiritual resources for grappling with her artistic and personal sense of estrangement. Here, she points to her inability to be a "joiner" as well as to the insider/outsider dilemma associated with her experience of gender and ethnicity, that is, of being a Jewish woman who represented "an involuntary act of rebellion"[13] in a land of brunettes ruled by Latin patriarchs. Finally, in terms of capturing the overall significance of Clarice Lispector's writing and its universal appeal, its metaphysics of difference and quest for identity, the words of the acclaimed Brazilian writer João Guimarães Rosa, a contemporary of Clarice Lispector, may serve as a fitting conclusion. In a conversation with Guimarães Rosa that she reproduced in one of her chronicles, he told her that the reasons he read her were "não para a literatura, mas para a vida"—not for literature, but for life (*Discovering the World* 194).

NOTES

1. I am applying to Clarice Lispector's experience with *galut* aspects of the following definition by Yitzhak F. Baer in *Galut:* "The word 'Galut' embraces a whole world of facts and ideas that have appeared with varying strength and clarity in every age of Jewish history. Political servitude and dispersion, the longing for liberation and reunion, sin and repentance and atonement: these are the larger elements that must go to make up the concept of Galut if the word is to retain any real meaning" (9). I am also taking into consideration Jacob Neusner's comment in his introduction to Baer's study: "The experience of exile and return forms the recurrent pattern of Jewish experience as that experience is put together and interpreted by diverse Judaisms from the beginning to the present" (ix). As a cultural paradigm, I am interpreting "exile and return" also as "exile and redemption."

2. For a more extensive treatment of Clarice Lispector's work in relation to her Jewish heritage, see the chapter, "Clarice Lispector: A Jewish Impulse and a Prophecy of Difference," in Vieira 100–150. Some of the information included in this study is based on the research completed for that book.

3. The tribulations of Lispector's emigration and her early years in Brazil's Northeast are detailed in Nádia Battella Gotlib's literary biography of Clarice Lispector, *Clarice: Uma vida que se conta* (1995).

4. This reference to Clarice Lispector's childhood is made in the 1976 interview held at the Museu de Imagem e Som in Rio and repeated in others as well as in various articles such as the one by Lígia Monteiro, "A saudade de Clarice e do seu amor pelo mundo" for *A Gazeta* (December 10, 1978).

5. This quote was reproduced in Monteiro's article.

6. See Earl Fitz's "A Discourse of Silence: The Postmodernism of Clarice Lispector" and his *Clarice Lispector,* 42.

7. The Jewish elements in *The Hour of the Star* were discussed in a review essay by Suzy Frankl Sperber in the *Suplemento Literário Minas Gerais* and in "Uma judia do Brasil: Clarice Lispector," a paper presented in the session "Female and Jewish in Latin America" at the 1990 NEMLA Convention in Toronto, April 6–8, 1990. Other studies touching on the Jewish element in Clarice Lispector are Sônia Régis, "O pensamento judaico em Clarice Lispector," *O Estado de SP* 7.408 (May 14, 1988): 8–9; Robert E. DiAntonio, *Brazilian Fiction: Aspects and Evolution of the Contemporary Narrative* (Fayetteville: U of Arkansas P, 1989), 162–74; and Nelson H. Vieira, "A linguagem espiritual de Clarice Lispector," *Travessia* 14 (1987): 81–95.

8. This interview conducted by Bella Jozef appeared as "A literatura, segundo Clarice," *Suplemento Literário Minas Gerais,* 3.109 (September 28, 1968): 8–9.

9. This is another version of a chronicle with the same title "Literatura e justiça," which appears in *A legion estrangeira,* 149–50, and in English translation in *The Foreign Legion,* 124–25.

10. For a succinct statement on the Golden Rule in rabbinic literature, see Holtz 11–12.

11. See Cohen 214–15.

12. Pellegrino's comment appears in an unpublished interview with João Carlos Horta, who began collecting material for his film *Perto de Clarice* at the time of her death. Parts of this interview were included as film voice-overs.

13. This phrase is found in the story, "Temptation," from *The Foreign Legion* (1986), a collection of stories and chronicles that was originally published in 1964. In this story about a young girl who has not come to terms with her difference, the phrase appears in the following context: "In a land of brunettes, to have red hair was an involuntary act of rebellion. What did it matter if one day this characteristic would cause her to raise a woman's head with an air of defiance?" (56).

REFERENCES

Araújo, Celso Arnaldo. "Uma escritora no escuro" (A Writer in the Dark). *Manchete* 3 May 1975: 48–49.

Baer, Yitzhak F. *Galut.* Trans. Robert Warshow. Lanham, MD: University Press of America, 1985.

Borelli, Olga. *Clarice Lispector: Um esboço para um possível retrato* (Clarice Lispector: A Sketch for a Possible Picture). Rio de Janeiro: Nova Fronteira, 1981.

Bosi, Alfredo, ed. *O conto brasileiro contemporâneo* (The Contemporary Brazilian Short Story). São Paulo: Editora Cultrix, 1975.

Cândido, Antônio. "No raiar de Clarice Lispector" (At the Dawning of Clarice Lispector). *Vários escritos,* 123–31. By Cândido. São Paulo: Livraria Duas Cidades, 1970.

Cohen, Percy S. *Jewish Radicals and Radical Jews.* London: Academic Press, 1980.

DiAntonio, Robert E. *Brazilian Fiction: Aspects and Evolution of the Contemporary Narrative.* Fayetteville: University of Arkansas Press, 1989.

Fitz, Earl E. *Clarice Lispector.* Boston: Twayne, 1985.

———."A Discourse of Silence: The Postmodernism of Clarice Lispector." *Contemporary Literature* 28 (1978): 420–36.

Gotlib, Nádia Battella. *Clarice: Uma vida que se conta.* 3d ed. São Paulo: Editora Àtica, 1995.

———. "Ser ou não ser autobiográfica (a propósito de Clarice Lispector)." *Navegar é preciso, viver: Escritos para Silviano Santiago.* Org. Eneida Maria de Souza and Wander Melo Miranda. Belo Horizonte: Ed. UFMG; Salvador: EDUFBA; Niterói: EDUFF, 1997. 314–22.

Helena, Lúcia. *Nem musa, nem medusa: Itinerários da escrita em Clarice Lispector.* Niterói: EDUFF, 1997.

Heschel, Abraham Joshua. *Man Is Not Alone: A Philosophy of Religion.* New York: Farrar, Straus and Giroux, 1951.

Holtz, Barry W. *Back to the Sources: Reading the Classic Jewish Texts.* New York: Summit Books, 1984.

Jozef, Bella. "A literatura, segundo Clarice" (Literature, According to Clarice). *Suplemento Literário Minas Gerais* 28 Sept. 1968: 8–9.

Lerner, Júlio. "A última entrevista de Clarice Lispector" (Clarice Lispector's Last Interview). *Shalom* 27 (June 1992): 62–69.

Lispector, Clarice. *Discovering the World.* Trans. and Introd. Giovanni Pontiero. Manchester: Carcanet, 1992.

———. *The Foreign Legion: Stories and Chronicles.* Trans. Giovanni Pontiero. Manchester: Carcanet, 1986.

————. *The Hour of the Star.* Trans. Giovanni Pontiero. New York: New Directions, 1992.

————. *A legion estrangeira.* Rio de Janeiro: Editora de Autor, 1964.

————. *A paixão segundo G. H.* Ed. Benedito Nunes. Paris/Brasília: Coleção Arquivos/CNPq, 1988.

————. *The Passion According to GH.* Trans. Ronald W. Sousa. Minneapolis: University of Minnesota Press, 1988.

————. *Selected Crônicas.* Trans. Giovanni Pontiero. New York: New Directions, 1996.

Lispector, Elisa. *No exílio.* 2d ed. Brasília: Ebrasa, 1971.

Monteiro, Lígia. "A saudade de Clarice e do seu amor pelo mundo" (Nostalgia for Clarice and for Her Love of the World). *A Gazeta* 10 Dec. 1978.

Rawet, Samuel. "A hora da estrela ou as frutas do Frota, ou um ensaio de crítica literária policial" (The Hour of the Star or Frota's Wormy Fruits, or an Essay on Literary Criticism as Criminal Detection). *Suplemento Literário Minas Gerais* 648 (1979): 8–9.

Régis, Sônia. "O pensamento judaico em Clarice Lispector." Paper presented in the session "Female and Jewish in Latin America" at the annual meeting of NEMLA, Toronto, April 6–8, 1990.

Ricoeur, Paul. "Narrative Identity." *On Paul Ricoeur: Narrative and Interpretation.* Ed. David Wood. London: Routledge, 1991

Sá, Olga de. "Clarice Lispector: Processos criativos" (Clarice Lispector: Creative Processes). *Revista Iberoamericana* 50 (January 1984): 259–80.

————. "Paródia e metafísica." Lispector, *A paixão segundo G. H.* 214–36.

Vieira, Nelson II. *Jewish Voices in Brazilian Literature: A Prophetic Discourse of Alterity.* Gainesville: University Press of Florida, 1995.

————. "A linguagem espiritual de Clarice Lispector." *Travessia* 14 (1987): 81–95.

Wood, David, ed. *On Paul Ricoeur: Narrative and Interpretation.* London: Routledge, 1991.

emigrant memory

JEWISH WOMEN WRITERS IN CHILE AND URUGUAY

Elizabeth Rosa Horan

The history of a nation, like the history of an individual, consists more of what's forgotten than of what's remembered.
JOSEPH BRODSKY, "PROFILE OF CLIO"

. . . what do these Jewish writers contribute towards building a stable bridge between being Jewish and being Latin American?
HAIM AVNI, "POSTWAR LATIN AMERICAN JEWRY"

This essay examines how Sonia Guralnik, Teresa Porzecanski, and Marjorie Agosín use memoir, writing the private history of individuals, to inscribe that *petit histoire* into the life of the nation.[1] They draw from the voices of emigrants to recognize the multiplicity of experience buried under the category of the national citizen. Their stories of Jewish immigrant experience reveal the instability of national identity, beginning with the years following World War I, accelerating in the post-Holocaust era, drawn into crisis under the military dictatorships that seized Chile and Uruguay in 1973. In the rootlessness and nomadism beginning with the early 1970s and extending into the 1990s, not land or possessions but memory has constituted the closest thing to an anchor.

These writers employ memoir and oral history to address gaps in traditional history and social science. They describe the ambiguous, often-contradictory welcome that the secular nation extends to immigrant Jews and their families, accepting them as citizens but not as Jews. Guralnik, Porzecanski, and Agosín bundle the hopes and sacrifices of the earliest immigrants with the disillusion and loss that they and their families experience, finding themselves repeatedly forced into the role of outsiders vis-à-vis the state, the lands of origin, and the adoptive lands. Against the role of outsider their work depicts the development of "double consciousness" amid multiple, provisional identities. One learns to play along, as Sonia Guralnik writes of her immigrant childhood: "Picardía: una palabra que encerraba el sentido de este país nuevo" (*Picardía:* a word that summed up the meaning of this new country") (*Recuento* 24).

sonia guralnik (chile)

Born in Russia in 1923 or 1925, Guralnik lived in the Ukraine near Kiev until age ten, when her family emigrated to Chile. Guralnik married rather than pursue a university education. She also worked as a professional chef while raising three children. Propelling her to write was the social unrest of the late 1960s, coupled with the bleak repression of the dictatorship. Guralnik, a housewife with substantial drive, some independent means, and grown children, enrolled in workshops that allowed her to develop her vocation as a writer. Guralnik's narratives have a strongly autobiographical, anecdotal aspect. Many are structured as dramatic monologues. Her first two collections of short stories, *El samovar* (1984) and *Relatos en sepia* (Stories in Sepia; 1987), were published by the small press Ergo Sum; her third, *Recuento de la mujer gusano* (Story of the Worm Woman), appeared with the more commercial publisher Sudamericana, in 1992.

A first-generation immigrant, Guralnik represents the living memory of Jews who settled in Chile before the Holocaust, as well as citizens who endured the seventeen-year Pinochet dictatorship. In interviews she has appealed to some aspects of the national mythology, for example, her recall of her parents coming to Chile fifty years ago as a place where "the land is green and the universities, free." Yet Guralnik's feminist sensibility rejects assimilation or categorization as a success-ful homemaker who incidentally writes stories full of grandmotherly wisdom. Replying to the question of whether her immigrant mother was likewise an excellent housewife, she states: "No, to the contrary. She kept the girls out of the kitchen, saying youth was a time for reading and study: 'You'll have plenty of time to learn to wipe, to cook, and wash up, whereas the time to learn is this moment, and what you learn now will last all your life'" (Torrejón F., Interview). Using the weapons of surface conformity, pleasantry, and slightly self-deprecating humor, she lures us in, pointing out the disparity between past ideals and present values.

teresa porzecanski (uruguay)

Born in 1945, Teresa Porzecanski spent her childhood in Monte-video, where she was raised in a traditional but nonetheless heterodox Jewish family: a father from the Baltics, a mother from a Sephardic family of Syrian emigrants. Trained in social work and in cultural an-thropology, Porzecanski has published academic studies, widely an-thologized fiction, and several novels. She has worked in Mexico and in Peru, and is currently a professor in the humanities faculty of the Catholic University of Uruguay. Her text *Historias de vida de inmi-grantes judíos al Uruguay* (Life Stories of Jewish Immigrants to Uruguay; 1986) masterfully deploys her skills in narrative, ethnography, and social analysis. She apparently compiled these sixteen oral histories from about 1978 to 1981, that is, during the worst years of military re-pression, when all of the Southern Cone nations were ruled by right-wing military dictatorships. Told in the first person, objectively, each history reveals the teller's private life, as part of a broader register of representative events, opinions, and experiences: "Cada Historia refleja lo acontecido a miles de personas en circunstancias similares" (Each History reflects what happened to thousands of people in similar circumstances) (Bronstein 24). While the span of time concentrates on the first two moments in the histories of the Jewish communities in Uruguay (from about 1905 to about 1947), the speakers' stories suggest numerous parallels between the conditions of Jews as outsiders to the state in Europe and the atmosphere of terror under the military dictatorship in Uruguay. Like Guralnik, Porzecanski mentions the gratitude of first-generation immigrants. Their emotion-charged description of the democratic Uruguay of old as a haven from the local prejudice and state-sponsored terrorism encountered in Europe constitutes an implicit criticism of the present-day Uruguayan state's failure to protect or recognize the rights of its citizens. The post-Holocaust significance of a dictatorship that separates women from their children and so destroys families presents a chilling element in the stories of "Sara" and "Isabella."

marjorie agosín (chile-u.s.)

Born to Chilean parents in Bethesda, Maryland, in 1955, Marjorie Agosín was raised in Chile, where her grandparents had emigrated from Odessa and Vienna in the early twentieth century. Her father, a doctor and research professor, brought the family to the United States in the early 1970s, taking up residence in Georgia. Agosín holds a Ph.D. in literature and teaches Spanish at Wellesley College in Massachusetts. Her earliest publications were in poetry: *Conchalí* (1980) is a book of poems named for the old Jewish cemetery in Santiago, where some of Agosín's uncles are buried. Subsequent volumes of poetry, criticism, and prose poetry are concerned with human rights: they bear witness to suffering. Feminism is key to her writing: exiles, recluses, and seeming madwomen are prominent in her catalog of heroes. Many of Agosín's books are organized around women's resistance to the tyranny of the military dictatorships ruling Argentina and Chile in the 1970s and 1980s, beginning, perhaps, with her account of the ordeal of Renee Epelbaum, a central figure in the Argentine Mothers of the Plaza de Mayo movement. Similarly, Agosín's *Scraps of Life* details the work of the Chilean *arpilleristas,* women whose craft work made public the devastating effects of the dictatorship on family life, thus contributing to the political opposition.

Neodemocracy in Chile, the exploration of ethnic identity among U.S.-based feminists, and work with orally based literary forms such as interviews and *testimonios* all provide a background to Agosín's memoirs of her parents' lives. The two volumes *A Cross and a Star: Memoirs of a Jewish Girl in Chile* (1994) and *Always from Somewhere Else* (1998) mix the writer's voice with that of her mother, father, grandparents, and others. The books recall four generations of Jews in Chile, from the earliest waves of immigrants and their attempts to make new lives in Chile, to the tensions that German-Jewish refugees encountered in their sudden, forced emigration, on to the ongoing experience of isolation for the grandchildren of immigrants, both in Chile and in subsequent emigrations to the United States and elsewhere.

historical contexts: the three moments of early,
holocaust era, and post-holocaust emigrations

One way to comprehend the work of these three, representative writers is to examine how their work with memoir relates Jewish to specific Latin American national identities. The twentieth century presents three defining moments for the emergence, realignment, and new understanding of these identities. The first moment opens with the earliest waves of emigration from Europe, during and after World War I. Each of the writers describes key aspects of the worlds that the earliest emigrants left behind. Guralnik describes the flight from Soviet Russia in terms of secrecy, the abandonment of household goods, the need to adopt disguises. Porzecanski and Agosín describe in human terms the close causal relationship between the political shifts in the Balkans, the Crimea, and the Ottoman Empire and the initial settlements of Jews in Uruguay and Chile.

As post-Holocaust writers, Porzecanski and Agosín detail how the second moment remakes Jewish identity in relation to the adoptive countries, a moment that opens with Germany's official persecution of Jews as a race, in 1933. A second round of war and forced deportations makes increasingly evident the profound instability of national identity, beginning with the absurdity of assigning an "innate" identity based on the place of birth, when national frontiers are political, not spiritual, boundaries, redrawn as often as four times in a decade. A particularly cruel paradox of identity faced Jews who escaped Hitler through flight to Latin America: German Jews and those from countries occupied by the Germans were deprived of citizenship, collectively accused of being Enemies of the State, yet in Chile they found themselves described as "German," the only criteria for nationality being the country of birth (Lachmann qtd. in Kleiner 45–46).

A third defining moment comes just as the post-Holocaust generation was entering adulthood. Uruguay and Chile, once stable democracies, fell under right-wing military dictatorships. Haim Avni remarks the irony of how "the post-Holocaust era, which brought the virtual destruction of European Jewry, marked Latin American Jewry's coming of age" (3). Another irony is added to this: the coming of age signals the return of state-sponsored repression, of the suspension of rights and disappearances of suspected opponents in an atmosphere of terror. In this third moment, however, the hypermasculine military dictatorships in Latin America unwittingly create a vast space of de facto feminine discourse. Making the military into the sole legitimate voice of national identity simultaneously forces all other speakers, potential or actual, housewives, intellectuals, mental patients, journalists, many clerics, into the category of outsiders.

The third moment marks an increasing skepticism toward national mythologies and the increased visibility of dissident writing, a phenomenon to which Guralnik, Porzecanski, and Agosín owe and contribute much. Refusing national myth, they refer us, instead, to local conditions, to feminized, nonofficial microspaces: the isolation of the kitchen, the slum, the temporary quarters of the summer house or the therapist's waiting room, the anonymity of the street corner, the doorway, the shop window, the beach at night, the sidewalk. They emphasize transitory, always tenuous survival. Drawing from an oral tradition that allows women to speak in mourning as mothers, Guralnik, Porzecanski, and Agosín represent the nation as a broken, dispersed family. Rejecting the warrior model, they choose anonymous or unlikely heroes, stressing survival in privacy, in freedom of thought and association.

first moments: toward transculturation

The men came first. Their mothers, wives, children might not come to the railroad station to say good-byes that would draw notice, and make leaving more difficult. Young men, boys really, were the first to leave, clutching one, perhaps two wicker suitcases, clambering onto wagons, boarding trains and ships.[2] The desire for education and economic opportunity was a factor in their emigration, as was flight from obligatory military service. Fight for or against the sultan, the czar, the Young Turks, or move beyond the Pale, cross the Caucasus, stow away for France, then the Americas.[3] The good-byes are forever. The best-case scenario: meeting again in the adoptive country.

Before the men reached Buenos Aires or Rio the rooms they had left behind changed hands, again and again, in Poland, Russia, the Baltics and the Balkans, in the old Jewish quarters of Turkey and the

Middle East. New rulers, new names: the old palace became the House of Culture. New rulers, same rules: a brief peace, more war, trains. Mass deportations. Armies leveled shtetls, and synagogues stood empty in the Mediterranean and southern Slav cities and towns that once welcomed Jews expelled from Spain. There were Ukrainians expelled from Romania, Russian political activists from Turkey, Syrians from Marseilles.

Uruguay welcomed immigrants even as neighboring Brazil and Argentina decreed national origins quota systems patterned after the United States, in the 1920s. Uruguay did not require a deposit of funds. To encourage colonization of the countryside the legislature authorized Uruguayan consuls to pay advance passages to immigrants. Immigrants did not have to present a certificate of good conduct for the past five years. Until 1918, most came by way of Buenos Aires, some from Brazil, a group of about 1,200, primarily single men, according to Porzecanski's introductory study to *Historias de vida de inmigrantes judíos al Uruguay.* Some of these now old men, grateful for the refuge they found, describe working in Uruguay just off the boat, not knowing a word of Spanish, sleeping in rented rooms located in the oldest parts of the city, rooms lined with mattresses, in six-hour shifts. They worked as peddlers, hoisting huge baskets of yard goods onto their backs, fanning from the city to outlying suburbs, sixteen-hour days. The names of their professions brought Yiddish into Spanish: *clápers,* salesmen who "clapped," that is, who knocked on doors, and *cuenteniks,* those who kept their own accounts, *cuentas,* selling on the installment plan. Many joined the working class, in construction and in the refrigeration industry. Others were nonspecialized workers in the garment industry, furniture making and shoe manufacture, streetcar conductors.

Chile demanded great stamina of the earliest immigrants, for the passage could be as long as traveling from Europe and back. By boat they would travel south from Buenos Aires, around Cape Horn, then north to Valparaíso. Others boarded the trans-Andean train. Unlike Buenos Aires and Montevideo, with its well-established Jewish neighborhoods of Barrio Once and Villa Muñoz, Santiago before World War II had only a few thousand Jews, mainly Ashkenazi, a few Sephardim. There were isolated families in the provinces, where the first generation set up as salesmen, shopkeepers, tailors.

UNEASY WELCOME:

JEWISH COMMUNITY AND LIBERAL SECULARISM

The presence of Jewish communities in Santiago and Montevideo develops from the process of nation building begun in nineteenth-century Chile and in Uruguay. Secularists looked to supplant the colonial identification of the Church as Teacher with the concept of the Estado Docente (State as Teacher). Secularists sought national institutions that would extend modern thought into philosophy, sciences, and theology. Public schools, lay cemeteries, and civil marriage all helped to establish the separation of church and state. Competition to the church appeared in the rise of international "brotherhoods" such as the Masonic order and, in the early twentieth century, theosophy.[4] Secularism and scientific education were linked with industrialization and efforts to engineer social reform in pro-immigration policies. In Uruguay, manufacturers argued that urban, industrial growth would strengthen the national economy. In Chile, the stimulus for immigration centered on the colonization and development of agricultural areas, to protect unstable borders, in lands recently taken from native inhabitants.

IMMIGRATION TO URUGUAY

The strict separation of church and state attracted Jews to live and work in Uruguay, but it provided a powerful disincentive to dying there. The creation of secular cemeteries (along with civil marriage and public schools) was one of liberalism's primary weapons in the consolidation of a new national order. The early-twentieth-century Uruguayan statesman José Batlle y Ordoñez championed this order, exhibiting an anticlericalism that veered into antireligiosity. As recounted from the memories of "Elías," one of the delegation of Jews who met and worked with Batlle, the anticlericalism of Batlle and his supporters presented an awful obstacle to establishing Jewish communal life:

> . . . él era muy inteligente y grandioso pero había una laguna en él que no la podía entender. Era tan antirreligioso, Batlle, sobre todo tan anticlerical, pero se expresaba y actuaba con un antirreligioso. Entonces dice '¿Cómo? En muchos países del mundo los echan en otros no los dejan entrar, o, si están adentro, los maltratan, acá los recibimos con los brazos abiertos. Viven igual que nosotros y no pueden morirse junto con nosotros?' Esa fué la frase de Batlle.
>
> [. . . he was very intelligent, a really great guy, but there was a blind spot in him, he couldn't understand it. He was so antireligious, above all so anticlerical, but he expressed himself and acted like someone who was against religion. So he said, "How's that? In many countries of the world they throw you out, they don't let you in, or if you're inside, they treat you badly. Here, we welcome you with open arms. You live just like we do but you can't die alongside us too?" This is what Batlle said.] (Porzecanski, *Historias de vida* 48)

Finally one of Batlle's lieutenants was convinced to allow the cemetery: "Le habían hecho creer que éramos muchos" (He was led to believe that there were a lot of us)(49).[5]

A primary purpose of *Historias de vida* (Life Histories) is to remember the origins of Jewish institutional life in Uruguay.[6] Synthesizing various years of research, the oral histories represent the diverse waves of immigration to Uruguay, beginning with the Sephardic Jews who arrived from the far shore of the River Plate in 1905.[7] There were few restrictions on granting visas, but Montevideo did not begin to attract immigrants directly from Europe until after 1918, when Argentina and Brazil reduced the number of visas granted to people born in Eastern Europe. A Uruguayan consul in Paris is supposed to have attracted many prospective immigrants because his offices, located across the street from the Argentine Embassy, stayed open while the competition closed for lunch.

On the whole *Historias de vida* suggests that the liberal state gave immigrants in the 1920s a very positive reception: thus the experience of "Leon," who describes selling notions—thread, ribbons—throughout the city. He rang the doorbell of a house in the Manga district. When President Batlle answered it, "Leon" was almost at a loss for words: "Yo ando vendiendo señor, perdóneme, señor Presidente" (I'm selling things, sir, excuse me, Mr. President). But the president answered, "I'm not the president here, I'm a man like you." After summoning his daughter to buy some notions, Batlle invited him in. "Me preguntó qué costumbres tenían los europeos. Yo dije: 'Mis costumbres son siempre tomando té.' Entonces Batlle mandó hacer un té, me sirvió la empleada y tomé un té, y estuve charlando con él como dos horas . . . " (He asked me what customs Europeans had. I said, "My customs are to drink tea, always." Then Batlle ordered some tea, the maid served it to me, and I drank tea, and was chatting with him for two hours or so . . .) (156).

The earliest immigrants express gratitude for the freedom and tolerance they found, leaving countries plagued by anti-Semitism, coming to Uruguay with its national constitutional guarantees. The memory of these early years produces what Porzecanski calls "an emotion bordering on devotion" in the immigrants interviewed, and she quotes: "La gente fue maravillosa. Nosotros, a quien cada mucha-chón polaco nos gritaba judío. Nosotros acá besábamos la tierra" (The people were marvelous. To us. In Poland every bully yelled Jew at us. Here, we were kissing the ground) (33). *Historias de vida* also records the immigrants' wonder at how cheap the food was: more than one recalls, sixty years later, going to buy meat at the butchers and getting for free good meat otherwise thrown away, for Eastern Europeans readily ate liver cooked with onions, almost every night. In Uruguay as in Chile, immigrants preferred to settle in the cities.[8] They formed a minute proportion of the rural population, where both the pressure to assimilate and the sense of being outsiders were that much greater.

IMMIGRATION TO CHILE

Chilean historians betray a tendency to push Jewishness from public view, beginning with the colonial period, to sketch out heraldic shields, ascetic priests, noble warriors, invisible native women.[9] Contradict-ing the national imaginary as homogenous, the historian Benjamín Vicuña McKenna caused a sensation when he revealed that the Lima-based Inquisition actively kept tabs on those suspected to be Jews, even in faraway Chile (Böhm vii).[10] Whereas community members in Lima were somewhat able to protect one another, the more iso-lated Jews in Chile were, by contrast, friendless when exposed: thus the physician Francisco Maldonado de Silva of Concepción, informed on by his sister.[11] While the Inquisition's efforts did not prevent Jews from coming to Chile, its zeal worked against the open practice of any non-Catholic faith, so that the 1809 census found only seventy-nine foreigners in Chile, and of those, only four non-Catholics.[12]

The coincidence of new, liberal governments, increased shipping, and problems in Europe led the way for the first Jewish settlements in

Chile, occurring between 1890 and 1920. In addition to Ashkenazi Jews from Russia, small numbers of Sephardim left old settlements in Serbia, Croatia, Macedonia, Greece, and some Arabic countries, as the Ottoman Empire fell. The Sephardic Jews were more likely to assimilate, yet there was also cooperation with the Ashkenazi Jews (Nes-El 33). The first Jew to establish himself in the newly founded town of Temuco left Monastir (Bitolj, in southwestern Macedonia, not far from Skopje) in 1900. He wandered Europe, came to Argentina, crossed the Andes, and became a tailor in Temuco, where he brought his brother to help him and made a fortune, quite possibly in the skill of "invisible mending" for which the Jews from the Monastir area were famous (Nes-El 34).[13] Valparaíso drew Jewish immigrants fleeing pogroms in Poland, Russia, and the Ukraine, before, during, and after World War I. Agosín's *A Cross and a Star* and *Always from Somewhere Else* describe the atmosphere in which the early immigrants lived and raised families, in the Central Valley and in the rural south.

THE GENDERED WORK OF IMMIGRANT IDENTITY

Work "gives birth" to the immigrant: it is through work that he exists. The immigrant whose work disappears, or does not exist, lives in shadows. Guralnik's stories carefully outline the economic aspects of domestic labor. The male speakers in Porzecanski's text take great care to describe their trades, dwelling on urban, street life. In Agosín's *Always from Somewhere Else*, a sign of Abraham Agosín's acculturation: everyone knows the Jewish tailor of Quillota. Work defines the immigrant's success, enabling *him* (in these texts, never *her*) to send for the families left behind, wives whose work the state does not recognize. Excluded from wage labor, the women did piecework at home, on sewing machines purchased on credit. Their invisible work supports family-owned businesses. Guralnik and Agosín explore how the elaborate middle-class facade of success, assimilation, beauty, and leisure, so integral to daily life, utterly depends on women's unrecognized work, "never done," because it is a complex, exhausting charade.

Work dominates the male immigrant's battle to win recognition, to step out of the shadows. Women, by contrast, are measured by their children's successful acculturation. They bear the burden at home. So Guralnik's allusions to her immigrant mother's overriding concern with her children's education, and so the sixteen oral histories that appear in Porzecanski's *Historias de vida:* the thirteen men, but none of the women, describe what it means to manufacture shoes, sell door-to-door, fight the Nazis. The labor of wives is noted only by those men who have worked in sales, especially in the provinces. The women interviewed, and only a few of the men, describe battling the shattering pressures that immigration and war bring to families.

In *A Cross and a Star* and in *Always from Somewhere Else,* Marjorie Agosín engages a primary concern of many Latin American feminists, Guralnik included, by making visible the behind-the-scenes work of the mother whose relation to the state is one of producing future citizens. The journey of Moises Agosín, future doctor, scientist, emigrant from Chile to the United States, involves traveling from the darkness of the house to the light of the laboratory. When he was a boy he played the piano in the darkness of the silent movie theater, in the provincial town of Quillota. Borne by the wings of music and the avatars of mathematics, his mother's faith, his father's labor, the teachers of the secular public school, Moises's belief in reason enables him to survive a medical training that smells more of alchemy in medieval dungeons than of science. He becomes, by turn, a doctor, a professor, a research biochemist. By contrast, his mother, Rachel, from Odessa and Sebastopol never steps into the light. She is associated with dusk. Trained as a cigarette maker, her work is obsolete before she even leaves Europe. At sunset in Quillota she draws the blinds of all three floors of her house, to celebrate Shabbat behind closed doors, apparently alone. The extensive notebooks that she keeps, composed in a Spanish-Cyrillic script, are a mystery that her grand-daughter cannot decipher. Rachel is a figure of pathos, returning to the shadows after she is called to sing in the town plaza, songs in Russian, Turkish, French. The only domestic work that the Chilean state seems to acknowledge is that of bearing children, future citizens: thus Russian Sonia, from *A Cross and a Star*. Standing under the bright Southern sky of Valparaíso, Sonia steps into the light boat that is republican motherhood, cutting through the waves to shore, six or seven barefoot children clinging to, hiding under her skirts. In Chile, she and other women will bear the burden of the family's assimilation as housewives and mothers.

Guralnik and Agosín show how women's isolation within the home leads them to view the world left behind in terms of a temporal, rather than spatial, loss. With every move there is precious little room for domestic items, mementos of feasts and fellowships: a tablecloth, a samovar, perhaps some sepia-toned photographs. For immigrant men living distinctly public lives in the store, street, or plaza, versus their private lives at home, there is more room to develop that split that W. E. B. Du Bois called the problem of "double consciousness." Du Bois points out that those who live in a creolized or hybridized culture stay true to an original identity while at the same time participating in a new identity, which then requires inventing a new identity. Confined to the house, women's interactions with the cultures of the adoptive land would involve charity work, some consumerism, and the need to educate their children.

While the male paradigm for "double consciousness" is invented out of the disjuncture between public/private life, the female double consciousness that Agosín and Guralnik represent arises from the disjuncture between past and present—houses left behind, houses to be filled anew. The double existence of men presents an abrupt divide between life on the outside as a solid citizen, even as a social activist, as opposed to the private individual, whose concerns with family and the life of the spirit are hidden from view. In Porzecanski's interviews this doubleness is manifest in male subjects who answer to different names depending on the context, for example, "Elias," a doctor born "Israel" and known by that name in the synagogue. The doubleness of women emerges from the chasm between memories of girlhood and the shadowy world of adult women who assemble and reassemble one house after another, all the while working to protect themselves, their children, and their spouses from attack by an outside world that regards them as foreigners.

"Double consciousness" refers to the individual's adjustment, while "transculturation" refers to the ethnic group in relation to the culture at large. The term derives from the Cuban anthropologist Fernando Ortíz:

> Cuando hablamos de transculturación nos referimos a los cambios sustanciales que ocurren a determinado grupo étnico, como producto de su dislocamiento geográfico, histórico o socio-cultural, y que convalidan formas de reajuste y readapción a un sistema social de coordenadas diferentes, resultando de este proceso, la invención más o menos abrupta de un estilo de vida novedoso. (Ortíz qtd. in Porzecanski, *Historias de vida* 49)

> [When we speak of transculturation we are referring to the substantial changes that occur to a determined ethnic group as a product of its geographical, historical, or sociocultural dislocation, and that summon up forms of adjustment and adaptation to a social system along different coordinates, with the result of this process being the more or less abrupt invention of a novel style of living.]

The memoir, done well, will reflect in brief how the immigrant destroys and constructs a form of living and a scheme of thought. If the self that is represented seems fragmented, it is because these tasks of destruction and creation imply an apprenticeship in new roles, an effort to personal adjustment that leaves its traces in the individual and group personality.[14]

second moment: remembering the holocaust

For all three of the writers discussed here, the act of speaking and writing is an act of remembrance, aiming to locate what has been forgotten. The primary model for that act of remembrance is the "nunca más" of those who have survived the Holocaust. This is evident in Guralnik's story "Bajando el Rhin" (Sailing Down the Rhine), which involves a group of elderly, German-speaking women who live together in a nursing home, the "Paradise Home." They very carefully embark for a boat trip along the Rhine. The women have misgivings about the trip ("The water isn't as clear as it was before. It's dirty . . . I get seasick). The director, a vigorous sixty-year-old named Frau Braun, orders them to board, even pushing them up the gangplank, despite the women's twisted, bowed legs, the legacy of concentration camp torture. The old women remain passive for the time being, each blaming herself when personal items they were carrying—eyeglasses, dentures—apparently disappear. One of the women, Madame Katz, wondering where she has seen the director, Frau Braun, before, suddenly realizes that Braun was a torturer in the concentration camps, who pulled her daughter away from her, and who continues her torture, stealing and throwing away the women's possessions. After Madame Katz recognizes Frau Braun, the other women join in, shouting out their own identities: the moment of recalling the nicknames of the camp guards who tortured and maimed them turns into a public recovery of their own identities and a refusal to accept continued tricks or victimization.

In Porzecanski, the will to record the circumstances under which Jews were stripped of their citizenship and forced to emigrate from Nazi-occupied Europe stands as a central aim of the oral histories. The precise language of *Historias de vida* reveals the considerations of gender that enter into a speaker's relations to the unnamed listener. For example, "Carlos," born in Bremen, Germany, in 1909, who left Germany in 1934, speaks of Montevideo of the 1930s in terms of what would be memorable to a female listener in the 1980s or 1990s:

> Yo no sé si Ud. sabe que aquí una mujer, en un café o en un boliche, era algo sumamente prohibido . . . Y cuando empezar a fumar un cigarillo las mujeres, entonces, fue el acabose. Y desde aquel entonces, todo cambió mucho y todo fue mucho más libre.

> [I don't know if you know that here a woman, in a café or in a bar, was something highly prohibited . . . and when women started to smoke cigarettes, that was incredible. And everything has changed a great deal since those days, and became much more open.] (132–33)

Awareness of history, of the scapegoating of Jews in Europe, is key to the substantial self-dramatization evident in the portrayal of "Heinz," born in Berlin in 1913, active in the anti-Nazi resistance from 1933 to 1938:

> Yo mismo, veinticuatro horas después que Hitler subió al poder, yo tenía una especie de presentimiento por los conocimientos de historia, y me di cuenta de lo que podía pasar. Era veinticuatro horas después que Hitler subió al

poder. Todavía estaban en mi mente las canciones y las palabras de odio de los nazis contra los judíos . . . fui a la calle y observaba el centro de Berlín . . . pensaba que yo tengo que hacer algo contra eso. Ya había pasado bastante en la historia medieval.

[I, myself, twenty-four hours after Hitler came to power, I had a kind of premonition because of what I knew about history, and I realized what could happen. It was twenty-four hours after Hitler came to power. The songs and hate-filled words of Nazis against Jews were still in my mind . . . I went out to the street and watched the center of Berlin . . . I was thinking, I have to do something against this. Plenty of it had already happened in medieval history.] (147)

The last, longest, and most powerfully written chapter in Porzecanski's book of oral histories attempts to describe the life of the Holocaust survivor, Isabella, concentrating on her experience of World War II. Its representation of memory breaks from the pattern of the previous stories, narrated in the past tense, with a formulaic opening stating the city and year of the speaker's birth. Isabella's life breaks in two, a "before" and an "after." Her "birth" is the outbreak of war in Satu Mare, Romania, even though she is fifteen years old at the time. The radical alteration in her identity can be expressed in familial terms: the third-oldest of six children, only she, a sister, and two uncles survive the round of ghetto, starvation, deportation to camps. The past tense appears only to describe the years before the war: "Nuestros mayores se sintieron siempre húngaros, se criaron en Austro-Hungría, y la mayoría de ellos, ni siquiera habla el rumano" (Our elders always felt themselves to be Hungarians, they were raised in Austro-Hungary, and the majority of them don't even speak Rumanian) (186).

Required to wear the Star of David, "Isabella" is left outside all law. Her words are a stark reminder of the brutality of ethnic and racial categories: "for us there is no defense from the police, even when they kill us in the street"(192). The trains with their human cargo come by. When the ghetto is emptied, they are sent to Auschwitz, the last time she sees her mother, sister, and brothers. The woman in charge of their barracks tells them: "See this smoke? That's where your parents are" (203). The memory of war and loss becomes the defining aspect of her ongoing, present consciousness, years later, marking forever her act of writing: "Después de tantos años, el recuerdo corta mi alma como un cuchillo y siento que mi corazón nunca dejó de sangrar. Cuántos años tuvieron que pasar para poder escribir de todo esto, y cómo sigue doliendo!" (After so many years, the memory cuts my soul like a knife and I feel that my heart never stopped bleeding. How many years had to pass to be able to write all this, and how it keeps on aching!) (204). "Isabella" is the only story in Porzecanski's text that does not offer the editor's reportage.

Auschwitz creates in the writer a knowledge that endures into the present, a knowledge that no one can "report" for her: "El ser humano soporta mucho más de lo que cree posible, de lo que nuestra mente es capaz de imaginar . . . todo esto lo escribo para que quede testimonio y no se pueda negar, como pretenden hacer ahora los nuevos nazis" (Human beings can put up with more than it's possible to believe, than what our mind is capable of imagining . . . I write all this so that it stands as testimony and cannot be denied, as the new Nazis are now trying to do) (205, 208–9). Neither the writer's knowledge nor her associated memories end with the war: as the soldiers flee the work camp, armed local citizens come in and set fire to the camp hospital: "We see the fire and we hear the desperate screams. One could live a hundred years and never forget those screams, desperate" (223).

The continual return to memory produces further knowledge, as in the writer's awareness that immediately following the war, their former captors continued to take advantage of them, charging them for donated goods: "Hoy pienso que todo esto nos pasó por ser tan intimidables, tan asustadas todavía del uniforme alemán" (Today I think that all that happened to us because we were so easily intimidated, still so terrified of the German uniform) (230). Among the worst horrors of war and of the Holocaust: coming up against brutality so unspeakable that words cannot express it, and the sense that the survivors are less fortunate than many of those who died. It is this psychic pain that seems to lead Isabella to observe: "Mi suerte en particular no fue muy grande" (My particular luck wasn't very great) (242).

FLIGHT FROM THE HOLOCAUST TO THE NEW WORLD

Anti-immigrant sentiment was part of national politics in both Uruguay and Chile during the economic crises of the 1930s.[15] The rise of exclusivist nationalism in Uruguay brought increasing restrictions on immigration from 1932 to 1945. Registration papers in 1935–36 noted, for the first time, "religion" as a classification for immigrants (Kleiner 13). By the following year, one of the few sure ways to bring one's family members to Uruguay from Europe was to find a landowner to guarantee the new immigrant employment as an agricultural laborer (Porzecanski, *Historias de vida* 78). Even legally admitted immigrants, as well as new immigrants with visas, could be expelled, measures that hindered the entry of refugees from Europe. The notorious *Conte Grande* steamship incident took place in February 1939: refugees from Europe seeking to land in Brazil, Uruguay, or Argentina had their Uruguayan visas declared null and were returned, where most of them died.

The outbreak of war transformed the nature and size of Jewish communities in Chile, as Steiner observes: "El número de nuestros correligionarios en Chile aumentó en un solo año hasta quedar casi duplicado" (The number of those who shared our religion in Chile increased in a single year to almost double its size) (22). Twelve thousand refugees arrived between 1938 and 1943, bringing to 20,000 the number of Jews in Chile (Kleiner 52). Estimating Santiago's Jewish population at 18,000 in 1941 would make it a little more than 2 percent of the city (Cohen 62). They worked in light industry as manufacturers and merchants, and about 1 percent were professionals.

New social organizations were established to assist this new generation of immigrants. Most were urban, educated older people. Some were allowed to stay with relatives who had pledged to pay all their expenses: such would be the case of the older women described in *A Cross and a Star.* They came almost empty-handed, expelled from Europe, facing a new climate, a new language, life in the rainy forests of southern Chile. The relation to home and community differed according to the kind of work, family members, and surroundings that the newest group of immigrants found. The arrival of so many new immigrants surely transformed the consciousness of those who had come prior to the Nazis: the Instituto Hebreo, the first Jewish school, was founded in Santiago in 1933, certainly through the contributions of earlier immigrants keen to rising anti-Semitism. Eight years later, the Instituto had several hundred students (Cohen 63).

Agosín's texts describe the contradictory welcome that refugees from Hitler's Germany encountered in Chile. In *Always from Somewhere Else* Agosín tells of doctors, highly trained specialists, coming as refugees to Santiago over the protests of the local medical establishment, which demanded that the new arrivals be sent off to the provinces. For Ana Morgenstern, from *A Cross and a Star,* there is forced assimilation. Employed by an old Chilean family, "to teach them strict German discipline and the wisdom of Goethe," they change her name to Fraulein Douglass. Or forced assimilation can be posthumous, as in a case that Agosín describes, of the unnamed Christian or goy wife of a grandfather's brother, who "made a bonfire of memories by burning all the photographs of the Russian ancestors and thus trying to eradicate all the evil spirits of the Jewish race" (101).

Given the increased number of refugees seeking asylum, a national origins quota system took effect. Still, Chile accepted Jews from Germany even as the two nations continued their long-standing economic ties (Cohen 140). Nazis campaigned within Chile even as the government sought to maintain "a generally neutral attitude" (Cohen 140). Nazi-fascist sympathizers "carried on anti-Semitic street propaganda" and declaimed slogans, "that Jews were coming to take away the bread from Chilean workingmen" (Cohen 134, 137). Here echoes a refrain appearing throughout Agosín's memoirs of her parents' and her own lives in Chile: "quien tomó el pan del horno? el perro judío, el perro judío."

Little has been published, and much could be told, of the complex relationship between Chile and Germany, during and immediately following the war. The role of Nazis within the military and in enclaves such as Colonia Dignidad needs investigation (Kostopulos-Cooperman, Prologue, A Cross and a Star). Sociologists have yet to study the ambiguous status of Jews in Chile's hyperstratified class system, a topic that Agosín's two texts often mention. The problem for scientific study would be the historical moment coupled with the investigator's own status in Chile. Thus Jacob X. Cohen, a visitor from the United States in 1941, confidently writes that "Jewish descent is marked in much Chilean high society" (64). Yet Günter Böhm, writing in Chile in the 1980s, is more cautious, ascribing rapid assimilation of conversos to the fear of reprisal in the colonial period (ix). It is no accident that Chilean historians begin exploring surnames and elaborating genealogies just as mass emigration to Chile became a real possibility, following World War I. When the prominent historian Luis Thayer Ojeda announced, in 1917, that he had found 447 Chilean surnames that were Hebrew in origin, his work was greeted by a public outcry. "La lista de apellidos no se atrevió a publicarla nunca" (He never dared publish the list of surnames) (Böhm 97, 98). The absolute reluctance to accept Jews as equal citizens is all the more perplexing when so many non-Hispanic surnames feature in the country's oligarchy, Edwards and Subercaseaux, for example.

Throughout all descriptions of the lands left behind in the first and second waves of immigration there is in Guralnik, Porzecanski, and Agosín a shared sense of the impossibility of regarding national identity as innate, for it is based on accidents of birth and politics. Guralnik uses a collection of hyphens to identify herself, Russian-Jewish-Chilean, and her stories engage settings as diverse as early Soviet Russia, Chile, and Israel. Porzecanski's interviewees name and describe the places where they were born, villages destroyed by advancing armies, towns and cities that were part of the spoils of war, and thus changed hands, from Poland to Germany to Russia, for example. The story of "Jaime" describes his using an ambassadorial reception in the 1950s to poke at the question of where he is from, since his natal city of Shemenig was Russian when he was born, Polish when he left Europe, and most recently occupied by Russia. The ambassadors decide that he is Polish because he came to Uruguay on a Polish passport (Porzecanski, *Historias de vida* 107). *Always from Somewhere Else* jokes that Moises Agosín is a Provençal gentleman because he was born in Marseilles of parents from Odessa.

third moment: post-holocaust identities
HISTORICAL CONTEXTS

Political involvement could be an indicator of Jewish assimilation. In Uruguay, the heritage of political activism and trade unionism expressed in Porzecanski's text became a distinctive aspect of cultural expression. By the end of the 1960s, however, Uruguay like Chile and other Southern Cone nations found itself in a state of profound social unrest. The military coup of 1973 initiated a period of neofascist repression, the very antithesis of the nation's earlier reputation as "the Switzerland of Latin America." Much of the intelligentsia was forced into exile, breaking cultural production in two. Abril Trigo's descriptions of the effects of the military dictatorship in Uruguay have a strong parallel with the situation for Chile:

> a culture of exile, which, cut loose from its moorings, drifted between a nostalgic longing for the no longer visible Model republic, and its own enrichment through marginality in other hegemonic environments. The counterculture of inxile, a culture of endurance due to repressive military politics under neofascism, was forced to resort to non-canonical artistic and literary means. (Trigo 39)

In Chile, the national divisions following the 1970 presidential election of Marxist Salvador Allende likewise split the Jewish community: "Centenares de personas y entre ellos muchos correligionarios deciden emigrar de Chile y esta migración provoca, en cierto modo, una paralización de vida societaria" (Hundreds of people and among them many who share our religion decide to emigrate from Chile, and this emigration provokes, to some extent, a paralysis of societal life) (Nes-El 213). Sephardic Jews found themselves on opposite sides, one elected general secretary of the university, another made president of the Counsel for Defense of the State (Nes-El 214). The ongoing political crises of the 1970s became worse, dividing parents, children, siblings, evident in Guralnik's story "Sabados gigantes," a chilling evocation of the insanity of the 1980s. Guralnik depicts a feuding family set against the weekly four-hour spectacle of Chilean-German Mario Kreutzberger, aka television game show host "Don Francisco." The first-person narrator unconsciously duplicates Don

Francisco's frenzied orchestration of unity, prosperity, and good cheer.

Sweet Revenge: Sonia Guralnik's Satires of Assimilation

The work of Sonia Guralnik offers an interesting example of the means by which a member of various groups previously excluded—an older woman, just entering publishing, a Russian-Jewish Chilean— can cultivate a place in the national literary scene by combining humor with social commentary. Telling the story, lightly, with humor, is her sweet revenge, in strongly domestic narratives that reveal the concerns of middle-class Chilean women, housewives who from the outside would seem privileged, even pampered. Precise and deftly humorous, her tales shed their light on that vast machinery, teetering on breakdown, that the well-to-do housewife employs to maintain the requisite surface of healthy children, husbandly comfort, and great fun for all. A feminist sensibility inspires her rebellion against the exploitation that the women of Chile's so-called *clase acomodada* ("comfortably well-off class") endure. There is self-mockery in depicting the maniacal effort to play the perfect wife and mother, a role that requires ignorance above all: first to ignore one's own potential, channeling it into exquisite pastries and three-sauce entrées; second to stand impervious to the effects of the macho mandate, which requires a mindless promiscuity in men. The stories reveal that the "comfortable" housewife in fact lives in no leisure at all, in summer houses with exploding septic tanks, dutifully taking care of a paralyzed mother-in-law, uneasily coexisting with the woman engaged to take care of the mother-in-law, and cowed by the imperious, all-seeing housekeeper, who's the first to know of the husband's current, cheerful adulteries.

The perfect wife's self-mocking, willed optimism is countered by her intellectual pessimism about the degrees of love that her marriage offers. Recently widowed, she visits Israel, where her brother urges her to marry one of the wife-hunting men who haunt the public parks: what do they want? "It's not easy for a single man to get housing" (*Historia de la mujer gusano* 124). Sizing up the situation, she declines to relinquish her new freedom.

In general Jewish women's traditions are presented in Guralnik's work as fully positive. A parade of students carrying candles brings to mind her mother lighting the Shabbat candles:

> Mi madre en vez de amilanarse o de llenarse de malos augurios, como hicieron otros emigrantes, armó un nuevo hogar, sacó brillo al samovar, vistió la mesa con su hermosa carpeta verde y encendió las velas de shabat. Vio en esto una nueva etapa, una nueva apertura, una nueva vida en América.

> [Rather than being cowed or glooming over with evil omens, like the other emigrants, my mother assembled a new house, brought a high polish to the samovar, covered the table with her beautiful green tablecloth and lit the Shabat candles. She saw in this a new stage, a new opening, a new life in América.] (*Recuento* 35)

Humor and optimism make it easier to survive the disappointment of the woman who has sacrificed perhaps too much to the role of good wife. It also works through and against the outsider status that the majority Catholic culture confers on the Jewish emigrant to Chile. One critic, A. E. Torrealba, has described as "humorous" the drama of the Jewish girl in Catholic surroundings in Guralnik's story "Con flores amarillas" (With Yellow Flowers). Humorous to whom? Certainly not to the parents of such a girl, or to the observant Jew. Guralnik's humor recalls writers like Erma Bombeck: a retrospective account of unavoidable pitfalls.

The story "Paris" offers a specifically feminist sensibility. The narrator is a businessman, off for a conference in Paris. He shrugs off his "hysterical" wife, "My poor Tita, so ridiculous and insignificant," who wants to go. The illusions of his egotism are immense: "Life for a successful executive begins at fifty, now the Frenchwomen will see what a 'Latin lover' can do." He takes off for an encounter with "my little French girl," who offers him a novelty: she wants to be pursued on roller skates. Finally she takes off his skates and does him, laughing at him all the while. In bad French he manages to summon up the spoken endearments that he imagines she wants. When he goes off drinking the next day with other businessmen, the culmination of the party involves a private showing of a videotaped sex act whose opening scenes the businessman recognizes all too clearly from the previous evening (*Historia de la mujer gusano* 120).

Such humor provides both an escape from and a confrontation of reality. The fact of narrowed options for escape rules the lighthearted comic description of rejecting a would-be, early adolescent boyfriend, the red-headed Tito Ruiz de Gamboa in "Pastillas de anis" (Licorice Candy). Her preference for life at the movies offers more to the imagination and provides an alternative to the prospect of total assimilation that "la pandilla"—"the gang" of adolescent girls, her chums—is inclined to demand.

HOW MEMOIR NEGOTIATES IDENTITY: LITERARY CONTEXTS

Guralnik, Porzecanski, and Agosín all focus on emigration and the role of memory, with a documentation of changes in women's familial and national roles that bridges Jewish with specific national identities. In Guralnik's stories the writer's subjectivity speaks directly, with little apparent mediation. In Porzecanski's fiction, as in her oral histories, the sensibility of emigration coalesces with that of the city. Dominant in Agosín's texts is the individual writer's meditative engagement with memory. For all writers the effort of pulling fragments into a temporary whole is an act of will and desire that shores up links between the Old World and the New, and between different sites in the Americas.

Latin American women choosing to work with memoir tread the edge of what has been a primarily male preserve in the history of Latin American letters, encompassing biography, journalistic essays, and history. Women have created a space for themselves in the memoir by stressing the association with speech. A far cry from the *Ego sum* of the semiretired military leader, women have been instrumental in creating and promoting testimonial literature and oral history. Speaking through others, or letting others speak through them, they have been rememberers, editors, translators. These modest, unassuming acts of remembrance have thus been an inherently collaborative enterprise, as distinct from the "supreme I" of the masculine bildungsroman or "Memorias."

A major choice in memoir is how the writer acknowledges (or not) her own subjectivity. Guralnik's, Porzecanski's, and Agosín's work each represents a distinct approach to the question of self-representation. Guralnik, the writer of her own story, chooses satire and humor to describe the dilemmas of assimilation. Porzecanski and Agosín are more consciously engaged in social history, which involves adopting another person's life and voice. In *Historias de vida* Porzecanski's editing creates the impression of subjects engaged in direct address. The transcribing writer's presence is kept to a minimum, although aspects of that presence are evident through the conspicuous omission of references to writing and occasional textual aspects signaling the interview situation. Porzecanski does not use this method of writing for another in the last, longest, and most disturbing of the stories. "Isabella," a Holocaust survivor, writes directly in her own words of her entire experience from the moment that the war begins, including in her commentary the difficulty of writing about her unmediated experience of the unspeakable.

Just as there can be no doubt that reading the direct testimony of survivors is a highly effective way to ensure that the Holocaust will not be forgotten or denied, the genuineness of that narrative renders dubious the imaginative appropriations of the ex-slave's or survivor's story. Texts such as William Styron's fictionalized *Confessions of Nat Turner,* or texts in which writers project their consciousness into that of the Holocaust survivor, the inmate of Auschwitz or the prison camps of Latin America, may do more harm than good. The imaginative account threatens to usurp the already-tenuous voice of the survivor. Further ethical questions come into play when the publication of testimonios, such as the stories of favela-dweller Carolina de Jésus, or of union organizer Domitila Barros de Chungara, or of survivors' stories, brings in substantial profits. The multiple reprinting of such texts have made international audiences aware of the desperate poverty and violence facing the majority of Latin American women, yet it is far from clear what happens with the profits realized from the sale of those stories.

Porzecanski: The Writer's Witness to Spoken Memory
The telling of the story may be set in the past, but the pleasure of telling it, of being listened to, belongs to the present and to the future, as in Porzecanski's "Issac":

> Yo creo que podría estar cuarenta, sesenta, noventa, ciento ochenta días hablando de cosas que podría interesar mucho porque mi vida de noventa y tres años que vine de mi país a la edad de once, pasé ochenta y dos años en América. ¿Puede imaginarse lo que son ochenta y dos años?

> [I believe that I could be here forty, sixty, ninety, a hundred and eighty days speaking of things that would be re-

ally interesting because my ninety-three years of life, coming from my country at eleven years of age, I spent eighty-two years in America. Can you imagine what eighty-two years are?] (*Historias de vida* 104)

In Porzecanski, scrupulous documentation makes possible the act of remembrance that sets the writer's personal sensibilities aside. Her fictional *Invención de soles* and *Ciudad impune* share the documentary sensibility of *Historias de vida*, likewise combining the personal and impersonal, recording a voice or an unnamed individual's experience. The detail, sparseness, and timing of her narratives all enhance their allegorical quality, which turns them from individual lives into fables of a general applicability. The allegory is a speaking otherwise, multileveled, as becomes evident from the composite effect of the interviews in *Historias de vida*. As the text moves in on present time, it becomes increasingly obvious that these stories from the first half of the century stand for and in relation to the nation's current political circumstances. Moving from the patriarchs who worked with and sometimes in spite of the legacy of Batlle to the toil of the *cuenteniks* and the *clápers* to the 1930s era refugees to the wartime terror, Porzecanski's construction of national history implicitly comments on the presence or absence of these aspects in the contemporary nation.

Turning to Porzecanski's interviews with women, two stories particularly stand out as drawing implicit parallels between the devices and effects of the Nazis and other military dictatorships: the story that Sara tells and the final, longest, grueling story, written by Isabella, a survivor of the ghetto, of Auschwitz, of a slave labor camp in Germany, of tuberculosis. The loss of children becomes part of what women in particular share: when one woman learns of the death of her only child, her screaming awakens in other women an awareness of their own vulnerability:

Siento su dolor en mi alma, como un presentimiento, que
un día yo también voy a padecer el mismo sufrimiento, el
mismo cáncer me va a corromper el alma hasta el final de
mi vida. En otras circunstancias, yo también pierdo mi
única hija, mi único amor, a la edad de 18 años.

[I feel her suffering in my soul, like an omen, that one day
I too will endure the same suffering, the same cancer will
corrupt my soul until the end of my life. In other circumstances I too lose my only daughter, my only love, at 18
years of age.] (*Historias de vida* 235)

That ache of loss is evident in the story of Sara, born in the city of
Vilnius in 1918 (which was Polish until 1943, then part of Russia during the Hitler-Stalin pact, then Lithuania from 1945 onward). Sara
describes the ghetto formed three months after war broke out, in September 1941. After her husband was taken away, Sara left the ghetto,
taking her year-old daughter with her. A family in the countryside
gave them shelter, but because the child's crying aroused the suspi-
cions of neighbors, she left, and decided to head back to the ghetto
and leave her child at the door of a convent: " . . . yo escribí el nombre y el apellido de ella, pero le di un nombre polaco. Y siempre yo lo
tenía puesto en la garganta, porque yo pierdo la memoria, para acor-
darme cómo se llamaba" (I wrote her name and surname, but I gave
her a Polish name. And my throat is always stuck, because I lost my
memory, I can't remember what I called her) (118). Returning to Vilnius after the war, she finds that only a few of the people she had
known had survived and that the convent where she had left her
daughter was no longer there: because it was Polish, everyone was
suddenly, forcibly evacuated at night, by train, to another city, no one
knew where: "Ud. sabe cómo es, cuando quieren hacer algo, ellos hacen
de noche para que nadie vea" (You know how it is, when they want

to do something, they do it at night, so no one will see) (125). Her commentary on the effects of terror echoes in a similar observation by Itzhak: "Todas las familias tenían a alguien preso o muerto y eso era la vida. Lo que nosotros empezamos a sentir y nos empezó a extrañar, ese miedo que se sentía, que no se podía hablar" (All the families had some one imprisoned or dead and that's how life was. What we began to feel, and how we began to miss it, feeling that fear, that one couldn't talk about) (176).

Always Between: Marjorie Agosín

Marjorie Agosín's as-told-to biographies of her parents, *A Cross and a Star* and *Always from Somewhere Else*, are mixed texts, emerging from the spoken testimony of the subjects, the reflections of the writing subject, and the work of the gifted translator, Celeste Kostopulos-Cooperman. Examining manuscripts, the translator works in collaboration with the author to produce a print-ready version of the whole. In the earlier stages of writing *A Cross and a Star*, the daughter has made her contemplation of the material part of the construction of the story. What has been overheard or recalled is mixed in the text with what has been said directly. This seamlessness remains as the text moves from one draft to the next, from Spanish-language manuscript to English-language print version. Given the roles of voice and memory in the construction of the text, the need to establish historicity is strong. A textual function of the book's family photographs, like prologues written by the translator or another party, is to establish historical parameters, to counter those who would dismiss the memoir as wholly imaginative.

In *Always from Somewhere Else*, the story of the father takes precedence. The writer's will to separate is clearer, which consequently strengthens the strictly narrative aspect of the text. Where the earlier memoir concentrates on girlhood, ending with marriage (as girls' narratives do), the representation of the father's journey takes on wider dimensions. As the family's representative in the world, his figure is heroic, traveling outward, from the provinces to the city and from there to battle: as one of three Jewish students at medical school in 1938, he was forced to carry a knife in self-defense. He returns, years later, to the scenes of his early struggles. The hero's return does not, in this case, offer reintegration, for the text suggests, in a multitude of examples, that the Chilean medical establishment never accepted him, even though they professed friendship.

The daughter who writes the story describes the far past as if it were halfway between remembered and imagined, but the stories of the more recent past, particularly the stories of ostracism in the United States, of being a blue-eyed Jewish-latina teenager, are written in the voice of a girl who is sharing, for the first time really, her mother's isolated, home-confined, emigrant existence. In both texts the attitude toward childhood mingles nostalgia for a specific locale with a refusal to idealize, or to dismiss past slights.

The narratives of A Cross and a Star and Always from Somewhere Else move beyond the personal by representing the lives of at least three, even four generations—as many generations as any living human being is likely to know. By spanning the range of known lives, Agosín's work with memoir, like Porzecanski's and Guralnik's, provides insight into questions of continuity from one generation to the next. Each writer registers the qualitative changes occurring in Jewish and national life as identities and allegiances shift, from the immigrants' generation to those of their children and grandchildren.

The span over several generations allows Guralnik and Agosín, descendants of Russian Jews who settled in Chile, to comment on Chile's long-standing affinity, even identification with, Russia's peripheral relationship to Europe, its feudalistic, agrarian legacy, its industrial expansion, its division between poets looking to the land and the spirit and the voices calling for modernization. Chile has had its

theosophists and back-to-nature Tolstoy enthusiasts in the early twentieth century, Shangri-la guru followers in the 1960s and 1970s, or
those fleeing the urban sprawl today. Yet that engagement, even wor-
ship of the countryside that is a hallmark of national writers throughout the twentieth century is only intermittently present in Jewish
writers in Chile: the provinces are hardly synonymous with tolera-
tion, and anyone who has ever lived in a small town will know the
truth of the old proverb, "pueblo chico, infierno grande"—little
town, big hell. Rather than escape to the countryside, Agosín looks
to the sea, like Neruda and Mistral, and above all to the past as a site
from which identity emerges gradually.

The bridge between being Jewish and being Latin American can
lead to new emigrations. *Always from Somewhere Else* uses the perspective of secularism to contest the priorities of a country more inclined to restore its thousands of churches than to design, build, and
equip its teaching hospitals. After all, the wealthy go to private clinics
or abroad for their medical treatment, while the rest do not matter.
The attempt to deal with such twisted values is a recurring problem
of Latin American identity, which the secular idealist will most
acutely perceive. Because the Moises Agosín who emerges from the
pages of *Always from Somewhere Else* is a secularist in the best tradition of the Enlightenment, it is those ideals, more than politics or religion, that motivate his relocation to the United States.

Contemporary Diaspora

Joseph Brodsky argues that the modern exile is the child of privilege,
whose act of boarding the airplane is a kind of homecoming: "what
takes place is a transition from a political and economic backwater
to an industrially advanced society with the latest word on individual liberty on its lips. . . . [Taking] this route is for an exiled writer,
in many ways, going home—because he gets closer to the seat of the

ideals which inspired him along" ("Condition" 24). Discarding as fuzzy-minded romantic assertions the idea that civilization begins in agriculture and in home, Brodsky asserts that nomadism is at the core of civil life. Whether we agree or not, it is certain that the relocation of Latin American Jews to the United States and Europe, perhaps to Israel, demands a new understanding of the phenomena of exile and of home.[16]

Modern diasporic emigration is motivated by a search for what Federico R. Lachmann, paraphrasing Nietzche, calls the "país de los hijos" as opposed to the "patria," the country in which our fathers lived. This is the searched-for country, where we might live in peace, and to which we could adapt, so that our children might live in peace and security, enjoying an equality of rights and educational opportunity, living and working in a "natural" way (Lachmann 49).[17] The insufficiency and failure of the patria—one's fathers' land—echoes throughout Agosín's and Porzecanski's work, in the state's failure to guarantee the equality of its citizens' rights, in the actions of military regimes that suspend the legal rights of citizens, as part of a war against so-called subversives. The insufficiency, or failure, of the idea of "patria" results in what Trigo calls "the cultures of exile and inxile."[18]

Conventional associations of exile with suffering and isolation are likewise insufficient to sketch out the consequences when the children of immigrants subsequently emigrate, putting aside the expectation, if ever it existed, of acceptance as full-fledged citizens in the countries that were and weren't their fathers', in which they were born. Even as that expectation is pushed aside, however, a great number of authors who reside abroad through forced or voluntary exile continue writing in the Spanish language of their childhood and youth, strengthening not only their identity with their country, but with other Spanish speakers, at the same time as they reaffirm their links with Judaism and explore the dilemma of emigration and acculturation.

The nomadic life can lead to multiple new modes of identification, as James Clifford points out:

> Decentered, lateral connections may be as important as those formed around a teleology of origin/return. And a shared, ongoing history of displacement, suffering, adaptation, or resistance may be as important as the projection of a specific origin. . . . Positive articulations of diaspora identity reach outside the normative territory and temporality (myth/history) of the nation-state. . . . Diaspora cultures thus mediate, in a lived tension, the experiences of separation and entanglement, of living here and remembering/desiring another place. (306–7, 311)

The multiple identifications of Porzecanski, Agosín, and Guralnik as Latin American Jewish women who write in Spanish reach far beyond their association with the particular nations of Uruguay and Chile.

The memoir and compilations from oral history are good places to begin looking for that bridge between Jewish and Latin American identity that Avni challenges us to find, thus selecting what is truly memorable as literature. What is interesting about Guralnik's and Agosín's texts is that they mediate those "experiences of separation and entanglement" on a familial level—as the texts of immigrant women writers so often do—Anzia Yezerska, Maxine Hong Kingston, and Jamaica Kincaid come to mind. Looking out from between the curtains women are not fooled by public shows: their gossip is a running commentary on the facades that each family erects in its efforts to preserve face among other members of the community. Thus Sonia Guralnik's description of the in-laws whose strategic window onto the entrance of the Union Hebrea provides the women of the house with the opportunity to comment on the disjunction between each family's prosperous facade and their scantily hidden economic distress.

The writers here represented are more consciously global in their outlook than are many of their counterparts in Chile and Uruguay. Despite the transnationalism of literary theory, studies of Jewish life and culture in Latin America have so far centered primarily on single nations, as if these were stable, fixed entities.[19] Furthermore, as Darrell B. Lockhart explains, "Latin American national identities have traditionally been formed around the ideas of cultural hegemony in which the collective takes precedence over the individual" (xi). Guralnik, Porzecanski, and Agosín all refuse the strictly national. Encompassing several generations of stories of emigration and memory, their work exposes the improvisational nature of "home." Not land or possessions but memory constitutes the closest thing to an anchor. In their use of multiple voices they present a new way of understanding not just memory but the construction of texts based on the confluence of memory and speech. This confluence gives the language of the text a personal, spoken quality.

To set the memoir in the context of historical conditions ultimately requires understanding the social and technological conditions of writing that produce these books, that contribute to women's emergence and expression as speaking, historical subjects. The literature of women in Latin America shares with Jewish Latin American writing a common orientation in that both are primarily twentieth-century phenomena. Women's emergence as writers historically connects to a tolerant government, education, leisure time. The security of a fixed residence and an income turns out to be a prime condition enabling the writing of the three women discussed here, oddly counterpoised to their interest in migration and in people living at the margins, economically. Holding a pension or a university position allows them to discover, looking back, the contradictory aspects of immigrant success. The children are grown, in Guralnik's case. There is the luxury of household help.

Participation in writing workshops during the later years of the dictatorships has been decisive in the emergence of Sonia Guralnik.[20] Her writing suggests a sympathy with the social unrest that came to affect every aspect of day-to-day, urban life in Chile, as opposition to the dictatorship gained momentum, from 1984 onward. The literary workshops in which Guralnik enrolled once her children became adults speak directly of the countercultural world beyond that of the university and the news media, providing an outlet for social discontent. Workshops can be seen as community based, or they can be seen as a group that has formed around a leader, usually a writer with an established social and artistic following. Whether the gathering serves the leader or its members, whether its designs are therapeutic or complements to educational problems, the better workshop urges its members to transform personal experience into artistry. Workshops are "a way to make literature and arts accessible to a wider range of people and to encourage them to write about their local history" (de Costa 19).

Both Guralnik and Agosín explore the multiple ambiguities that being Jewish creates for their class status, in terms of their relation to wealthy non-Jews and to "puertas adentro," live-in servants. In her short story "Surnames," for example, Agosín relates how members of Chile's traditional, Hispano-Catholic landholding class can comfortably denigrate an equally wealthy descendant of Jewish immigrants, by dismissing the latter's surname. A *Cross and a Star* alludes to the complex domestic relationships, in the South, between the fair-complexioned Jewish girls and women who, while impoverished and discriminated against, belong to the race and class of those whom native and mestiza women serve as domestics. If, in *Happiness*, Agosín's short story "Slaves" satirizes the class roles that the employer and domestic servant play out, another short story, "An Enormous Black Umbrella," sentimentalizes the nanny figure, making her radically other, a person against whom the child narrator defines herself even as she declares eternal allegiance.

Discarding the myth of the solitary artist, inspired by the muse, and examining instead the book as a collaborative enterprise, we get a clearer idea of the circumstances allowing the emergence of Jewish women as writers. Representatives of the generation born in Chile and Uruguay following World War II, Agosín and Porzecanski were raised amid Jewish social institutions. University trained, they are conscious of an international audience. Their writing, editing, and publishing activities are necessarily collective enterprises if they are to reach that international audience. Appearing in translation, in a variety of countries, and with the support of various communities, as their work takes social conscience as a central theme, introspection or nostalgia diminishes. There is less interest in activist organizing, so far, in the work of the youngest generation of writers, which would include Shlomit Beytelman of Chile and Julia Schercherner of Uruguay, binationals who have resided for substantial periods of time in Israel yet who choose to work in Spanish.

For Porzecanski and for Agosín, it is but a short step from the effort to depict social reality to seeking social change. Each author's widest audience comes through texts best described as collaborative products between two (more) communities. The book is itself a microspace, in which editors and translators play key parts, as does institutional support, in the form of direct and indirect funding. Also relevant are the networks of national and international distribution that reinforce the author's decisions to write about multiple cultural identities.

Returning to Avni's challenge, quoted in the opening epigraph, I am arguing that books are produced in and for local, national, and global contexts. In Chile as in Uruguay the restoration of neodemocracy has given way to a proliferation of literary subcultures, the emergence of new cultural practices and discourses. This multiplicity has enabled the ongoing questioning of national identity. Minority voices, such as Jewish writers, indigenous and mixed-blood peoples, and gays, have substantially contributed to this process. Understanding what the book contributes to the construction of a stable bridge between Jewish and Latin American identities depends on how such books are produced, what sort of writing communities they emerged from, how they were financed and by whom, how they were distributed, who bought them, and so forth. In the end, the nature of the identity that memoir shapes depends on how it comes to print and for whom and on what readers and other writers make of it.

NOTES

1. I wish to thank Ledig House International Writers and Artists Colony in New York for the fellowship that enabled me to write the first draft of this chapter and particularly Kathleen Lynch Baum and Irit Ziffer, who provided much useful help. In Arizona, I thank Lisa Cornell Bower and Susan McCabe for their valuable comments on an early draft.

2. At the borders of czarist Russia an ever-tightening web of legal, educational, and occupational restrictions were directed against Jews. Officials encouraged acts of violence against Jews: expulsions from the cities and pogroms in the countryside distracted attention away from social change. More than a million Jews left Europe between 1881 and 1914 (Porzecanski, *Historias de vida* 16).

3. Abel M. Bronstein argues that Jewish emigration differs from all others, in that it has been neither voluntary nor spontaneous but motivated by the risk to their existence as individuals and as communities and that in the Jewish Diaspora, the words "immigrant" and "refugee" are more or less interchangeable, indicating the impossibility of return to the country of origin.

4. In Chile, the founder of the first Masonic Lodge was Manuel de Lima y Sola, a Sephardic Jew born in Curaçao.

5. The establishment of burial societies was the earliest form of Jewish institutional life in Uruguay. "La muerte se constituyó en el elemento gravitante del primer impulso de aglutinamiento judío. Es que el judaismo le da a la vida una importancia capital a tal punto que en la muerte también proyecta la vida" (Death constituted the gravitating element of the first impulse of Jewish cohesion. It's that Judaism gives such a capital importance to life, to such an extent that life is also projected into death) (Bronstein 5). In Uruguay, the first cemetery consecrated according to Jewish ritual was opened in November 1917.

6. Jews coming from Eastern Europe transported self-governing models such as the Kehillah as early as 1918. *Historias de vida* amply documents the ideological and ethnic diversity of Uruguay's Jewish community, which included, by 1930, Zionists, a Jewish Workers' party affiliated with the Uruguayan Socialist party, a cultural center with a leftist orientation, and the Yiddish-Socialist Bund. By 1941 the divisions between the new, German-speaking versus second-generation Ashkenazic and Sephardic Uruguayans living in Montevideo troubled Jacob X. Cohen, a visitor from the World Jewish Congress, who commented that "all efforts for a union of the three groups have been fruitless" and estimated that Jews made up 5 percent of the urban population, 2 percent of the nation, and 1 percent of the population in the Uruguayan countryside (Cohen 32).

7. Although the situation of the first immigrants from Eastern Europe to Uruguay, arriving right after World War I, was "miserable and extremely difficult," they could immigrate there "without difficulties," that is, with minimal paperwork and funds, and "many of them have used Uruguay only as a trampoline, to go on travelling to neighboring countries" (Kleiner 11–12, 15). In *Historias de vida* Porzecanski states that about 70 percent of the Jewish community in Uruguay derives from Eastern Europe and 15 percent from Western Europe, and about 12 percent are Sephardic and 3 percent are Hungarian.

8. These contrasts are confirmed on comparing the data and impressions appearing in Cohen and Kleiner.

9. Accompanying Diego de Almagro to Chile when he left Cuzco in 1535 was Rodrigo de Orgoños, from Toledo, a *converso* born in 1505. "Conversos" or "New Christians"—Jews or the children of Jews who converted to Christianity when faced with the alternative of death, expulsion, or baptism into the Catholic faith—formed a significant part of the second expedition, led by Pedro de Valdivia, who traveled with 11 men, 6 of them conversos or the sons of New Christians and at least 2 of them condemned by the Inquisition for professing Judaism (Böhm 19–21). It is no coincidence that the complex theme of Marranos, "Portuguese Jews," "conversos," and "New Christians" comes to the awareness of historians such as Vicuña McKenna just as the nation experienced its first significant wave of colonization since its independence. It is the arrival of new colonists from Europe that prompts a renewed interest in the idea of colonial Chile as more broadly European than previously imagined.

10. Studies of the Inquisition and inquiries into the origins of surnames in colonial Chile, begun by Vicuña McKenna and continued by José Toribio Medina, Tomás Thayer Ojeda, Luis Thayer Ojeda, Günther Böhm, and Günther Friedlander, have revealed the forgotten heroism of the crypto-Jews

and in general the Jewish presence during the colonial period. As Nes-El points out, the earliest Jews in Chile are variously described as "crypto-Jews," "Portuguese," "conversos," "New Christians," and "Marranos." "Portuguese" was a term often used to describe Spanish-speaking Jews who had fled to Portugal around the time of the 1492 expulsion, subsequently settling in Brazil and other parts of the Americas.

11. Böhm's study tells much of Maldonado, who was born of mixed parentage in Tucuman in 1592 and who saw his father condemned by the Inquisition as a Jew. After the father had confessed and was relieved of his property, Francisco left the area and went off to practice medicine in Concepción. His sister, living in Santiago, discovered her brother's adherence to Jewish beliefs and practices and denounced him to the Inquisition. The Inquisition seized his property and held him in prison for twelve years in an attempt to convert him, and he even tried to starve himself to death, but finally he was burned at the stake as a heretic.

12. Writers describing the Sephardic communities of Chile have noted the presence of small communities of crypto-Jews, for example, in the rural community of Cunco, near Temuco, whom Nes-El and Testa regard as possible descendants of early Jewish settlers. Twenty-nine of these congregations, known as the Iglesia Israelita del Nuevo Pacto, exist mainly in isolated villages of the south, "integradas por artesanos, obreros, campesinos y en general por gente muy honorable, de quehacer humilde . . . " (Nes-El Testa 12). Böhm suggests that there are less than a thousand members of the Iglesia Israelita throughout Chile, and he traces their origin to a Chilean admirer of U.S. Supreme Court Justice Louis Brandeis (Böhm 125).

13. Monastir was founded as Heraclea Lynquestis. The expulsion of Jews from Spain coincided with Turkish rule, which was far more favorable to Jews. Emigration from the area began with a big fire of Jewish houses and businesses in 1863 and increased when a railroad connected the town to Salonica. The Sephardim who came from communities such as Salonica and Monastir to Temuco were not especially prosperous. Like all residents in Chile they were very hard hit by the 1930s depression. Nes-El describes how they sought to dissuade friends and family back in Monastir from emigrating, sending circulars to be posted, stressing how hard life was here, that agricultural labor was difficult, and that employment possibilities were very limited. Emigration to Chile, the United States, and Israel from the Jewish communities of Salonica and Monastir continued during the Serbian annexation and World War I. Nazis deported the remaining members to the death camp at Treblinka in World War II.

14. Rapid acculturation of the early-twentieth-century immigrants that all three writers mention was rooted in part in the challenge of a country on the edge of industrial and commercial development which needed semiskilled labor. Uruguay and to a lesser extent Chile assumed modernization by way of liberal, laicizing politics, offering some protection and integration, social security systems, and a degree of vertical mobility thanks to free education. The formation of a middle class, characterized by the access to previously unavailable or prohibited goods, came about by novel forms of commerce. The system of buying in installments, which Jewish peddlers used in the outlying areas of the city and in the suburbs, allowed families to acquire household items that they previously had been unable to purchase. Also significant to immigrants and their children was progressive legislation protecting workers and retired people. While freedom of religion and access to education made it possible for immigrants to integrate into the national life, the threat of authoritarian interventions in politics brought restrictions on immigration in the 1930s, which interrupted the tendency to accept and integrate minorities into the society as a whole.

15. Porzecanski remarks that in Uruguay the center to right wing, seeing themselves as the upholders of tradition and custom, has generally opposed immigration, while the left has been more open to it. The situation in Chile was complicated in the 1930s by the rise and fall of the Popular Front.

16. "Becoming a nomad again, a man could think of himself as imitating history, since history, in his eyes, was itself a nomad" (Brodsky, "Profile of Clio" 124).

17. "El hecho natural de ser el país en que vivieron nuestros padres fué sustituído, una vez más, por la busca del País en que pudiéramos vivir nosotros mismos en paz y al cual pudiéramos adaptarnos, y más allá, en el sentido de la diferencia formulado por Federico Nietzsche, la busca del 'país de los hijos,' país en que nuestros hijos pudieron vivir en seguridad y naturalidad, que para nosotros habían sido suspendidas y rotas de modo tan horrendo" (Lachmann 40).

18. By the criteria appearing in William Safran, "Diasporas in Modern Societies," the communities of Jews in Uruguay and in Chile are not entirely diasporic:

> 1) They or their ancestors have been dispersed from a specific original "center" to two or more "peripheral," or foreign, regions;
> 2) they retain a collective memory, vision, or myth about their original homeland—its physical location, history, and achievements;
> 3) they believe that they are not—and perhaps cannot be—fully accepted by their host society and therefore feel partly alienated and insulated from it;

4) they regard their ancestral homeland as their true, ideal home and as the place they or their descendants would (or should) eventually return—when conditions are appropriate; 5) they believe that they should, collectively, be committed to the maintenance or restoration of their original homeland in one way or another, and their ethnocommunal consciousness and solidarity are importantly defined by the existence of such a relationship (83–84).

19. Haim Avni, a founding scholar of Latin American Jewish studies, has specifically called for more comparative work, for side-by-side analysis, and for attention to the less-frequently studied, although important, Jewish communities (6, 10, 13).

20. A generational counterpart to Guralnik is the Uruguayan writer Julia Galemire (see Lockhart) who likewise turned to writing after retirement, was involved in workshops during the dictatorship, and has published three very well received books. Galemire's publications begin after her retirement from the nursing profession. Both women published their first books during the closing years of their country's military dictatorships, and each continues to publish, employing a polished and exact language for their carefully crafted texts.

REFERENCES

Agosín, Marjorie. *Always from Somewhere Else/Siempre de otro lugar*. Trans. Celeste Kostopulos-Cooperman. New York: Feminist Press, 1998.

———. *A Cross and a Star: Memoirs of a Jewish Girl in Chile/Sagrada Memoria*. Trans. Celeste Kostopulos-Cooperman. Albuquerque: University of New Mexico Press, 1995.

———. *Happiness/Felicidad*. Trans. Elizabeth Horan. Fredonia, NY: White Pine Press, 1993.

Avni, Haim. "Postwar Latin American Jewry: An Agenda for the Study of the Last Five Decades." *The Jewish Diaspora in Latin America: New Studies on History and Literature*. Ed. David Sheinin and Lois Baer Barr. New York: Garland, 1996.

Böhm, Günter. *Historia de los judíos en Chile*. Santiago: Andrés Bello, 1984.

Brodsky, Joseph. "The Condition We Call Exile." *On Grief and Reason: Essays*. By Brodsky. New York: Farrar, Straus and Giroux, 1995.

———. "Profile of Clio." *On Grief and Reason: Essays*. By Brodsky. New York: Farrar, Straus and Giroux, 1995.

Bronstein, Abel M. Prólogo. *Historias de vida de inmigrantes judíos al Uruguay*. By Teresa Porzecanski. Montevideo: Kehila—Comunidad Israelita del Uruguay, 1986.

Elizabeth Rosa Horan   159

Clifford, James. "Diasporas." *Cultural Anthopology* 9.3 (1994): 302–38.

Cohen, Jacob X. *Jewish Life in South America*. A survey study for the American Jewish Congress. Foreword Stephen A. Wise. New York: Bloch, 1941.

Costa, Elena de. "Workshops." *Encyclopedia of Latin American Literature*. Ed. Verity Smith. London: Fitzroy Dearborn, 1997.

Guralnik, Sonia. *El samovar*. Santiago: Ergo Sum, 1984.

———. *Recuento de la mujer gusano*. Santiago: Sudamericana, 1991.

———. *Relatos en sepia*. Santiago: Ergo Sum, 1987.

Kleiner, Alberto, comp. *Informe* presentado en Argentina por la Sociedad de Socorro a los judíos de habla alemana respeto a la inmigración de judíos alemanes a la República de Chile, 1943. Buenos Aires: Instituto Hebreo de Ciencias, 1985.

Lachmann, Federico R. "La nueva inmigración judía y sus problemas en la América Latina." Kleiner 37–49.

Lockhart, Darrell B. Introduction. *Jewish Writers of Latin America: A Dictionary*. Ed. Darrell B. Lockhart. New York: Garland, 1997.

Nes-El, Moshé (Arueste). *Historia de la comunidad israelita sefaradí de Chile*. Prólogo Enrique Testa A. Santiago: Nascimiento, 1984.

Porzecanski, Teresa. *Ciudad impune*. Montevideo: Monte Sexto, 1986.

———. *Historias de vida de inmigrantes judíos al Uruguay*. Montevideo: Kehila— Comunidad Israelita del Uruguay, 1986.

———. *La invención de los soles*. Stockholm: Nordan, 1979.

———. *Mesías en Montevideo*. Montevideo: Signos, 1989.

Safran, William. "Diasporas in Modern Societies: Myths of Homeland and Return." *Diaspora* l.l (1991): 83–99.

Steiner, Carlos. *Informe*, comp. by Alberto Kleiner 5–35.

Trigo, Abril. "Uruguay." *Encyclopedia of Latin American Literature*. Ed. Verity Smith. London: Fitzroy Dearborn, 1997.

venezuelan jewish women writers and the search for heritage

Joan Esther Friedman

The Venezuelan women writers considered in this chapter are descendants of wandering Jews who arrived in Venezuela from Turkey,
Greece, Rhodes, and Morocco and other places in North Africa and
who were in turn descendants of those who had left the Iberian Peninsula in 1492. For the Sephardic Jews, Ladino, or Judeo-Spanish, facilitated adaptation to the new environment. But for the Ashkenazi
Jews, who arrived from the shtetls that once populated Central
Europe, where they were prohibited from attending school, *el dulce
iddish*, which they brought and passed on to their children, made survival harder. Thus language both facilitated and hindered the making of a new identity.

Jews came to Venezuela before and during the two world wars, the
Spanish Civil War and after, and on the heels of the Cuban Revolution and the dictatorships in Chile and Argentina. The writers I discuss here are immigrants and children of immigrants. Their ancestral

history is their inspiration. However, often these authors belong more to a past they are connected to than to the majority culture that surrounds them. This is the internal struggle. Through their works each of these authors reaches a unique balance between past and present, Spanish and Yiddish, pain and pleasure. Yet all of their individual struggles have similar elements as well. They must ultimately confront *the* question: ¿Qué es ser judío? What does it mean to be a Jew in Venezuela?

The playwrights Elisa Lerner and Blanca Strepponi, the novelist Alicia Freilich de Segal, the short story writer Lidia Rebrij, and the poets Jacqueline Goldberg, Sonia Chocrón, and Martha Kornblith all expose their Jewish souls in crisis. They bring the Jewish Diaspora into the mainstream of contemporary Venezuelan and Latin American literary culture.

The harsh dictatorial rule of the 1930s, 1940s, and 1950s controlled every aspect of Venezuelan life and accounts for the dearth of literary production. The fall of the dictatorship of Marcos Pérez Jiménez in 1959 brought about a booming political activism, reflected in a free press and the rebirth of literary creativity. With the integration of women into all levels of work and study, liberated women began to write.

The 1960s bring to light works by women such as Alicia Freilich de Segal and Elisa Lerner who write as a way to understand their past and establish a place in the present for themselves: an identity. These works are very Jewish in style and most of the time in content as well. These women translate or express themselves through a *periodismo de opinión* (a more subjective form of journalism) and *crónicas,* ways in which Jews traditionally maintained ties with each other and shared news. As Elisa Lerner reminds us:

> . . . ¿Cómo se comunicaban nuestros antecesores, los que
> yo vi? . . . leyendo el periódico iddish . . . de una forma

ilusoria e hipotética pienso que me van a volver a leer mis padres, o porque me van a leer otros padres, o los hijos de esos padres. Porque el judío ha sido un lector de periódicos . . . yo sé que puedo escribir crónicas, porque eso está dentro de una costumbre muy casera nuestra. Es una literatura casera, es algo que me pertenece.

[How did our ancestors communicate, the ones I saw? . . . reading the Yiddish newspaper . . . in an illusory and hypothetical way I think my parents will read me, or other parents, or the children of their parents. The Jew has been a reader of newspapers . . . I know I can write chronicles, because this is something familiar. It's familiar, it's something that belongs to me.] (*Yo amo a Columbo* 82)

As Jews and Venezuelans, these writers inhabit a place in between. They live neither as fully Jewish nor as fully Venezuelan. Identity is a search beyond the present, through the alleyways of the past. The pasts of these women are not what came before them; rather, their pasts define who they are in the present. They must redeem their pasts to find themselves. This is what their Jewish *herencia*—their centuries-old inheritance—is. It is what Marianne Hirsch terms "postmemory":

. . . a powerful form of memory precisely because its connection to its object or source is mediated not through recollection but through an imaginative investment and creation. . . . [It is] the experience of those who grow up dominated by narratives that preceded their birth whose own belated stories are evacuated by the stories of the previous generation, shaped by traumatic events that can be neither fully understood nor recreated. ("Past Lives" 684)

Freilich de Segal, Kornblith, Chocrón, Goldberg, Lerner, and Strepponi have an urgent need to create history anew for themselves, one that is based on a memory. This is a history that they have never experienced firsthand. From a memory they create their reality in the present. Implicit in their texts as well as articulated in their conversations with me is the theme of their Jewish "herencia," as Lerner calls it. This herencia hinders them from creating an identity as women and as Jews in a Catholic and *machista* society. They all share the weight of the past as a postmemory, a vivid present.

As a Latin American Jew born in China of German and Russian parents who found a haven in that very same Venezuela, I identify very closely with the words of these authors. In them, I hear my own herencia. These authors empower me with special and deep insights into their worlds. To preserve the beauty and integrity of these works, I have included many passages from the original sources, hoping to whet the reader's desire for more while begging indulgence for their unworthy re-creation in my translations. The Venezuelan Jewish writers you are about to meet do not have *one* country, *one* place, *one* loyalty. They have only their words to express their ineffable singularity.

blanca strepponi

In Blanca Strepponi's unpublished one-act play, "Silencio en la pecera" (Silence in the Fishbowl), dramatizing the unbreakable and ancient bonds that weave together the members of an assimilated Viennese Jewish family, she pays homage to Marie Langer (1910–87), one of the most remarkable women of our times. Langer studied with Freud, was a Communist party member, joined the International Brigades against Franco, and when forced to leave Spain, emigrated to Argentina. In Buenos Aires, Langer founded the Argentinian Psychoanalytical Association, which had great influence on the direction of psychoanalysis by stressing the need to combine the insights of analysis with those of Marxism and feminism. Continuing her lifelong fight for human rights, she was once again exiled, because for the Argentinian generals "subversión y derechos humanos, es lo mismo, para ellos es lo mismo" (there is no difference between subversion and human rights, to them, it is all the same). Marie Langer ended up in Managua, Nicaragua, where, already in her late seventies, she was a group organizer in the Sandinista movement.

The one-act play in two *cuadros* opens onto a darkened space as three characters address the audience. Isaac and Raquel (Marie's parents) answer the Maestra's question:

> Maestra: "¿Tú? ¿Qué eres? No seas tonta, ¡responde! ¿Tú qué eres?"
> Isaac: "María, hija, te preguntaron si eres judía o católica? . . . Eres judía."
> Raquel: "Hija, nunca me atreví a bautizarte, pero elegí para tí el nombre más católico: Marie."
>
> [M: "You? What are you? Don't be silly. Answer! What are you?"
> I: "María, my child, they asked if you were Jewish or Catholic . . . you're Jewish."
> R: "My child, I never dared baptize you, but I chose the most Catholic of names for you: Marie."]

Immediately after, the rest of the stage is lit by a very large and overly decorated Christmas tree that will be the backdrop for the entire play. There is also a life-size Nativity scene.

The events of Marie Langer's life emerge with the "lighting" of the gigantic Christmas tree, which darkens when we are returned to the present of the action. Marie's aristocratic young cousin Leo, impeccably dressed in riding gear, finds his cousin with a *refugiada* from Russia who is touching the Nativity scene:

> Leo: "Ven aquí Marie. ¿Cómo te atreves? Una judía no toca mi pesebre."
> Marie: "Papá me dijo que yo soy judía."
> Leo: "Tu papá ¡bah! ¡Que diga lo que quiera! En todo caso yo no soy judío . . . "
> Marie: "¿Qué es ser judío?"

> [L: "Come here Marie. How dare you! A Jewess, touching my Nativity scene?"
> M: "But, Papa told me I was Jewish."
> L: "Your father? Forget it! Who cares what he says? Anyway, I'm not Jewish!"
> M: "What's Jewish?"]

This question is returned to her in the last scene of the first cuadro, at which time the Christmas tree is covered by an enormous yellow Star of David. Cousin Leo aproaches slowly, touches the star, and arrogantly yells: "¡Salgan de mi casa! ¡Fuera de aquí!"

> Oficial: "Ya no tienes casa, ¿ves? (Blandiendo la llave) Los judíos no tienen casa."

> [Leo: "Get out of my house! Out!"
> O: "You got no home, see? [showing the key] Jews don't have homes."]

In Cuadro II Leo appears emaciated. Liberated from a camp and in his riding gear, now gray and much too big on him, Leo returns to the eternal question, the one Marie put to him at the beginning of the play:

Leo: "Los americanos vomitaban cuando entraron al campo. . . . Dios me tomó por el cuello y me hizo pedazos. . . . ¡Marie! ¡Marie! ¿Qué es ser judío?"

[L: "The Americans vomited as they entered the camps. . . . G took me by the neck and tore me up in little pieces. . . . Marie! Marie! What's Jewish?"]

To be a Jew in a Catholic country is the struggle of Blanca Strepponi's characters. Leo, who has been baptized in order to escape his herencia, is nevertheless sent to a camp with all the other Jews. In a tight theatrical space, Strepponi asks the audience: How do I escape a past I did not choose? A life that is not mine? Is a Jew one who simply practices rituals, or does being Jewish signify that one is condemned to an herencia? Is assimilation salvation?

Strepponi is not only a child of immigrants, she is an immigrant herself. Her memory is not only one imagined or created through her words, a postmemory, she herself is a wandering Jew. Her works reflect her personal search for an elusive identity, as in this passage from *Poemas visibles:*

> . . . *a los 24 años emigré*
> . . . *que curioso itinerario familiar*
> *siempre vinculado al Avatar*
> *Histórico*
> *Lituania, Reggio Calabria, Buenos Aires*
> *soy muy típicamente Argentina*
> *es decir, judeo-italiana*
> *y como amo el desatino*
> *soy también venezolana.*
>
> [. . . *at the age of 24 I emigrated*
> . . . *what a curious family itinerary*
> *always tied to historic*

reincarnations
Lithuania, Reggio Calabria, Buenos Aires
I'm typically Argentinian
by that I mean, Jewish-Italian
and as I love irrationality,
I'm also Venezuelan.] (12)

Born in Buenos Aires, Strepponi considers herself a Venezuelan writer because her artistic consciousness and her entire artistic production have taken place here. She has published poetry, plays, short stories, newspaper and magazine articles, and two film scripts. She has been invited to speak about her work at the Universidad de Buenos Aires and at the Instituto Caro y Cuervo in Bogotá as part of the Congreso de poesía escrita en lengua española desde la perspectiva del siglo XXI, and in 1996 represented Venezuela at the International Book Fair in Germany. She is a founding member of the publishing house Pequeña Venecia and currently is director of publicity for Fundarte.

elisa lerner

The search for identity in Elisa Lerner's work, whether inherited or created, forces her into constant "translation" and into a very particular view of reality. Starting from a "soy lo que no soy"—I am what I am not—she gives an interesting twist to the concept of Other. Her words could have been articulated by any of the writers discussed in this chapter:

> Definirse a partir de lo que no se es, de observarse en la mirada acusadora de los otros implica relacionarse con el mundo como un ser ajeno, como un extranjero.
>
> [To define yourself based on what you're not, to see oneself in the threatening stares of others, implies relating

to the world as "other," as foreign.] (*Crónicas ginecológicas* 192)

A lawyer by training, Lerner had her first theatrical piece, "Una entrevista de prensa o la bella de inteligencia" (A Press Interview, or A Woman of Intelligence), performed in 1960, and in 1964 she received the Ateneo de Caracas Ana Julia Rojas prize for her poetic play "El vasto silencio de Manhattan"(The Vast Silence of Manhattan). Her "Vida con Mamá" (Life with Mother), a play in two acts, was first performed in 1975, received the Premio Anual 75 as best theatrical production of the year, and earned her the Juana Sujo award for outstanding Venezuelan playwright of 1975. All playwrights expose themselves to immediate criticism because the impact of their words on the audience is so direct. Few writers have had such a profound impact on Venezuela's literary and cultural scene as has Elisa Lerner. Her success is all the more impressive when we consider the machista values against which she pits her unhappy and unfulfilled women.

In Lerner's work, the *unmarried woman* and the *mother* are the key elements in Jewish life. Her women are unhappy because they can never be what they should, what is expected of them, married and mothers: "Para los judíos el no casarse es sobrellevar una culpa, estar en rebeldía . . . "(315). Rosie Davis, the forty-something character who wears a pink hat and who carries apple pies to her mother in "The Vast Silence of Manhattan," is a professionally accomplished and intelligent woman; nevertheless, she is a failure. She is not what she should be, and of course the fault is hers: "Sin duda algo marchaba mal en mí: toda soltería tiene que ser silenciosa, muda" (Obviously something was wrong with me: spinsterhood should be silent, mute) (313).

Rosie Davis has no control over her life and is helpless in the face of historical forces: "con la Depresión los hombres se marcharon del pueblo" (with the depression men left the village) (300). If there were men around, if she could marry, she would become Mother, controller of memory and dreams, of everything. Such a Mother is the one in "Life with Mother." In this play the daughter is forced to tell her mother stories, and if she does not or does not tell them the way her mother wants to hear them, she is punished. The punishment is that her mother withholds descriptions of *the* wedding gown. Only the Mother can evoke that memory:

> Madre: "¡Irresponsable! Mas nunca volveré a hablarte del blanco y nupcial traje que aparece en mis sueños."
> Hija: "No puedes hacer eso. El traje es mío. Me pertenece."
> Madre: "Irrespetaste el trato. No has contado lo convenido. Me desharé del sueño. Me desharé del traje."
> Hija: "Tú deber es cuidarlo. Es lo único que tengo."

> [M: "You irresponsible creature! I shall never again tell you about the white wedding dress that appears in my dreams."
> H: "You can't do that! The wedding gown is mine. It belongs to me."
> M: "You broke the deal. You did not tell the story we agreed on. I will get rid of my dream. I'll get rid of the gown."
> H: "But your duty is to take care of it. After all, it's all I've got."]

In fact, the Hija does not have even that. The Madre's duty is to care for and pass on the tradition—the two candelabras that she polishes constantly. In not sharing them with her daughter, she refuses to pass on that herencia to someone not prepared for it—as an unmarried and never-to-be-a-mother person, the Hija becomes doubly dispossessed of her herencia. As in Strepponi's play, it is memory that connects and binds.

In this play of very little action and a great deal of nostalgia, Lerner tells us that a Jew is someone who is not. Someone who is not married, not a wife, not a mother. Someone who will never be able to possess the candelabra.

Lerner says very clearly that it is her Jewish herencia that causes her to write:

> Tengo una urgencia casi periodística de decir las cosas, por una culpabilidad existencial. Es la herencia judía: sentir que vengo de inmigrantes, de gente que tuvo que sobrevivir. Me sentía culpable de una vocación literaria cuando era más solidario con mi origen, con mis padres, tener un oficio más pragmático. . . . En mi sentido del humor está manifiesta mi singularidad de judía dentro de la sociedad venezolana. . . . Mi humor está encadenado a una reflexión y a una narración . . . [a] un argumento de la literatura. . . . Pienso que me viene . . . de mi padre. . . . [E]n él había un testimonio conmovedor porque venía de una experiencia, había dejado atrás una tierra y se había abierto a la herida del océano hacia América. . . . [P]ienso que a mí me diferencia [de otros autores venezolanas] . . . un dolor, el dolor como fue un dolor muy cercano que me viene del dolor de mi padre. . . .

> [I have an almost journalistic urgency to say things, perhaps because of an existential guilt. It's my Jewish heritage: to always feel I came from immigrants, from people forced to survive. I used to feel guilty about my literary vocation when it would have been much more in keep-

ing with my origins, with my parents, to have a more prag-
matic profession. What sets me apart from others within
Venezuelan society is most obviously my sense of humor.
It is deeply connected to reflection and narrative . . . to a
discussion of literature. . . . I think I get it from my father.
. . . [H]is was a very moving narrative because it came out
of his experience. He left behind his home and laid himself open to the hurt of the Ocean leading him to America. . . . I think what separates me [from other Venezuelan
women writers] is a pain, a hurt that comes from very
close, from my father's pain.] (Freilich de Segal, *Legítima
defensa* 37)

alicia freilich de segal

In 1987 Alicia Freilich de Segal published her first work of fiction,
the beautifully evocative novel *Cláper* (Clapper). She had, like Lerner,
a prolific and successful career as a journalist and teacher. The very
week of *Cláper's* publication, the French Press International News
Service referred to her as the third most read author in Venezuela.

"Cláper," a term coined by the author and now part of the Venezuelan lexicon, refers to the man who peddles goods (clap, clap) from
door to door and on credit. Although he travels on foot bearing a
heavy load, he is firmly supported by an inner strength derived from
the legacy of Talmudic wisdom. The cláper, in turn, will hand down
this wisdom as part of that never-changing internal baggage that is
the Jewish culture.

The novel is a fictional account based on actual conversations held
in Yiddish between one such cláper, Freilich de Segal's own father,
Max, and herself. It is fictionalized autobiography, history, and ultimately another moving story of displacement in the long history of

the Jewish people. It is narrated by two voices chatting away in the timeless realm of the imagination. This structure authentically reproduces the never-ending dialogue that goes on between parent and child, between humans and God, and within humans themselves. Tight, unadorned, and simple, the style ranges from the romantic lyrics of Latin *boleros* to centuries-tested Yiddish parables that give the work a poetic and spiritual undertow. In both narratives readers hear, taste, and smell local life. Enchanted by the aroma of humble cabbage soup and the juiciness of ripe mangoes, our attention sways between the sinister and ever-present sound of Cossack boots and the hot sensuality of salsa and mambo rhythms; between the moving solemnity of a Shabbat dinner, where there is only water to share with the guest, and a bottomless cornucopia of luscious fruits with unpronounceable names, vegetables and flowers with which the sensuous and colorful Caribbean welcomes the immigrant in black suit and hat.

Max's narrative is steeped in sage Talmudic teachings, Yiddish bittersweet humor, and ancient superstition, full of the life-giving and life-nurturing strength that survived for centuries in the thousands of shtetls that once populated Eastern Europe. It is the idiom of people who hungered for food and desperately needed the most basic human comforts, but who were never needy of spiritual connectedness, familial warmth, or faith in a God who, to paraphrase Martin Buber, was not to be talked *about* but to be talked *to* and *with*. Max the cláper always speaks to his particular god (with a g, never G). His narrative is the history of the persecution of the Jew, starting from the Middle Ages and generously sprinkled with moving and humorous tales of the Ashkenazic and Sephardic voyages, up to his arrival in America. Alicia, this cláper's Venezuelan-born, university-educated, strong and independent-minded daughter, writes in a sophisticated and literate Spanish. Her voice is cosmopolitan, elegant, and redolent of the feminist psychoanalytic, Marxist, Zionist, intellectual, and political jargon of her milieu. In her narrative one sees the important changes that Jewish immigration brought about, including a new awareness of the outside world. It is a rich source of cultural and political history of Venezuela from the 1940s to the 1970s. Freilich de Segal is a woman struggling to find her place, a woman who loves and respects the traditions of her upbringing, even as she struggles to break away from them.

In her second work of fiction, *Colombina descubierta* (Colombina Discovered), she takes up again the theme of our immutable bonds to the past. The novel earned her the prestigious Fernando Jeno International Literary Prize in Mexico, where it was selected unanimously from among texts published in Spanish, Yiddish, and Hebrew in 1990–91. The selecting jury stated:

> [Alicia Freilich de Segal] reaches the reader, his very fiber, with an innate linguistic clarity, an accurate intuition and an imaginary power capable of suggesting the most unconventional settings and situations, in which as if by magic, clues, enigmas and mysteries are intertwined much as they were in Columbus himself.
>
> *Colombina descubierta* leaves an indelible and very unique imprint on the world of creative Jewish Literature of our time. (*Nuevo Mundo Israelita*, Nov. 1992)

Freilich de Segal weaves a labyrinthine tale of Columbus, the expulsion of the Jews from Spain, the terror of the Inquisition, the encounter with the New World, and the complex issue of *marranismo* from a feminist perspective. She creates a vast physical and emotional tapestry that intertwines past, present, and future.

The narration takes place simultaneously in the fifteenth and twentieth centuries, and the reader is witness to and participant in this meandering compelling story. Here Freilich de Segal searches in prose for what Goldberg, Kornblith, and Chocrón search for in verse: an individual and collective Jewish identity accompanied by the inevitable and weary search for a primary space. In *Colombina descubierta*, Freilich de Segal explores this theme by means of an elaborately introspective literary process, one that digs deep into our conscious and subconscious memory and demands a confrontation with what is found. One is forced to confront truth and conjecture, tradition and adventure, to both cover and discover. The fast-moving text requires a reader willing to be engaged in uncovering the most incredible of all cover-ups: whether Columbus's journeys were wanderings, adventures, or flights. A Columbus who is now Colombina: a woman.

The novel is divided into four chapters or monologues, as the author calls them: (1) En el nombre del Padre (In the Name of the Father); (2) Y del Hijo (And the Son); (3) Y del Espírito Santo (And the Holy Ghost); (4) Santísima Trinidad (Holy Trinity) and Amén, a prologue. It narrates two very intriguing and long journeys to the unknown, two that perhaps always were the same. One is that of a persecuted Jewish Columbus looking for safe lands for himself and his people; the other is that undertaken five hundred years later (or is it?) by Biná Colom, who, like the cláper's daughter, struggles to find her *casa* in the world, and, like Columbus, is the subject of many myths. In the course of these monologues, Biná Colom splits into several personalities—Cristina, Paloma/Colomba, and Colombina.

As the novel unfolds, Colombina is a sad old woman talking to the moon on a beach in Barcelona, Spain. The time is October 12, 1992. It is the eve of lavish festivities celebrating the 500th anniversary of the Encounter. The moon and the lyrical prose mesmerize the reader into forgetting that the novel was published in 1991, long before the narrated events take place.

As the novel ends, the relationship between Columbus the subject and the Spanish queen, his ruler, takes on a charming and ironic twist as Freilich de Segal changes it into the quintessentially modern relationship of patient and therapist. Here Doctora Isabel del Castillo is an ambitious and ruthless professional, indifferent to the "real" needs of her patient. Colombina as Paloma peacefully accepts the many roles life has forced on her, including that of "navigator." Her narrative is as simple and direct as navigational charts, one might even say, a diary. Colombina is a child of the world of being and seeming to be. She is a vital Jewish character pushing to reach "los límites de lo imposible" (the limits of the impossible). She is one and many, and so epitomizes the issue of multiple Jewish identities that we see in the writings of Jacqueline Goldberg, Sonia Chocrón, and Martha Kornblith.

lidia rebrij

Lidia Rebrij, whose work has appeared in several anthologies of Venezuelan short stories, was born in Argentina but like Strepponi has realized all her artistic work in Venezuela and considers herself "de esta tierra." In addition to her short stories, she has published *La pintura americana: Venezuela, Chile y Colombia* (American Painting: Venezuela, Chile and Colombia; 1977), which is used as a textbook.

In answer to my question of what, if any, were the Jewish elements in her writing, she mentioned how surprised she was when the Venezuelan writer Humberto Mata said of her book *Con los besos de su boca* (With the Kisses of Her Mouth): "Es un libro muy judío" (It is a very Jewish book). In my interview with her in summer 1996, she said she has asked herself over and over again what he meant by that, but she has no answer.

> Para entonces yo era demasiado joven y demasiado feliz como para comprender la dimensión exacta de aquella afirmación. Hoy sé que apuntaba a los elementos esenciales de la idiosincrasia judía que Mata supo reconocer mucho antes que yo misma, y que hoy compruebo como constantes en mis libros.

[In those days I was much too young and too happy to understand the exact weight of those words. Today I know that it referred to the essential elements of Jewish idiosyncrasy that Mata was able to recognize long before I could, and which today I can accept as constants in my books.]

Rebrij's main theme in all her short stories, five in *Con los besos de su boca* and eleven in *El dorado vino de tu piel* (The Golden Wine of Your Skin), is the "minucia diaria" (detailed diary) of the lives of lonely and alienated women, for whom she re-creates a poignant and pessimistic reality. In both collections we follow the solitary lives of unrealized women, married or not, who seem to be discarded and abandoned by the masculine historical events surrounding them. In *Con los besos de su boca* the story "Del brazo del papá" the character is "Nena," who was never allowed to grow up because her father took care of all the details of life for his fragile daughter. Another is "Eloisa," who is unhappy with the lack of love in her marriage but can only break away from it by getting sick. The texts are woven together by a thread of profound sadness: stories of hopeless women of "pueblitos pequeños" (small villages), stories of suspended lives.

In "El dorado vino de su piel," the story that gives its title to the collection, the narrator, like a movie camera, presents a story that seems to come out of a collective memory. Quick visual images show us Greta, to whom nothing happens until love comes along. Then she changes. The narrator is an adolescent boy in love with her who sees that she is able "abrir sus alas y batirlas contra el viento" (to open her wings and flap them against the wind). But love does not set her free. She must pay for her transgression, for her search for realization, and she falls. Her husband forces her to remain by killing her lover.

The story "Falsa piel" (False Skin) is a wonderful epistolary narration in which a young girl describes how she goes through the motions of a striptease to aggressively punish those who think they are enjoying the spectacle.

Rebrij creates precise and delicate short stories about the stifling and unendurable situation of women for whom life is an eternal open wound, women incapable of changing their lives and whose endings are always violent and sad: murder, sickness, alcoholism, promiscuity.

According to Rebrij, the Jewish elements in her works are that her characters have a very tragic sense of life mixed with a ready ability to laugh at themselves; that they have a tremendous will to live and survive no matter what tragedy befalls them; that in all of them there is a feeling of commitment to a destiny that has been foretold; that they all are conscious of our human fragility in the face of historical events; that she has a tendency to see the universal in terms of temporal and spatial discontinuities; that she feels tied to a "memoria activa de la diáspora judía" (an active memory of the Jewish Diaspora); and, most of all, that in her works there is a very strong sense of what she terms *desarraigo,* an interesting word that in English can mean either "uprooted" or "eradicated."

jacqueline goldberg

The poet Jacqueline Goldberg understands what it means to be bound to "la condena indecible / de su memoria" (the unpronounceable chain / of her memory) (*Luba* XXII), to be forced by that herencia to be part of "una raza de mujeres / que se destruyen" (a race of women/ who destroy themselves) (*A fuerza de ciudad* 220).

In the thirty delicate, dense, and exquisite poems that make up *Luba* she sketches a picture of her *raíz,* her root. Searching for the answer to who and what she is, she finds herself in her grandmother. Unlike Strepponi but like Lerner and Chocrón, Jacqueline Goldberg is not herself a wandering Jew. She was born and raised in Venezuela—

a *criolla*. Yet she must wander through her mind, listening to the narratives of her grandmother, and with her own words create a memory. She takes on the destiny that her heritage has prescribed for her, a heritage that stigmatized her and condemned her to feel the pain all over again:

> *Luba*
> *diálogo*
> *de pasillos diurnos*
> *Raíz*
> *Memoria que soy.*

> *[Luba*
> *conversations*
> *in daylong corridors*
> *root*
> *the memory I am.] (III)*

> *Cambia*
> *de sombra*
> *para obligarme*
> *a padeder*
> *una herencia . . .*
> *Con el cuerpo a cuestas*
> *intentando siempre*
> *un segundo desvelo*
> *Una estancia*
> *en otro lado.*

> *[She changes*
> *like shadows*
> *to force me*
> *to suffer*
> *an inheritance . . .*

Carrying her body
always searching for
a second unveiling
A room
in another place.] (VII)

Tomo
su herencia
de edades en quiebra
los oficios tristes
del abandono
Sus muertos. . . .

[I take on
her inheritance
of crumbling ages
the sad tasks
of abandonment
her dead ones. . . .] (II)

Duelen
estas ganas de luto
De amanecer recogiendo
plumas
en patios ajenos
Ganas de ser ella.

[There is hurt
in this desire for mourning
for waking up
nesting
in someone else's yard
Desire to be her.] (XX)

Goldberg takes on the same face, the same wound, as that of the character she has created. She takes on her grandmother's past. Finally and inevitably the poet becomes her grandmother. Her "post-memory" forces her to become Luba, to relive Luba's nightmares and through her rescue all the Lubas that suffered the "viajes incompletos," the incomplete journeys, of our Jewish history:

> Soy oficiante
> de sus incendios
> Sábado merodeador
> que no se asusta
> ni grita.
>
> [I am the keeper
> of her fires
> Saturday's plunderer
> who does not fear
> or scream.] (I)

The poet travels and returns to her grandmother's past:

> Viajo en sombra
> Recorro
> los techos de sus pesadillas
> mi palabra
> no logra detenerse
> ando de cicatriz
> en cicatriz
> buscando algo
> que nos duela.
>
> [I travel in shadow
> wander over
> the roofs of her nightmares
> my word
> cannot stop
> I go from wound
> to wound

searching for
a pain of my own.] (XXIII)

Goldberg uses "my word" to speak of the ancient pain at the same time that through those words she claims ownership over her life:

> *Más ebria*
> *y más sola*
> *sufriendo*
> *viajes incompletos*
> *distancias*
> *que no resisten*
> *otra calle*
> *su puño agotado*
> *su país ardiendo.*

> *[More drunk*
> *and more alone*
> *suffering through*
> *unfinished journeys*
> *distances*
> *that cannot endure*
> *another road*
> *her fist exhausted*
> *her country in flames.] (I)*

The reader of Goldberg's poems is left with a deep desire to know more, to go on reading, to know things perhaps not said, to clear up shadows and questions, to go farther into the dark and intentional, volatile and allusive, references that the poet offers us and that seem to evaporate in our hands.

Luba, a petite and very intimate poem, requires a sensitive and intelligent reader, one able to appreciate its genesis, testimony, love, pain, and rebirth. With and through it Goldberg honors and connects herself to her *herencia*.

The sadness that pervades the poems that constitute *Luba* is a sadness of not having a life, of having to live out and erase the past pain. The suffering of survival is Goldberg's way of paying homage, by remembering and recovering all the Lubas—all the Jewish women who were dispossessed of their infancy, adolescence, youth, and hope. Women who survived the Holocaust and who survive.

> *Luba*
> *asiste*
> *a cuanto soy*
> *Detiene*
> *sus raíces*
> *Sufre de nuevo.*
>
> *[Luba*
> *through me*
> *holds on to*
> *her roots*
> *she suffers anew.] (XXX)*

In an interview with the author in summer 1996, Goldberg said her "extraña condición ruso-polaca-francesa-judía-maracucha-caraqueña-latinoamericana" is what makes her write. And because as a Jew she is

> todo y nada. Por mirar desde un territorio múltiple y ajeno. Porque la identidad es un imaginario desde donde trazo conexiones con el paisaje, la lengua, con los otros que siento y presiento cercanos. Identidad que asumo, copio, creo y repito. Identidad a medias, a conveniencia quizás.

> [everything and nothing. Because I look from and through a multiple and "other" perspective. Because identity is an image from which I trace connection to the land, to the language, of those whom I feel and sense to be close. An

identity that I assume, copy, create, and repeat. A semi-identity, one of convenience, perhaps.]

Jacqueline Goldberg was born in Maracaibo, Venezuela. She is co-founder of the literary magazine *Babilonia*, editor of the publishing house Séptimo Sello, and director of publications for the Dirección de Cultura Luz. She says of herself:

> *Me hago a fuerza de extenderme*
> *por donde nadie pasa ya.*
>
> *[By unfolding myself*
> *I go to places where people no longer go.] (Luba XXI)*

She writes as a Jewish-Venezuelan woman because

> una mujer salió en 1933 de Druskininkai, a orillas del río Neman, en la Rusia Blanca . . . porque un hombre y una mujer abandonaron Kazymierz en Polonia . . . [porque] mi madre nació en Maracaibo, mi padre en Paris . . . yo, al final de este destinado árbol, nací en Maracaibo . . . aprendí a leer el complicado alfabeto de un hebreo que ya no entiendo, encendí velas los viernes, culminé el bachillerato en un colegio de monjas. . . . leí a Paul Celan y Octavio Paz.

> [in 1933 a woman left Druskininkai, on the shores of the River Neman, in White Russia . . . because a man and a woman fled Kazymierz in Poland . . . [because] my mother was born in Maracaibo [Venezuela], my father in Paris . . . and I, at the end of this fated tree, was born in Maracaibo . . . learned to read the complicated Hebrew alphabet which I no longer understand, lit candles on Fridays, grad-

uated from a parochial high school . . . read Paul Celan
and Octavio Paz.] (11)

Goldberg has published eight books of poetry. The poems are short,
ranging from fifty to seventy words, deeply emotional and darkly ex-
pressive.

martha kornblith

Martha Kornblith in her poetry collection *Oraciones para un dios
ausente* (Prayers for an Absent God) echoes Lerner's words about "el
dolor de mi padre" and Goldberg's "sufro de nuevo" when she writes:

> No hay nada que me duela más
> que el dolor de mis padres
> por sus padres muertos. . . .
>
> [Nothing hurts me more
> than my parent's pain
> for their dead parents. . . .](14)
>
> Me acordaré que me contaba
> cuentos sobre su mamá que a mí me aburrían . . .
>
> [I shall always remember her telling me
> stories about her mother that bored me so much. . . .] (16)
>
> Yo estaré alerta de rescatar . . .
>
> [I will be in charge of rescuing . . .] (16)

She tries to rescue herself by searching through the dark alleys of
her memory: "Vagar como un fantasma ausente / en la conciencia de
miles sin cuerpo ni cara" (Wandering like an absent ghost / in the
conscience of faceless and bodyless thousands)(23). She is constantly

searching for her past, when "vimos por última vez a esos parientes. / Sé que es a ellos a quienes busco" (we last saw those relatives / I know it is them I search for)(24).

At the same time that Kornblith tries to uncover those memories, she knows they need to be annulled, annihilated, decapitated:

> A veces
> es preciso
> volver a los recuerdos
> para anular la memoria,
> aniquilar vestigios,
> otras vidas,
> saludar viejos lazos,
> decapitar antiguos papeles.
>
> [At times
> it's necessary
> to return to those memories
> in order to quiet memory
> to erase every trace
> other lives,
> greet old ties
> behead old characters you once played.] (39)

The Peruvian-born Venezuelan poet Martha Kornblith exiled herself permanently from this world in which she had felt so abandoned. She took her own life in July 1997. The fragility and loneliness of her disturbing poems were a warning. She had long ago and many times announced her death while exposing her soul in words:

> Estoy harta de esta manía de suicidarme
> en cada verso. . . .
> no he perdido mi hilo central,
> esa forma triste de desganarme
> en cada línea.

[I am sick and tired of this mania of mine
to commit suicide in each verse. . . .
I have lost my central chord,
that sad way of using myself up
in each line.] (55)

For Kornblith, poetry was "nuestra única, frágil cuerda"—was the only, fragile connection, the umbilical cord that not only tied her to her parents and her herencia, but through which her survival was nourished. Only by becoming a poet could she survive:

> *Por eso me volví poeta*
> *porque pasa lento el tiempo en la soledad*
> *¿No es apenas un peligroso instante*
> *lo que sostiene nuestra cordura?*
> *¿No depende la locura*
> *de nuestra única, frágil cuerda?*
> *¿No pende ella de un sólo término?*
> *del preciso término*
> *aquel que nos salva*
> *o nos condena?*

> *[That's why I became a poet*
> *because time passes slowly in loneliness*
> *Isn't it in fact just a dangerous instant*
> *that sustains our sanity?*
> *Doesn't madness depend on*
> *our inimitable single, fragile chord?*
> *Doesn't it just hang on one word?*
> *On the only word*
> *that saves*
> *or condemns us?]* (58)

The moving confessional poems of *Oraciones para un dios ausente* are about mental sickness, love, suicide, orphanhood, abandonment;

they are about a death wish, about being lost in a "casa [que] se re-siste a sus habitantes—house that rejects its inhabitants: because when we die as Jews, "los espejos nos esperan ansiosos," mirrors await us anxiously. Her roots are different from those of others. She under-stands and recognizes that she comes from "una legión distinta de ganadores" (a legion distinguished by winners)(109) in a world where she is a loser, where all that remains is "la costumbre de la angus-tia"(27)—the habit of suffering—because "el perdedor se lo lleva todo" (loser takes all)(108).

Kornblith's image of viaje/journey, includes places, calles/streets, roads, países/countries, and rooms:

> *Una vez viví en esos países*
> *donde ahora habitan*
> *hombres que ya han muerto.*
> *Los veo como afirmación*
> *pero son sólo una metáfora,*
> *los quiero pero no me reconocen*
> *veo el cuarto*
> *pero esos cuartos*
> *ya tienen huésped.*
>
> [*Once I lived in those countries*
> *inhabited now by*
> *men who have already died.*
> *I see them as an affirmation*
> *but they're really only a metaphor,*
> *I see the room*
> *but those rooms*
> *already have other guests.*] (37)

The God of the title is someone who does not hear her prayers, someone who does not want to know that

que aún hay seres
que en las madrugadas
maúllan al unísono
llamando a sus madres.

[that there are still beings
who in the early hours
meow in unison
calling their mothers.] (69)

At Kornblith's burial, her friend the poet Rafael Arraiz Lucca said:

Sus poemas tienen el extrañísimo poder de la iluminación:
a medida que discurren van como arrojando luz hacia
adelante. . . . [V]an rescatando de las sombras la materia
del pasado. Evocan sin ser sólo evocativos; reconstruyen
sin abusar de la fuerza reconstituyente de la melancolía;
sorprenden sin proponerse encadilar al lector. . . .

[Her poems have the very strange power of illumination:
as they roam they shed light before them. . . . [I]n shadows they rescue the subjects of the past. They evoke without being just evocative; they reconstruct without abusing
the reconstructive power of melancholy; they surprise the
reader without blinding him. . . .]

Kornblith searched for an identity and found it in her poems:

. . . en estas calles
donde yo busco una nueva dosis de inspiración
para amparar a mis poemas de la muerte
y a mí de la muerte por los poemas.

[. . . along these streets
where I search for new doses of inspiration

> *to protect my poems from death*
> *and me from the death over my poems.] (51)*

How clearly Hirsch's postmemory applies to the work of this poet. Like Goldberg, Kornblith's words flow from narratives that precede her existence, and because she is so dominated by these traumatic narratives, she cannot conceive her stories.

sonia chocrón

The poet Sonia Chocrón is of Sephardic descent and admits that she always felt that she was not alien to the Hispanic reality because it was an integral part of her traditions and her ancestry. For her, her language is the most important part of her Jewish heritage. She takes great pride in the fact that *her* language is the one that was used to translate, *ladinar*, the Holy Scriptures into Spanish. In her only book of poetry, *Toledana*, we see her delight in handling language. It is a beautifully melodic work that celebrates the love between Alfonso VIII of Spain and a Jewess named Raquel. The music comes from the exquisitely woven synthesis of a spoken thirteenth-century Spanish, a literary seventeenth-century Spanish, and colorful contemporary Latin American metaphors.

Chocrón shares a common immigrant heritage with the criollas Goldberg, Freilich de Segal, and Lerner. The ancestral memories of this "hija pródiga de mi raza," prodigal daughter of my race, pull her into an infinite number of women displaced through an infinite number of times:

> *Soy Raquel la toledana*
> *y cada mujer en mí es*
> *pues yo soy una soy cinco soy diez*
> *Soy Eva desterrada*
> *y soy Rut la moabita*

y soy la reina de Saba
y Esther y la noche y Heloisa
Al fin que soy quien esto escribe
tierra de siembra vigorosa
y leve.

[I am Rachel from Toledo
and each woman is in me
because I am one I am five I am ten
I am Eve the exile
and I am Ruth the Moabite
and I am the Queen of Sheba
and Esther and the night and Eloise.
In the end
I am the one who writes this
Land of vigorous and subtle seed.] (17)

Chocrón admits to "un sentimiento místico arraigado" in the poemario. In fact she says that returning to the Old Testament in Aramaic with its very unusual syntax, after several years of rejecting everything not only Jewish but religious, was the inspiraton for *Toledana*. In these poems and by recapturing that Judeo-Spanish identity she reencounters through family history and the diasporic inquiry her own identity in her writing: "soy quien esto escribe" (I am the one who writes this) (49).

By looking back on her rich cultural heritage, deeply into the pain of loss and the lack of belonging, Chocrón fears:

Temo que me suplanten
seguramente otra podría rubricar mi nombre
cien veces con sonoridad
y escribir como mi hablar diciendo
Esta soy yo
la bendicha al ser nacida

por Sará Rebeca y Lea
para ti . . .

[I am afraid of being replaced
surely another could sing my name
a hundred times with great sonority
and write the way I speak saying
This is I
the blessed one to have been born
of Sarah, Rebecca and Leah
for you. . . .] (43)

The evocative language of the poem is the glue that binds Chocrón
to the Iberian Peninsula, to Morocco where her father was born, and
ultimately to her present in Venezuela.

Alicia Freilich de Segal and Lidia Rebrij in their prose, Sonia Chocrón,
Martha Kornblith, and Jacqueline Goldberg in their poetry, Blanca
Strepponi and Elisa Lerner in their plays struggle to grasp the complex issues of historical origins. They speak of the conflict between
old roots and the culture one belongs to by birth, language, and choice.
They write about what it means, and has always meant, to be the
exile, the uprooted, the dispossessed, the one struggling to come to
terms with an identity that is many-cultured as well as assimilated
into the dominant culture. Theirs are familiar names to the Venezuelan reading public, only a small percentage of which is Jewish. They
have all been accepted and celebrated as writers who happen to be
women and who happen to be Jewish.

The writers presented in this chapter pose the questions What
does it mean to be a Jew in Venezuela at the dawn of the twenty-first
century? Is our Jewish herencia some form of genetic information we
are programmed with so that we are always as Jacqueline Goldberg
says "al borde de lo presentido"—at the edge of what is felt (Luba XII)?
The answer to the second question is yes. The answer to the first

is to be found in the past and their reconnection to it. Their mournful journeys rescue the past not through recollection but through an imaginative investment and creation—their writings. As their own stories are overshadowed by those of powerful events that preceded their births, they rescue and are rescued as they mourn, remember, and create.

The Brazilian-Jewish author Clarice Lispector says: "I don't want beauty, I want an identity." For an immigrant, and a Jew, the desire to belong is somewhat contradictory. There is not one but many places one belongs to. Identity is a vague term and a vaguer reality. Our identity is us, but it also follows and accompanies us. It is both the pleasure and the fear of walking along an unknown road. It is the inexplicable nostalgia for boiled potatoes with onions and sour cream. It is the intoxicating sensation of drinking strong coffee in an elegant Berlin room full of books and a Bechstein piano. It is being profoundly moved by the lyrics of a song from the Middle Ages sung in Ladino. It is the word "NONE" in Chinese next to the line requesting "Nationality."

REFERENCES
PRIMARY SOURCES

Sonia Chocrón (1961-)
Toledana. Collection of poetry. Caracas: Monte Avila, 1991.

Martha Kornblith (1959–97)
Oraciones para un dios ausente. Caracas: Monte Avila, 1985.
El perdedor se lo lleva todo. Caracas: Fondo Editorial, 1997.

Elisa Lerner (1932-)
Carriel número cinco (un homenaje al costumbrismo).
    Crónicas. Caracas: El Libro Menor, 1983.
Crónicas ginecológicas. Caracas: Unea, 1984.
Una entrevista de prensa o la bella de inteligencia. Monólogo. Caracas: Monte
    Avila, 1959.

La envidia. Teatro. Caracas: Monte Avila, 1975.

Jean Harlow. Monólogo. Caracas: Monte Avila, 1962.

La mujer del periódico de la tarde. Monólogo. Caracas: Monte Avila, 1976.

El paí odontológico. Monólogo. Caracas: Monte Avila, 1966.

Una sonrisa detrás de la metáfora. Crónicas. Caracas: Monte Avila, 1968.

El vasto silencio de Manhattan. Teatro. Caracas: Monte Avila, 1971.

Vida con Mamá. Teatro. Madrid: Centro de Documentatión
      Teatral, 1976.

El último tranvía. Monólogo. Caracas: Monte Avila, 1984.

Yo amo a Colombo o la pasión dispersa. Crónicas. Caracas: Monte Avila, 1979.

Blanca Strepponi (1952–)

Adela tiene el pelo rojo y cree en los espíritus. Narrativa. Caracas: Centro de
      Estudios Romula Gallego, 1982.

"Bírmanos." Teatro. Caracas: Fondo Editorial, 1991.

Diario de John Roberton. Poesía. Caracas: Fondo Editorial, 1990.

El jardín del verdugo. Poesía. Caracas: Fondo Editorial, 1992.

Poemas visibles. Poesía. Caracas: Fondo Editorial, 1988.

Las vacas. Poesía. Caracas: Casa de la Cultura, 1995.

Lidia Rebrij (1948–)

Con estos mis labios que te nombran. Caracas: Fundarte, 1993.

Con los besos de su boca. Caracas: Editorial Planeta, 1990.

Cuerpo de Venus, Corazón de Rockola y otras historias más. Caracas: Secretaria de
      la Cultura, 1984.

El dorado vino de tu piel. Caracas: Fundarte, 1990.

Fastos y oropeles de la carne. Monólogos teatrales. Caracas: Fundarte, 1992.

La nostalgia vestia chaqueta militar. Caracas: Editorial Planeta, 1985.

Jacqueline Goldberg (1966–)

POEMARIOS

De un mismo centro. Caracas: Monte Avila, 1986.

En todos los lugares, bajo todos los signos. Caracas: Monte Avila, 1987.

A fuerza de ciudad. Caracas: Tierra de Gracia, 1989.

Insolaciones en Miami Beach. Caracas: Fundarte, 1995.

Luba. Caracas: Editorial Séptimo Cielo, 1988.

Mascaras de familia. Caracas: Fundarte, 1992.

Mi bella novia voladora. Poemario infantil. Caracas: Monte Avila, 1994.

Una señora con sombrero. Poemario infantil. Caracas: Monte Avila, 1993.

Trastienda. 1991.

Treinta soles desaparecidos. Caracas: Secretaria de la Cultura, 1985.

Alicia Freilich de Segal (1939-)

NONFICTION

Cuarta dimensión. Caracas: Biblioteca Nacional, 1975.

Entrevistados en carne y hueso. Caracas: Librería Suma, 1977.

Legítima defensa: Comentarios y polémicas. Caracas: Seleven, 1984.

Triálogo. Caracas: Editorial Tiempo Nuevo, 1973.

La Vendemocracia. Caracas: Monte Avila, 1978, 1981.

FICTION

Cláper. Caracas: Editorial Planeta, 1987.

Colombina descubierta. Caracas: Planeta Venezolana, 1991.

SECONDARY SOURCES

Baskin, Judith R., ed. *Women of the Word: Jewish Women and Jewish Writing.* Detroit: Wayne State University Press, 1994.

Canetti, Elias. *The Conscience of Words.* Trans. J. Neugroschel. New York: Seabury Press, 1979.

Glickman, Nora, and Robert DiAntonio, eds. *Tradition and Innovation: Reflections on Latin American Jewish Writing.* Albany: State University of New York Press, 1993.

Dimo, Edith, and Amarilis Hidalgo de Jesus, eds. *Escritura y desafío: Narradoras venezolanas del siglo XX.* Caracas: Monte Avila, 1996.

Hirsch, Marianne. *The Mother-Daughter Plot: Narrative, Psychoanalysis, Feminism.* Bloomington: Indiana University Press, 1989.

————. "Past Lives: Postmemories in Exile." *Poetics Today* 17.4 (Winter 1996): 659–85.

Hoffman, Eva. *Lost in Translation: A Life in a New Language.* New York: Penguin Books, 1989.

Langer, Marie. *From Vienna to Managua.* Trans. M. Hooks. London: Free Association Books, 1989.

Medina, José Ramón. *Cincuenta años de literatura venezolana.* Caracas: Monte Avila, 1969.

Miranda, Julio. *Poesía en el espejo: Estudio y antología de la nueva lírica femenina venezolana 1970–1994.* Caracas: Fundarte, 1995.

Rosen, Norma. *Accidents of Influence.* Albany: State University of New York Press, 1992.

Rotker, Susana. *Isaac Chocrón y Elisa Lerner.* Caracas: Fundarte, 1991.

Zago, Angela. *Aquí no ha pasado nada.* Caracas: Editorial Planeta, 1990.

in search of the cuban
jewish woman writer
A TRIALOGUE/UN TRIÁLOGO

Ruth Behar, Ester Shapiro Rok, and Rosa Lowinger

The Jewish presence in Cuba was brief, like a candle lit in the wind, and left few traces. The most visible signs of that presence are the cemeteries: the Ashkenazic and Sephardic cemeteries in Guanabacoa, just outside of Havana, and the provincial cemeteries in Santa Clara, Camagüey, and Santiago de Cuba. Then there are the synagogues: four in Havana and one in Santiago. If you go to Cuba now looking for the Jewish presence, that is what you will find: cemeteries and synagogues. Little else that is palpable remains. The thousand Jews left on the island, most of whom are desperately seeking ways to leave, maintain Jewish traditions, for the time being, with the aid of humanitarian gifts from Jews in Latin America, Canada, and increasingly, the United States, Jews abroad who cannot yet bear to imagine a Cuba bereft of Jewish memory. If only there were a Cuban Jewish woman writer documenting all the loss, all the longing on the island today. . . . But no, I am told when I ask, there are no Cuban Jewish women writers; not one.

And yet Jews have been present in Cuba from the time of the conquest. The problem is that this presence always inscribed loss, for it remained hidden, repressed, disguised as something else. Christians of Jewish origin—"crypto–Jews" or *conversos*—came to Cuba fleeing the persecution of Spain's Inquisition. One of Cuba's earliest settlers was Luis de Torres, a Jewish convert to Christianity who spoke several European languages as well as Aramaic, Hebrew, and Arabic. He was sent to the island in 1492 by Columbus to gather information about Cuba's inhabitants, and it is said he remained in Cuba until his death a few years later.

A true unveiled Jewish presence did not take form in Cuba until the turn of the twentieth century when Sephardic Jews began to arrive, followed by Ashkenazim, coming in the 1920s when the United States restricted immigration, and followed, in turn, by Jewish refugees from Nazism. Jews found their way to the farthest corners of the island, but the Jewish community grew strongest in Havana, where Jewish day schools, newspapers, and businesses flourished and Ashkenazi and Sephardic Jews kept separate in their own neighborhoods and temples. But this Jewish world, like a dream, all too quickly vanished. Although the Cuban Communist party was founded by a Polish Jewish emigrant to Cuba, very few Jews chose to stay on the island after the Cuban Revolution of 1959. Their economic interests, mostly dependent on family–owned businesses, among those who prosper, and street peddling, among those who don't, were threatened by socialism, and most decided to emigrate and remake their homes in the United States.

Like their ancestors who fled Egypt too quickly to allow their bread to rise, the Jews who left Cuba did not find time to nourish any women writers in their midst. The first generation of young Jewish women to arrive in Cuba in the early decades of the twentieth century spoke Yiddish, Ladino, and a range of European languages; when they worked, they helped their husbands to run family-owned stores. Women did not write for the Yiddish–Spanish weekly, *Havaner Leben–Vida Habanera*, published between the 1930s and 1950s, which was a venue for the articles and testimonies of Ashkenazi male writers and also featured advertisements for Jewish businesses. Nevertheless, this generation produced a woman poet, Sarah Wekselbaum Luski, whose poems, written in Spanish, were collected and published in Miami by her children after they had emigrated to the United States. One of Luski's more strongly felt poems spoke of her nostalgia for Cuba, "¿Volveré a verte algún día mi Cuba querida / O en el exilio pasaré el resto de mi vida / Añorando tus cielos, tus playas hermosas. . . . ?" (Will I see you again dear Cuba / Or will I spend the rest of my life in exile / Longing for your skies, your beautiful beaches?) For, indeed, Cuba became a tropical paradise for the first generation of Jewish emigrants, who found on the island a degree of tolerance and openhearted kindness, as well as a measure of prosperity, that contrasted sharply with the legacy of anti–Semitism and economic duress they had left behind in Europe.

The second generation of Cuban Jewish women, born on the island and benefiting from the labor of their emigrant mothers, came of age in the conservative 1950s, experiencing upward mobility and feminine enclosure that came to be expressed in lavish *quinceañeras* (sweet fifteens) followed by even more lavish weddings. Most women in this generation were forming their own families when they found themselves having to pack their suitcases, as had their mothers before them, and embark on a new diasporic journey to the United States. Again, like their mothers, they had to learn a new language, English, and start from scratch, but this time in a new land that did not know what to make of the fact that they wore Jewish stars around their necks but Spanish flowed from their tongues, and rumbas, rather than horahs, rolled from their hips.

It is the generation of Cuban Jewish women who came to the United

States as children and were educated in English in American schools and universities who are now beginning to write the histories and stories of their double diaspora. This trialogue is the record of a conversation between three Cuban Jewish women writers who came of age in the United States and are just now, in our early forties, finding the self-confidence, strength, and sense of community to write the tales that still remain unwritten. This trialogue is part of an ongoing discussion, begun when we first met three years ago, about our lives, our struggles to become educated, and the way we have come to books and the desire to write them.

Each of us is a writer by calling, and yet none of us dared pursue writing as the profession by which to secure our livelihoods. Ruth Behar is an anthropologist at the University of Michigan in Ann Arbor, Ester Shapiro Rok is a psychologist at the University of Massachusetts at Boston, and Rosa Lowinger is an architectural conservator based in Los Angeles. In a three-way phone conversation one September morning, we tried to invent a genre as we spoke, a genre for an experience not yet scripted anywhere, a genre somewhere between sisterly commiseration, mutual therapy, historical testimony, the poetry of yearning, and theater in motion.

—*Ruth Behar*

Setting: Imagine three Cuban Jewish women, in Boston, Ann Arbor, and Los Angeles, with telephones pressed to their ears.

Ruth: Had we remained in Cuba together, the second generation born there, who knows? Without the abrupt dislocation of the Revolution and *el exilio,* we might have become Cuban Jewish women writers within a new generation, following on the hardships of the immigrant generation of our grandparents and parents. We might have been part of building a new community whose prosperity and stability might have supported an artist's way.

Rosa: Or we could have spent all our time shopping at El Encanto [the fancy department store in Havana] and having our eyebrows done.

Ester: In that lost island world that you idealize, Ruth, remember how deeply we were already in training to be good Cuban Jewish daughters. Piano lessons, ballet lessons. All the accoutrements of a well-established financial security can serve just as much as instruments of social control in our lives. Our lives as women could easily have been even more tightly scripted. We might have become women who would provide proper adornment for a successful businessman. Not that we wouldn't have been, all three of us, every Cuban Jewish family's nightmare daughter, *hijas atrevidas,* bold, intrepid daughters. Instead, we were destined to become immigrants, and as Jews we joined the Cuban exilio with our ancestral knowledge, so recently refreshed in the shadow of the Holocaust, that we must never settle down completely. We embraced our fates, coming of age between our Jewish, Cuban, and American worlds.

Rosa: You have to remember that we come from two of the most practically minded cultures in the world: the two together, Cuban and Jewish, *son como una bomba,* are like a bomb, in how they pressure you to do something from which you can at the very least make a living. Not that any of us chose the careers where you could make any real money.

Ester: Pero Rosa, that's *their* measure of our success talking, the really big money that builds pseudo–Italianate mansions on the beach. Remember, all three of us sought economic stability that might still secretly feed our soul's submerged longings for creative work. Look at how each of us has used our distinctive professional sensibility to both transform our fields and refashion a writer's life.

Rosa: Our jobs are not conventional and safe.

Ester: We couldn't play it safe if we wanted to.

Rosa: We tried to fit into the mold.

Ester: And then we broke the mold.

Ruth: For us, the passion for writing seems closely linked to a deep need to make shattered lives whole, to make connections out of rupture.

Rosa: I'm an art preservation expert, so what do I do? I fix things. I repair the unrepairable. You give me something in three hundred pieces and I'll make it look like it never happened. I never wrote anything until I was thirty. My art dream was to be an actress. My parents said, "¿Qué cosa? Eso es lo mismo que una puta" [What do you mean? That's like saying you want to be a prostitute].

Ester: Funny thing about that, *a mí me pasó lo mismo* [the same thing happened to me]. I was dying to play the slut in "David and Lisa" in my senior year play, and my father said the theater was for *putas y patos,* whores and homosexuals. And he didn't even know the part I was aching to play!

Rosa: That's why the visual arts are not threatening. Using your hands to make "beautiful" things is acceptable. It's not too far removed from embroidering Shabbos tablecloths. Works of representational art fit into this crafts category. Abstract stuff is less acceptable, but they don't understand the meaning enough to be threatened by it. And it doesn't threaten men, of course. "My wife is an artist" is nice and respectable so long as she cleans beneath her fingernails before a dinner party. That's where they pushed me, that's how I went into art preservation.

Ruth: So how did you start writing?

Rosa: I started by writing plays. Play writing was a good place to go because it's about the way people talk. I find it amazing to be able to use language as an artistic tool. I feel as if I'm cheating because the eccentricities of language actually enhance the power of a play. I had always avoided writing because I felt I didn't have a good enough command of the language.

Ester: Yes, there's the feeling among us that we haven't mastered one language, that we fluidly move through multiple languages for our images—Spanish, English, Hebrew, Yiddish.

Rosa: To quote my mother, "Se me está olvidando el español y todavía no sé el inglés. ¡Estoy muy jodida!" [I'm forgetting Spanish and I still don't know English. I'm really screwed up!]. When I was an adolescent my mom used to entertain me in the car by simultaneously translating *boleros* or *canciones de amor* [love songs] into Yiddish. It's quite a talent. In theater this talent is a gold mine. In my plays I tend to invert syntax, or use expressions and words inappropriately. In my first play, *The Encanto File,* the main character is a Cuban woman whose language is rich in malapropisms and odd syntax. She'll say things like "I'm not going to cut myself to spite my nose"—an expression I borrowed from my mother. This character's language is very funny and very powerful. The play is actually *about* language, about how people use words to conceal their true intentions.

Ester: I became a family therapist out of a deep impulse to heal my own family. Both my sisters are family therapists as well. Yet over and over again, I have had to face the fact that I cannot transform my family's struggles the same way I can be a healer to the strangers whose growth I guide. During my four years of psychoanalysis, the *gantze tzimmes* [whole thing], four times a week on the couch, I wrote a three-hundred-page manuscript of family stories because classical analysis had no place for these culturally informed narratives spanning continents and languages and revolutions and replete with as many characters as a Russian novel. For me, they were the sources where soul and voice began. Thanks to Ruth and the *Bridges to Cuba* project and the force of her obsession with gathering the scattered fragments of our community, her passionate need to connect with the island and the lost relationships that would have filled our Cuban Jewish lives there, we found each other and began the conversations that have nurtured our secret desires and creative strivings. And thanks to the *ejemplo* she offered in her essay "Death and Memory" [in her book *The Vulnerable Observer*] I began to tell my family stories in a new and deeper way.

Ruth: Well, Ester, I'm very honored by what you say, but you know how conflicted I am about the writing I've done as an anthropologist. I feel I've waited a long time to do the writing I've most wanted to do—the poetry I'm starting to write, the novel I still long to write. But perhaps to get here I had to take this long journey through anthropology, the journey that took me from Spain to Mexico to Cuba, from writing about land tenure among Spanish peasants to the Jewish rituals surrounding my own grandfather's death in Miami Beach. What drew me to anthropology was that I needed to understand the clash of cultures around me, not only Cuban, Jewish, and American, but the huge gulf between my mother's Ashkenazi identity and my father's Sephardic identity. I grew up within my mother's Ashkenazi family, hearing Yiddish and eating gefilte fish, and yet, always, I was reminded by my mother's family that I resembled my father's Sephardic family. I had dark curly hair, Frida Kahlo eyebrows, and large brown eyes that made me more like *el lado turco* [the Turkish side]. My temperament, too, marked me as *turca*. I had a terribly strong will, and I didn't forgive easily. But it was scary to be connected to the turco side, to those savage tempers. My father terrified me when I was young. I wore long bangs that he detested because they fell into my eyes, and once he threatened to cut them in my sleep.

Ester: What complete helplessness you must have felt—what a reign of terror.

Rosa: What else might he do, right? You know, my mother used to say, "If you're going to marry a Turk, you might as well marry a goy."

Ruth: Well, I took this sense of being "other" within the family very much to heart. I was drawn to the Spanish-speaking world from the time I was in high school and came into contact with a wonderful Spanish teacher who'd also emigrated from Cuba and encouraged me to study. I remember my Ashkenazi great-uncle telling me he didn't understand why I was spending so much time in Spain where the Inquisition had persecuted Jews when I could have been working on archaeological digs in Israel. But Spain touched a nerve in me—being there I connected with my Sephardic heritage in a strange way; like a *conversa*, I hid my Jewish identity in order to pass as Spanish, I felt the loss of Spain and the longing for it very deeply.

Rosa: Your father was poor, right?

Ruth: Yes, he was. My father grew up next to the Port of Havana, in a tenement, and he resented the fact that his father made him work days to help support the family and so he wasn't able to study to become an architect, which had been his dream. He had to go to night school, and the only thing he was able to study was accounting.

Rosa: My mother grew up very poor. My mother grew up in an orphanage. My mother, instead of being demure, she's like gang kids who are in your face because they're so hurt. My mother's just like that, because people have always judged her by how much money she has or doesn't have.

Ester: Cuban Jews are definitely the most mercantile. It's such a tiny enclave. It's so different from the Jews of the United States. Jews in the United States revere the intellectual.

Rosa: I grew up in a house that did not have one book in it. Not one book.

Ester: Absolutely. . . . I walk into the one cousin's house who has books, she has a clinical psychology degree, and when I walked into her house with her mother-in-law, the first thing she says is, *"Mira, otra loca con libros"* [Look, another nut who's got books]. You take someone who had a serious career, you marry her into my family, and all of a sudden she lives for those purses—the little jeweled purses that cost $10,000.

Rosa: They cost like $500.

Ester: Then they're not the Cuban Jew purses. These cost thousands of dollars. They're not insured, so they can't just leave them lying around on the table at bar mitvahs.

Rosa: Did you grow up with books, Ruth?

Ruth: A few books. In our house there were a few books about World War II and a couple of Cuban revolutionary pamphlets. My father brought with him from Cuba a first edition copy of Fidel Castro's *La historia me absolverá* (History Will Absolve Me). I still don't understand why he would have brought that with him.

Rosa: My mother used to say, as a joke, *"Yo creo que me cambiaron la hija en el hospital"* [I think they exchanged my daughter at the hospital]. Did any of you get in trouble for not watching television? Literally, I would get into trouble for being in my room instead of watching TV with my family.

Ester: *Me llamaban podrida* [They called me rotten fruit]. Because if you read a lot of books, *se te pudre la mente* [your mind gets ruined, spoiled]. You're not doing edifying things like watching television and going shopping.

Rosa: I wrote this article on the restoration of Old Havana for the magazine *Preservation* and my parents didn't show any interest in it until someone called to congratulate them. Then they asked for a copy. If that person hadn't called, they wouldn't have read it. But they read it and loved it. *"Oye, Rosa, mira lo bien que tú escribes y piensas"* [Listen, Rosa, you really do write and think very well]. I'm forty years old, when are you going to figure it out?

Ester: Every once in a while, there's a truth-telling moment. Fifteen years ago my father said that from the time I was two years old, I scared the family, because I was too smart. That's why I became a family therapist. I needed a system where I could see what I saw and not be labeled crazy. You become a psychopathology expert so no one can tell you you're crazy.

Rosa: When you said before that reading *te pudre la mente,* I find lately that I simply cannot read, it really hurts my brain, it clots me with other stuff. What I find most useful is just looking at things. Do you know what it's like to sit in an airport without reading? I was in an airport at Charlotte. It felt like Yom Kippur, I have to tell you. I had the same feeling—how many more days until I can't? Just like, how many more hours until I can eat? So I looked and looked. In an hour, I got an entire structure of a play. I got this whole play just sitting there. Images are really amazing. . . . I'm embarrassed to say this to both of you girls, but I know you'll understand. I'm really not an intellectual. I've never read Freud or Jung.

Ester: Mira, mi amor, no te preocupes, don't worry. I had to read it all as a teacher to know what is harmful, what to discard. I can teach you what's worth having in an hour. Like Rabbi Akiba's standing on one foot.

Rosa: It's actually Hillel who stood on one foot.

Ester: You know, you're right. You see, you read more than you think!

Rosa: To be an intellectual you have to read Freud and Jung, and also you have to be able to read some philosophy, without feeling you have to get up and put a bullet through your head. In college, I felt I really had to read these guys, it was excruciating, like having a root canal. I felt mad for not understanding. I was secretly embarrassed that I had to work so hard to understand it. I'm sure you guys don't have to work that hard to understand this stuff.

Ester: No, but we have the problem of the pretentiousness of the academy. The tyranny of texts. The dogmatic rituals. Ruth and I are very burdened by that. We have learned very well to do what our work demands of us. But following the Talmudic track can be very constraining.

Rosa: When I was in junior high school, I actually studied Talmud. The real McCoy, from the page. I adored that nitpicky discussion, what meant what. The discussion was interesting. The argument was interesting.

Ester: You don't read that much text—you read two or three lines and stay there forever. . . . In my Freud classes with Paul Lipman, we would take weeks on one essay, we'd study things line by line.

Ruth: I had a very strong passion for philosophy, but I didn't do well in college in philosophy courses. I was led to believe, by a woman teacher I greatly admired, that I wasn't smart enough to "do" philosophy. I went to graduate school in anthropology largely to prove to myself that I was smart. I allowed myself to be academically trained almost against my own will. I received my Ph.D. at the age of twenty-five, and had planned to quit and write novels, but I found that my imagination had been disciplined, brought under control. Now I'm struggling to free my imagination again, to unloosen it from its academic fetters.

Rosa: I think the place of writing for you and me, Ruth, is pretty clear, and what we see as the inching toward that liberation of the creative self, but I don't think I know so clearly about you, Ester.

Ester: I continue to see my writing as part of my project as a psychologist. It's a grandiose project.

Rosa: I don't think it's so grandiose.

Ester: Well, let me tell you and you'll see why it's so grandiose. I want to change the ways we practice to highlight positive forces for growth within ourselves, our families, and our communities. When I went to Clark University, I went into a developmental program. In psychology you choose between being a clinician and being an academic psychologist. I discovered at Clark a place where these approaches are very linked. I was encouraged to get clinical training. Things clicked when I went to Cuba. I began to think more deeply about the economic and prestige agenda of clinical psychology, the way healing takes place at great expense to the patient, instead of having things be accessible that can help people live their lives. My grief book [*Grief as a Family Process*] is about changing the models we work from. Now I want to write things that go directly to people. I want to speak against the materialism of what psychology has become as an industry. I agree with Paolo Freire, that it's all about education.

Rosa: Maybe you can write me a cartoon book on what I need to know.

Ester: The stuff is made obscure and mystified to give prestige to the profession. There is no reason why it can't be accessible, why there can't be more power-sharing. Going back to Cuba, I was searching for a way that I could make mine a revolutionary practice.

Ruth: And Cuba does revolutionary psychology?

Ester: They do with their family doctors. Psychologists are linked up to all the places where people live their lives, their family lives. The problem is when you get into social dogma in the practice of psychology. There it's oppressive. There's the danger of pathologizing what is socially unacceptable. Paolo Freire is not accepted in Cuba. He criticizes everything. . . . Dialogue is the great equalizer, Buber's idea of "I/Thou" dialogue, that's how you learn what you're imposing on somebody else.

Ruth: I still don't see exactly how Cuba figures in all of this.

Ester: Some of it is in the writing I did for my essay in your *Bridges to Cuba*, about exile, loss, and grief. But it's also in the memory of my father asking me how much money I'm making an hour and how many patients I'm seeing. He kept wanting to add up a total. I realized that my project as a psychologist was going to have to be a socially transformative one. Now you know why I called it a grandiose project.

Rosa: It is, *pero ¡qué coño!* I couldn't have come up with that in a million years. When I hear you talking about this, my vision of my novel appears to be so much fluff . . .

Ester: I like the way you write. I like the way you use images, that you trust images. The big fight between Freud and Jung was the Jew/Goy struggle. That Freud had picked for a son a goy who tried to destroy him. Freud used a Talmudic approach, but Jung was interested in eternal symbols, the archetypes tied to the very basic cycles of the earth and reproduction. The texts start with symbolic ritual images.

Rosa: Images are the only thing I can rely on.

Ester: Yes, and the image is what is *traif* in Judaism. That is what is most forbidden. . . . I feel that I've never been more Jewish than I am now, as I search for new ways to reinterpret Abraham's prohibitions against pagan images. I feel a need to connect with images that are animistic, with images from nature. You can find a way around the rules.

Ruth: Let's talk about the pull all three of us feel lately toward Afro-Cuban culture and religion.

Rosa: I'll start.

Ester: Yes, you have the kosher kitchen. We had to go make *mariscos* [seafood] at another person's house.

Rosa: I do have a kosher kitchen.

Ruth: You have two sets of plates?

Rosa: Not only that. I have two other sets of plates for Passover. Up-
stairs I have *cajones llenos de* (boxes full of) Passover dishes.

Ester: You were going to tell us something you hadn't told us.

Rosa: It embarrasses me in a strange way. I lead services a lot at High
Holy Days. I want to lead services in out-of-the-way places. In
Idaho . . .

Ester: I read services until puberty. I didn't have a bat mitzvah because girls didn't have them in my family. . . . My Jewish teachers wanted to send me to Hebrew High School where you
studied, Rosa. *Siempre no.* These people would come and try to
talk to my parents but they wouldn't budge.

Rosa: You were asking about Santería [Afro–Cuban religion]. For a
long time I avoided getting involved. When I started going to
Cuba, I kept seeing a lot about Santería. I saw how Americans
would come and put on *collares* [the necklaces with beads of
specific colors marking devotion to a particular saint]. I felt that
Santería had been used without authenticity, so I avoided it.

Ester: Santería was in the atmosphere for me all through my growing
up in Cuba and Miami. If you hang out with Cubans, it's always
there, in *referencias,* music. I encountered it when I visited Santiago de Cuba and when I saw rumba performed in Boston. One
set was dancing music, and one set was sacred music.

Rosa: I kept going to Cuba, I kept feeling the presence of Santería,
but I stayed away from respect. I have been to Cuba eleven times
since 1992, and this last time *me hice el Elegguá* [a first rite of
initiation through which the participant obtains access to the
primary deity who has the power to open and close the path-
ways of life].

Ruth: Me too, after just as many visits to Cuba, I received my Elegguá
and it has been a way for me to strengthen my connection to
Caro, the Afro–Cuban woman who took care of me as a child

and who has been the inspiration for the new writing I'm starting about how our Jewish diaspora story meshes with the African diaspora story of Caro and her family.

Ester: I'm reexamining why Jews left these animistic religions, and
I'm trying to understand what was lost in the process. I find Judaism so profundly sexist that it can't be my single religious
home. Consuelo, my aunt, coming of age in the small town of
Bolondron, in Matanzas, would sneak off with Afro-Cuban guys.
She would get caught and beaten. The family had to marry her
off. It haunted the family, the presence of all of these forbidden
traif men. And yet they fell asleep every night to the sound of
the Santería drums.

Ruth: Hearing you say that, I realize that the morning is ending. So,
what do you think? Can we fictionalize this conversation a bit
for the article?

Ester: Sure! I've come to believe in the importance of fictionalizing
in the name of a greater truth.

Rosa: You said it before I did. *Bueno, me duele el oído ya. Las dejo, seño-
ras* [My ear hurts already. I've got to go now, ladies].

epilogue

*November 12, 1997, Ruth's birthday. Rosa and Ester, who are together in
Los Angeles, call to give their* felicidades *to Ruth.*

Ruth: I just heard from Marjorie Agosín and she likes our triálogo,
but she thinks we need to add a conclusion. She wants us to say
something about how we are the keepers of Cuban Jewish
women's memory and have a responsibility as the next generation to keep alive the voices of our grandmothers and mothers.

Rosa: I think the triálogo ends nicely the way it is.

Ester: It is a conversation, after all.

Rosa: It ends, and then there's air behind it. You don't have to pummel the point. You leave a little space, because you don't know whether you're the keeper of anything when you're doing it. The Talmudic approach is to argue a point back and forth and in a circle for years without actually saying, "This is the conclusion." The law is made in the argument. Whether we're the keepers of anything is not for us to say.

Ester: We're making it up as we go along. We affirm ourselves and each other as writers in the conversation. That's why it's so precious to us. And since we're Cubanas, after all, *tenemos que cerrar con un relajo,* we have to close with a Cuban sense of teasing humor to leaven the serious Jewish stuff, to keep open the Talmudic circle.

Ruth: Well, you've both convinced me. What do you think, Marjorie?

 contributors

MARJORIE AGOSÍN is a Chilean poet, short story writer, and human rights activist. She is currently professor of Latin American literature at Wellesley College and chair of the Spanish Department. Agosín has received numerous awards for her writing. Among them are the Letras de Oro and the Latino Literature Prize, both in 1995. She was honored in 1998 with a United Nations Leadership Award in human rights. Her most recent publications include *Dear Anne Frank* (1998) and *Always from Somewhere Else* (1998).

RUTH BEHAR was born in Havana, Cuba, in 1956 and moved to New York in 1962. A poet, essayist, and ethnographer, she is currently professor of anthropology at the University of Michigan. She received a MacArthur Fellows Award in 1988 and a John Simon Guggenheim fellowship in 1995. Her books include *The Presence of the Past in a Spanish Village: Santa María del Monte* (1986, 1991) and *Translated Women: Crossing the Border with Esperanza's Story* (1993). She is also the co-editor of *Women Writing Culture* (1995). Her poems have been published widely, and her most recent publication is *The Vulnerable Observer: Anthropology That Breaks Your Heart* (1997), a book of essays.

DAVID WILLIAM FOSTER is Chair of the Department of Languages and Literatures and Regents' Professor of Spanish, Humanities, and Women's Studies at Arizona State University. He has written extensively on Argentine narrative and theater and has held Fulbright teaching appointments in Argentina, Brazil, and Uruguay. Among his publications are *Violence in Argentine Literature: Cultural Responses to Tyranny* (1995), *Cultural Diversity in Latin American Literature* (1994), and *Gay and Lesbian Themes in Latin American Writing* (1991).

JOAN ESTHER FRIEDMAN is currently a faculty member in the Department of Modern Languages and Literatures at Swarthmore College, where she teaches Spanish. The focus of her research is Venezuelan Jewish literature. She has contributed to *Latin American Writers: A Critical Dictionary* and the forthcoming work, *The Sign of the Star: Stories by Jewish Women Writers of Latin America.* Her translation of Alicia Freilich de Segal's *Cláper* was published in 1989.

ELIZABETH ROSA HORAN is Associate Professor of English (Comparative Literature) at Arizona State University. She is a poet, translator, and book reviewer. Her publications include *Gabriela Mistral: An Artist and Her People* (1994), an introduction to and translation of *Happiness* by Marjorie Agosín (1993), and essays in *Sulfur, Academia, Emily Dickinson Journal, and Taller de Letras.*

REGINA IGEL is Professor of Brazilian and Portuguese literature and an affiliate of the Rebecca and Joseph Meyerhoff Judaic Center at the University of Maryland. She has written extensively on Brazilian Jewish authors, especially women. Among her numerous publications are *Imigrantes judeus escritores brasileiros* (1996) and *Omas lins una biografia literaria* (1988). She is a frequent contributor to the *Handbook of Latin American Studies* and several Brazilian and Portuguese publications in Latin America, Europe, and the United States.

ROSA LOWINGER was born in Havana, Cuba, and arrived in the United States at a very early age. She studied art history and restoration. She presently lives in Los Angeles and is writing plays and working on a first novel.

MAGDALENA MAÍZ-PEÑA is Associate Professor of Spanish at Davidson College. She is the author of numerous publications exploring gender and autobiography in Latin America, specializing in Mexico. Among her recent works are *Identidad, nación y gesto autobiográfico* (1997) and *Modalidades de representación de sujeto auto/bio/gráfico feminino.* She is president of the American Association of Teachers of Spanish and Portuguese in North Carolina.

5 8 40

ESTER SHAPIRO ROK is a Cuban Jewish clinical psychologist, associate professor at the University of Massachusetts at Boston, and writer adept at living *entremundos*. After years of academic writing, including *Grief as a Family Process* (New York: Guilford Press, 1994) and professional papers on family transitions, she has begun writing her family stories, with and without accompanying recipes. She has helped complete *Nuestros Cuerpos Nuestras Vidas*, a translation and culturally sensitive adaptation of *Our Bodies Ourselves*, for use by the Latin American sisterhood in both hemispheres (New York: Ballantine Press, 1999).

ILAN STAVANS teaches at Amherst College. His books include *The Hispanic Condition* (HarperPerennial), *Art and Anger: Essays on Politics and the Imagination* and *The Riddle of Cantinflas: Essays on Hispanic Popular Culture* (both by the University of New Mexico Press), and *The Oxford Book of Latin American Essays*. He has been a National Book Critics Circle Award nominee and the recipient of the Latino Literature Prize.

NELSON H. VIEIRA is Professor of Luso-Brazilian Literature in the Department of Portuguese and Brazilian Studies and Fellow in the Program of Judaic Studies at Brown University. He is president of LAJSA and founding editor of the literary journal *Brasil/Brazil*. Recipient of National Endowment for the Humanities, Fulbright, and Rockefeller fellowships, among others, Vieira was also guest resident at the Ledig International Writers' Colony, Ghent, New York (1996). Besides articles and essays on modern Brazilian fiction, Vieira has the following among his recent titles: *Jewish Voices in Brazilian Literature: A Prophetic Discourse of Alterity* (1995), *Construindo a imagem do judeu* (1994), and *Brasil e Portugal: A imagem recíproca* (1991).